ARCHITECTURE *and* FILM

ARCHITECTURE *and* FILM

EDITED BY MARK LAMSTER

PRINCETON ARCHITECTURAL PRESS *new york*

PUBLISHED BY
Princeton Architectural Press
37 East Seventh Street
New York, NY 10003

For a catalog of books published by Princeton Architectural Press, call toll free 800.722.6657 or visit www.papress.com.

04 03 02 01 00 5 4 3 2 1
FIRST EDITION

BOOK AND COVER DESIGN: Sara E. Stemen

SPECIAL THANKS: Ann Alter, Eugenia Bell, Jan Cigliano, Jane Garvie, Caroline Green, Beth Harrison, Mia Ihara, Clare Jacobson, Leslie Ann Kent, Anne Nitschke, Lottchen Shivers, Jennifer Thompson, and Deb Wood of Princeton Architectural Press—Kevin C. Lippert, publisher

PRINTED AND BOUND IN THE UNITED STATES

LIBRARY OF CONGRESS CATALOGING-IN-PUBLICATION DATA
Architecture and film / edited by Mark Lamster.
p. cm.
Includes bibliographical references.
ISBN 1-56898-207-0 (pbk.:alk.paper)
1. Architects in motion pictures. 2. Motion Pictures—setting and scenery. 3. Architecture in motion pictures. I. Lamster, Mark, 1969–

PN1995.9.A695 A73 2000
791.43'657—dc21 99-057029

COVER: [Front] Publicity image for *Mr. Blandings Builds His Dream House* (1948), with Cary Grant and Myrna Loy. [Back] Still from Jacques Tati's *Playtime* (1967). Images Courtesy Photofest.

PAGE 355: Still from Jacques Tati's *Mon Oncle* (1958). Courtesy Photofest.

IMAGE CREDITS: Academy of Motion Pictures Arts and Sciences/Margaret Herrick Library: 100, 105, 107, 110, 113; Academy of Motion Picture Arts and Sciences/Margaret Herrick Library—Saul Bass Collection: 128; Ken Adam/Serpentine Gallery, London: 116, 123–5; Bob Craft: 140; © The J. Paul Getty Trust, 1997, 1999. Used by permission. All rights reserved: 88, 92, 94, 97; Courtesy Pennebaker Hegedus Films: 136; Photofest: viii, 10, 37, 50, 76, 148, 170, 196, 206, 242, 245, 255; Photo © Julius Shulman: 163; Maggie Valentine: 152.

CONTENTS

PART II: BEHIND THE SCENES

PART III: VISIONS OF THE WORLD

INTRODUCTION

MARK LAMSTER

THE ARCHITECT AND the filmmaker have much in common. Their professions demand a combination of courage, determination, and hubris that allow them to impose a personal vision on an often unreceptive world. Both practice synthetic arts, where collaboration and compromise are rules rather than exceptions and where clients have financial—if not creative—control. Orchestrators of complex productions, they require a supporting cast of able craftsmen who must carry out their tasks with creativity, intelligence, and practicality. If they don't, if a project fails to live up to expectations, the principal alone will take the blame. Conversely, it is the heroic *auteur* who will bask in the adulation of any grand success, the role players fading quietly into the penumbra. We should all know better.

Filmmakers, with the help of production designers, art directors, location managers, and countless other members of cast and crew, insert architecture into their films. On a practical level, architecture sets a scene, conveying information about plot and character while contributing to the overall feel of a movie. In more discreet ways, filmmakers can use their cameras to make statements about the built—or unbuilt—environment, or use that environment to comment metaphorically on any of a variety of subjects, from the lives of

OPPOSITE: **Partygoers inspect a model apartment tower in King Vidor's *The Fountainhead* (1949).**

the characters in their films to the nature of contemporary society. Architects, for their part, create not only the structures that appear in films but the structures in which films appear—theaters—and the very infrastructure that supports the film industry.

As arguably the defining art form of the twentieth century, film has had a profound effect on both the way architects envision their work and the way the public consumes architecture. Today, we often hear of architecture that is "cinematic"—that is, theatrical in effect and thematic in nature; the vast hotels of Las Vegas, the new Times Square in New York, and the seemingly ubiquitous theme restaurants scattered across America are prime examples. The New Urbanist movement of planning and design finds its picket-fence paradigms in Hollywood's depictions of small-town America. Meanwhile, a number of avant-garde practitioners have sought more abstract inspiration from the medium of film, finding in its use of montage, sequential progression, and spatial composition devices applicable to their own work.

An examination of any one of these convergences would make fine fodder for a book in its own right. But that is not the intention here. Eschewing a narrowly focused theme or theoretical agenda, this collection seeks only to suggest a few of the many different ways to think about the entwined subjects of architecture and film, and to do so in a thoughtful and engaging manner. If there is a shared conviction among these writers, it is simply a commitment to both architecture and film along with the belief that these two art forms exert a profound influence—sometimes positive, sometimes not—on the way we live.

This book is divided into three parts. The first, "Architects on Screen," examines the depiction of architects in both fiction films and documentaries. Part II, "Behind the Scenes," explores the process of creating on-screen architecture, focusing on the professionals who are responsible for putting it there and its effects on the way we perceive our environments. The essays in Part III, "Visions of the World," show how filmmakers have used the built environment to reflect their ideas about the societies in which they live.

What better place to begin than with a look at the evolution of the on-screen portrayal of the architect? While researching her essay on this subject, "Tall Buildings, Tall Tales: On Architects in the Movies," Nancy Levinson quickly realized that architects are few and far between in major motion pictures—a reflection of the relative invisibility of the profession in the popular imagination, but also of the fact that the architectural career doesn't suggest the *frisson* of danger and crusading righteousness we have come to expect from doctors, detectives, politicians, spies, and even lawyers in the movies. The architects that filmmakers have created are almost invariably distorted characterizations, but, as Levinson writes, these distortions, "like jagged views reflected by a cracked mirror, contain disconcerting shards of truth." Although on-screen architects have served predominantly as window dressing—well-appointed minor players, Renaissance men (they are always men) equally at home in the worlds of art and business—a handful of films have featured architects as primary characters. From *The Fountainhead* to *Indecent Proposal*, Levinson tracks the "mystique" of the profession over the course of a prolonged, downward trajectory from Messianic figure of prodigious creative and sexual vigor to impotent and lowly cog in a hollow consumerist economy.

How exactly did this come to pass? Philip Nobel explores this question in his essay, "Who Built Mr. Blandings' Dream House?" He finds the answer in the reorganization and redefinition of the profession in the face of World War II. Nobel documents the vain attempts made by architects to contribute to the war effort, their rejection by a technocratic government that perceived them as mere aesthetes, and the subsequent corporatization of the architectural profession.

Documentary filmmaker Bob Eisenhardt addresses the portrayal of a particular architect—and a major work of architecture—on screen in his frank account of the production of *Concert of Wills*, a film that he edited. More than a decade in the making, this *cinema verité* chronicle of the marathon design and construction process of the Getty Center in Los Angeles is unique among documentaries about architecture. As Eisenhardt writes, "The focus was on the actual process of making architecture," rather than the hagiographic treatment of client and architect typical of such films. Eisenhardt, who trained as an architect and received an Academy Award nomination for his 1983 film *Spaces: The Architecture of Paul Rudolph*, suggests that the process of making a film is, in fact, quite similar to that of constructing a building.

The inherently collaborative nature of filmmaking is a fact that is made explicit at the close of every movie, when a seemingly endless stream of cast and crew names scrolls up and off the screen. Nevertheless, we often forget that there are professionals besides the director who are responsible for the look of a film. Part II begins with appraisals of two such figures, the art directors Cedric Gibbons and Ken Adam. Though Gibbons' career was coming to a close just as Adam's was beginning—indeed, Adam is still working today—and their personal histories and stylistic proclivities are wildly divergent, both not only gave shape to the individual films on which they worked, but influenced countless others.

As head of the Metro-Goldwyn-Mayer art department, Gibbons defined the look of Hollywood's Golden Age, a look that offered stylish escape for Depression-weary audiences. For such early talkies as *Our Dancing Daughters* and *Grand Hotel*, Gibbons pioneered the use of fully three-dimensional stage settings to augment the dramatic effect of sound. But most significantly, as Christina Wilson points out, he was the first to introduce the modern—generally in deco form—into the Hollywood film. During the course of a career that garnered an astonishing twenty-nine Academy Award nominations, his nuanced handling of space and decoration received wide coverage in the press (particularly in women's magazines), sparking a variety of trends in interior design.

Now in his sixth decade of professional practice, Adam is the *éminence grise* of art direction, a man equally at home designing for thrillers, comedies, dramas, period productions, and children's stories. Described by Donald Albrecht as the "Frank Lloyd Wright of decor noir," Adam translated the expressionist aesthetic of the twenties and thirties into the postwar era, creating stylized settings for such films as *Dr. No* and *Dr. Strangelove*, *Chitty Chitty Bang Bang* and *Addams Family Values*. He remains best known for his designs for the James Bond series—he art-directed seven of the films, making him, in Albrecht's words, "the real-life Q" responsible for Bond's gadget-infested autos as well as his rivals' secret lairs, designs that have left an indelible mark on both the film industry and the public's imagination.

Like art directors, film title designers rarely appear on the popular radar—no small irony given their role in doling out credit. Yet these architects of graphic information are responsible for the opening segments of a film, which establish a tone for what will come. Peter Hall examines the fertile period between 1955 and 1969, when, in the hands of such designers as Saul Bass and Steve Frankfurt, this "bastard child of the medium" came of age.

In a darkened theater, with our disbelief suspended, we are prone to forget that even the most prosaic settings depicted on screen have been carefully chosen, vetted, and choreographed. How are these spaces selected? Such is the purview of the location manager, whose responsibilities include scouting locations, negotiating filming rights, and ensuring that a production runs smoothly in the field. Bob Craft, revered for his keen eye and political acumen by such directors as Quentin Tarantino, Andrew Niccol, Nicholas Roeg, and Diane Keaton, describes the ins and outs of this invaluable but largely invisible profession while telling of the trials and tribulations imposed by small budgets, leaky roofs, bizarre requests, and Mother Nature.

In "Escape by Design," Maggie Valentine also deconstructs the world behind the screen, reviewing the history and ersatz nature of the studio set. She argues that the ever-increasing artificiality of the film industry has thoroughly saturated a contemporary American landscape in which pleasure parks and planned communities are avatars of Hollywood-inspired dreams.

Joe Rosa looks at how Hollywood films have colored the way we receive our environments. In "Tearing Down the House," he reviews Hollywood's history of stereotyping and stigmatizing modern domestic design, in opposition to more traditional revival forms, which have long been used to symbolize stability and harmonious family life. He finds it to be a trend that is accelerating, despite the ever-growing fascination with modern design in our conspicuously consumptive age. As he writes, "Bad guys may no longer wear black, but they do live in white-walled modern homes."

Part III of this volume opens with essays by Joan Ockman and Mitchell Schwarzer on the filmmakers Jacques Tati and Michelangelo Antonioni, directors for whom architecture and landscape serve as primary elements—practically characters in and of themselves. Both use physical environments as metaphors for and embodiments of societies they wish to critique, though their visions could hardly be more different. Antonioni's films use architecture to describe, in Schwarzer's words, "the turbulence, tedium, and sublimity that make up the modern age." Looking at Tati's classic film *Playtime*, Ockman shows that this filmmaker's vision is altogether more optimistic. His ever-oblivious clown, Mr. Hulot—whose distracted persona becomes an exemplar for the way we receive both Tati's film and our own architectural environments—presents us with a happy-go-lucky spirit that is adaptive, resilient, and humane.

If Antonioni's landscapes are characterized by what Schwarzer describes as an "enervating numbness," the spaces in the films noir Jonathan F. Bell examines in his essay about "rural noir" are fraught with danger. Bell demonstrates that in the fatalistic world of noir, the ostensibly placid countryside offers little escape from the travails of the city. Produced in a postwar period when both city and country were being abandoned in favor of a homogenized suburbia, these films reflect contemporary anxieties about crime-ridden urban spaces and the deserted wastelands connecting them.

The cities of George Lucas's *Star Wars* films, the subject of my contribution to this volume, are similarly places of danger and corruption. Time and again in this series we see the forces of good finding respite in the natural world while their evil foes build ever-more-elaborate urban monstrosities—machines not for living, but killing, and killing on a grand scale. Between these poles are a series of retro-futurist cities of great physical beauty but dubious moral character, reflections of Lucas's own ambivalent feelings about urban space.

It is fitting to end this collection with Eric Rosenberg's "Bursting at the Seams: Architecture and the Films of the Beatles," an essay whose very subject is termination. Rosenberg traces the Beatles' evolution through the architectural spaces of their films *A Hard Day's Night, Help*, and *Let It Be*, which he describes as "parables of the band's maturation." Rosenberg reveals how architecture at first fails to satisfy the group's constant need for shelter, but eventually becomes a suffocating hermetic container that leads to the band's dissolution.

We all have our favorite architectural movies and movie moments. For anyone growing up in New York in the seventies and eighties, it was impossible not to be captivated by Woody Allen's romantic visions of the five boroughs, especially Manhattan. And films like *Dog Day Afternoon* and *Taxi Driver* captured the lurid nature of the city with equally memorable images. The introduction of the VCR was a revelation. While other teens were out experimenting with forbidden substances and exploring the downtown club scene, my small group of friends spent weekend nights rotating among each other's apartments, gorging ourselves on double features, pizza, and microwave popcorn. Our urban experience was, to a rather disturbing degree, vicarious.

Things haven't changed all that much in the intervening years. Woody Allen continues to produce a movie just about every year, and a rental and a pizza is still my idea of an evening well spent. For better or worse, this collection is a product of that adolescent fascination with film and the city, a fascination that happily continues unabated.

PART ONE

ARCHITECTS *on* SCREEN

TALL BUILDINGS, TALL TALES: *on* ARCHITECTS *in the* MOVIES

NANCY LEVINSON

PICTURE THIS: A film festival consisting of movies in which one of the characters is an architect. It would be a curious cultural event, featuring major stars and has-beens, towers in the sky and conversation pits, dedicated designers who triumph over Herculean obstacles and defeated idealists who can hardly bear the burden of their blank sketchpads. The festival would not appeal to all cinéastes, certainly not to those who reserve their viewing hours for artistically significant films; for this festival would showcase neither neglected masterpieces nor minor sleepers but rather the sort of overwrought melodramas and glandular comedies that seem destined for videotape obscurity or oddball cult status. However, moviegoers who can savor the frothy pleasures of certain dream-factory products would find these films a distinct treat, as would anyone who wishes to see how architects have been portrayed in the most popular and influential art form of the twentieth century.

What images of architects and their profession have flickered across the screens of movie palaces and art houses during the past half century? To answer this question, I engaged in that pleasant activity that once would have been considered a loungy pastime but can now be deemed research: I spent many hours lying on the sofa

OPPOSITE: **Kirk Douglas as architect Larry Coe in *Strangers When We Meet* (1960).**

watching movies. The visions of architecture that took shape were, not surprisingly, diverse; but many of them exhibited an intriguing contradiction. Most screen presentations of the architect's life distort those aspects that can be labeled "realistic." The movies have no use for that workaday professional world whose too-common characteristics are long days and lean paychecks, teamwork and compliance, creeping frustration and mid-life disillusion. Instead, they display a tenacious fascination with the more ethereal aspects of the architectural career. Far from underpaid draftsmen or overage apprentices, most architects in the movies are inheritors of the heroic modernist mission (or at least its aura), formgivers honored by society, disciples of an ancient craft, artists with steady funding and stylish quarters, creative and sexy free spirits pursuing enviably unfettered lives. The movies are captivated by certain dreams, ideals, and even fantasies that have come to characterize the architect's image—the *mystique* of the profession to those outside the discipline and sometimes even, against considerable odds, to practitioners themselves. And as is so often the case when comparing the movies and "real life," the question of cause and effect is impossibly complex. The movies seize upon our fantasies and project them back to us, larger than life in the intimate dark, thereby intensifying and perpetuating them.

PLAYBILL

What movies might make up the architects film festival? My selection methodology was unscientific but energetic: I queried friends and colleagues, searched the Internet, consulted film histories and historians, and even got the film snobs in my local video store intrigued with what they saw as a quirky project, involving the voluntary viewing of many mediocre movies. No doubt the playbill is incomplete. It is limited to English-language films, both because I am more familiar with them and because it is always harder to catch the nuances of films viewed with subtitles and to understand cultural references when the culture is not one's own. Thus I do not discuss the only great film I know to feature an architect as a character: Michelangelo Antonioni's 1961 masterpiece *L'Avventura*.

Nor does this essay address two of the more lurid movies with architect characters, both of which dramatize the 1906 sex scandal that ended in the public shooting of Stanford White by Harry Thaw, husband of White's mistress Evelyn Nesbit. This scandal is the subject of *The Girl in the Red Velvet Swing*, a little-remembered 1957 movie that starred the young Joan Collins as Nesbit and the too-stolid Ray Milland as White. I saw this as a teenager on late-night television, registering even then its silliness, and might have included it here had it been available on video. *Ragtime*, the film adaptation of E. L. Doctorow's novel, is of course available on video, but the Nesbit story is just one of many in this sprawling narrative and not central to the main action. Suffice it to say, though, that the casting of the orgasm-obsessed writer Norman Mailer as the notoriously roving White is suggestive.

A chronologically organized festival might begin with two very different Hollywood productions of the late 1940s. In *Mr. Blandings Builds His Dream House*, Cary Grant and Myrna Loy play Jim and Muriel Blandings, gullible Manhattanites who wish to depart the blaring metropolis, where the view from your hopelessly cramped apartment is the window of your neighbor's hopelessly cramped apartment, and lay claim to a patch of rustic Connecticut. In pursuit of their exurban dream, the Blandings bump up against the arcane expertise of laconic rural contractors and the country-gentleman bonhomie of their budget-oblivious architect. The best thing about this wry but predictable comedy, released in 1948 and directed by the obscure H. C. Potter, is the rollicking title. A topical response to the postwar housing shortage that would produce a veritable nation of dream houses, the movie gives its tweedy, bow-tied architect, played by the British actor Reginald Denny, very little screen time. For the most part, the story details the mock horrors of the construction, not the design, of the Blandings' neocolonial mini-manse. Released a year later, *The Fountainhead* (1949) also shuttles between teeming New York and country-house Connecticut. However, *The Fountainhead* is not a light comedy but an earnest adaptation of Ayn Rand's improbable cult classic about the impossible Howard Roark, architect of genius and pillar of integrity in a world of spineless mediocrity. Directed by King Vidor, with Gary Cooper as an iron-jawed

Roark and Patricia Neal as his demon-goddess lover Dominique Francon, the film is true to its literary origins, managing to convey the novel's mix of monomaniacal characterizations, heavy-handed plotting, speechifying dialog, sadomasochistic sex, proto-fascist politics, sub-Nietzschean philosophizing, and architectural clichés.

Twelve Angry Men is a gimmicky but effective drama from 1958, directed by Sidney Lumet. The gimmick is that the action takes place in real time, in one room, as twelve jurors assemble in a Manhattan courthouse to decide their verdict on the case of a young man accused of robbery. The defendant is Hispanic, and the class-sensitive screenplay has dutifully cut a demographic cross section through the American society of its day. One of the men is an architect and, played by Henry Fonda, the hero of the film. The only juror willing to explore the proposition of "reasonable doubt," he persuades the others, one by one, to vote "not guilty." Moreover, the architect-hero occupies the highest rung of the socioeconomic ladder of the film. His intelligence and compassion, king's English and dignified restraint, are contrasted with the crudeness of the others, who are blue-collar drudges or desk-jockey bureaucrats and thus, in the schematic logic of the story, bigoted, hotheaded, bored, and obscenely concerned with wrapping up jury duty in time for the opening pitch at Yankee Stadium.

Next on my schedule was *Strangers When We Meet.* An independent release of 1960, produced and directed by Richard Quine and based on a novel by Evan Hunter, this CinemaScope production was in its day the kind of "prestige" picture that confronted "adult" themes and sophisticated situations, keeping one eye on the censors and the other on the *Kinsey Report.* The drama revolves around the professional and personal dilemmas of a Los Angeles architect, played by Kirk Douglas, who resolves creative frustration through a plum commission from a rich client and marital *ennui* through an adulterous affair with a voluptuous neighbor, played by Kim Novak. Artistically clumsy but psychologically insightful, *Strangers* is one of the few films I know that explores architectural practice in any nuanced way. It benefits from a strong performance by Douglas, who, with his square jaw and crew-cut hair, looks more than a little like the late Paul Rudolph.

Adultery mixes with architecture in another 1960s picture, *Two for the Road* (1966), directed by Stanley Donen, written by Frederic Raphael, and starring Albert Finney and Audrey Hepburn. In this witty romantic comedy, the young Finney portrays a recognizable type of successful architect: good looking but not slickly handsome, eternally boyish, keen on cars and gadgets, incurably flirtatious. As the kind of woman such a man would marry, Hepburn is not only sleekly decorative but also intelligent and acerbic. The film follows the ups and downs of the couple's marriage over the course of a decade by focusing on their summer holidays, during which they travel through the French countryside, first hitchhiking, then driving a series of increasingly posh cars. More about *amour* than *travail*, *Two for the Road* is interested less in its hero's profession than in the swinging-sixties, *La Dolce Vita* lifestyle—pretty settings and pampered people—that it believes the profession makes possible.

The disaster genre that now threatens to annihilate the film industry had its cheesy beginnings in the 1970s and is represented here by *The Towering Inferno* (1974), produced by the impresario of the field, Irwin Allen, who had previously concocted *The Poseidon Adventure*. Given the stakes in more recent disaster marathons—usually on the order of galactic destruction—*Inferno* looks, in retrospect, like a baby's first step. Its animating crisis involves neither multinational madmen with nuclear contraband nor long-slumbering prehistoric creatures who wake up hungry, but a comparatively dinky building fire in a San Francisco high-rise—"the world's tallest building," needless to say—that threatens to asphyxiate and incinerate a large ensemble of actors, led by Paul Newman as a virile architect and Steve McQueen as an equally virile fire chief. (The cast also includes a young O.J. Simpson, fresh from the NFL, as a gentle security guard who spends the entire movie attempting to rescue a pussycat.) One can perhaps watch this awful film today as an unselfconscious artifact of seventies style (compared, say, to recent films like *The Ice Storm* or *Boogie Nights*, which labor mightily to recreate the decor and outfits of the era); but architects will note the ambivalence, even disapproval, with which the movie views its central prop, and indeed the profession of architecture itself.

Deathwish, also of 1974, was the first in a series of action pictures in which Charles Bronson plays a middle-class New York architect. After the brutal murder of his wife and the rape of his daughter by a trio of hoodlums (one of whom is played by the young and bizarrely miscast Jeff Goldblum), he becomes a heat-packing vigilante, obsessed with vengeance. Made during a period when New York was widely pictured as the inner circle of urban hell, *Deathwish* focuses mainly on the dangers that lurk around every dimly lit corner and hardly at all on the avenging architect's career; in any case, this designer wields not a Rapidograph but a revolver.

Two films of the 1980s feature architects as minor but attractive characters, the casting equivalent of the "extra man" at an old-fashioned dinner party. Woody Allen's 1987 *Hannah and Her Sisters*, for which the writer-director created one of his familiar ensembles of exceedingly privileged and verbal New Yorkers, includes Sam Waterston as an exceedingly presentable and eligible architect, whose bachelor status provokes among certain female characters all but Pavlovian quivers of flirtatious anticipation. As this worldly-wise film makes plain, an essential part of the man's charm, is his career, which appeals instinctively to the artistic-creative types who roam the lofts and supper clubs of Allen's Manhattan. Social cachet and career choice are explored more directly in the 1988 independent release *Mystic Pizza*. This well-observed and skillfully acted Cinderella story, directed by Donald Petrie, anatomizes class lines and loyalties in two communities on the Connecticut coast of Long Island Sound, here personified by working-class town girls (Lili Taylor, Annabeth Gish, and pre-*Pretty Woman* Julia Roberts) and their Social Register suitors. Among the latter is a thirtyish, Yale-educated architect, whose lifestyle accoutrements are clearly intended as class signals, circa the late eighties—khakis and horn rims, Volvo wagon and shingle-style house.

One film of the eighties features an architect as a major character. With *The Belly of an Architect* we move from the multiplex at the mall to the art-film screening room. This 1987 film is English writer-director Peter Greenaway's exegesis on many subjects, including architecture, art, success, failure, sex, reproduction, photography, food, indigestion, impotence, cancer, and death; these subjects are also worked into the various themes that bubble up from the turbid waters of the plot, including the death of the author, the decline of the West, the Old World versus the New, the renewal of life, the fascination of death. The biggest belly in the film belongs to Brian Dennehy, as a Chicago architect who travels to Rome with his wife to design an exhibition commemorating the work of his hero, Étienne-Louis Boullée. There the American discovers that New World size and enthusiasm are no match for the continental strategems and diabolical finesse of his Italian hosts. Like much of Greenaway's work—including *The Draughtsman's Contract*, *A Zed and Two Noughts*, and *The Cook, The Thief, His Wife, and Her Lover*—*Belly* is not a film that inspires neutral responses. Or even consistent ones: with its innocent Americans, exaggerated staging, and evocations of famous paintings by artists from Jacques-Louis David to Giorgio de Chirico, the film seemed on first viewing impossibly pretentious, as if a novella by Henry James had been crossed with the French New Wave and storyboarded by a garret of art students. By the second and third viewings, though, the art and sex and food and death began to seem like parts of a coherent whole. Like much of Greenaway's work, it deals squarely with the plight of the artist, offering a memorable portrait of the architect as a dying man.

More than half the movies I watched date from the past decade. If not a staple character—architecture entails far too little entertaining danger to attract much film financing—the architect has nonetheless appeared frequently in recent films. I suspect this is due to the growing cultural interest in design —an interest that some might applaud as evidence of increasing visual sophistication, and that sterner critics might decry as the latest outbreak of commodity fetishism and conspicuous consumption. In any case, an incidental pleasure of these films—and in a few cases the chief interest—is their pastiche of trendy design. In fact, some recent movies seem eerily like animated shelter magazines, as if the spirit of Martha Stewart, like a succubus of gentry-style good taste, had taken possession of the set dressers. The similarities are undoubtedly intentional, given the intensifying pressures of "product placement," on the one hand, and global corporate "synergy" on the other.

In *Intersection*, Richard Gere plays a successful Vancouver architect who spends much time in his two-seater silver Mercedes, speeding dreamily between the whackingly big and beautiful Dutch Colonial where he once lived with his estranged wife—played by Sharon Stone with blonde hauteur and perfect posture—and the ritzy places where he trysts with his brainy sexpot girlfriend—played by the red-haired Lolita Davidovich. The drama centers on this emotionally untidy triangle—a "bad design," as one character puts it. Directed by Mark Rydell and based on a French novel and film of the 1960s, this 1994 movie generated little attention in theaters. Yet *Intersection* is not so much a bad film—it is well acted and often sharply written—as a fatally dated one. This brand of domestic drama, once known as the "woman's picture," rarely attracts much notice in today's gadgety and aggressively populist movie culture. But *Intersection* is not helped by the ways in which it exploits the professional identity of its hero and the lifestyle he enjoys—by its almost obsessive evocation of an impossibly prettified milieu.

Fearless (1993), directed by Peter Weir, locates its hero in another urbane and fashionable Pacific city. Jeff Bridges plays a San Francisco architect who survives the devastating crash of a commercial airliner, only to discover that survival exacts its own unexpected penalties. He returns home and moves numbly through a life that seems once to have been fine and full, defined by a successful career and by marriage to a beautiful ballet instructor, played by Isabella Rossellini. Like *Intersection*, *Fearless* is mostly a domestic drama—although the crash-survivor theme gives it some primal edge—and it too can be watched for the artfulness of the interior *mise-en-scène*, in particular the funky-elegant North Beach townhouse in which the architect and his family live, which is filled with Asian antiques and iconic modern furniture.

The only crash in *Indecent Proposal* is financial. This 1993 movie is the work of Adrian Lyne, the British director whose résumé, which includes *Flashdance*, *91/2 Weeks*, *Fatal Attraction*, and a recent adaption of Vladimir Nabokov's *Lolita*, suggests a weakness for what might be called "hot-button" stories. Woody Harrelson plays a young up-and-coming Los Angeles architect whose career is derailed by the real estate recession of the early nineties; Demi Moore plays his wife.

To recoup their losses and finance their Santa Monica beachfront "dream house," which they believe will establish his reputation and reclaim their future as entitled Angelenos, architect and wife make a desperate trip to the casinos of Las Vegas. There destiny hands them not a winning way with roulette but a fateful encounter with a Trump-like plutocrat, played by Robert Redford. Itchy for the architect's shapely wife, and used to getting whatever he wants, the billionaire makes the titular proposal: one million dollars for one night with the wife. *Indecent Proposal* is unrelievedly offensive and extremely watchable. Architects in the mood to be alternately appalled and amused—or appalled and amused at the same time—will find its glimpses of the profession grimly fascinating.

After the West Coast *gestalt* of Vancouver, San Francisco, and Los Angeles—lifestyle meccas fringed with splendid landscapes—the fractious New York of *Jungle Fever* is a bracing change. Since this 1991 film was written and directed by Spike Lee, the sources of contention are racial, ethnic, sexual, cultural, and economic—almost anything that can make any of us seem, to those who think in such grooves, less individual than stereotypical. The main racial-ethnic-sexual drama hinges on an adulterous affair between a married, upper-middle-class African-American architect, an associate in a big firm, played by Wesley Snipes, and his young, single, Italian-American secretary, Brooklyn-bred and working class, played by Annabella Sciorra. As in most of his movies, Lee seems less interested in exploring and developing character and milieu than in scoring polemical points. In *Jungle Fever*, to accentuate what the filmmaker sees as his hero's tenuous racial solidarity, the architectural profession has been understood—or misunderstood—as a well-appointed nook of the corporate master class: the smug white partners of the firm, who wear suspenders and sip *vin blanc* at meetings, have apparently modeled themselves on the reptilian tycoon played by Michael Douglas in *Wall Street*.

Several romantic comedies of the nineties feature an architect as a leading character. *Sleepless in Seattle* (1993) stars Tom Hanks as a widowed architect who, as the movie starts, is in mourning for his wife but by the final fadeout has fallen in love with Meg Ryan, whom he has met courtesy of a personal ad placed on a lonely-hearts radio show by his enterprising son. That a young boy who has recently lost his mother would act as matchmaker for his father is only the silliest notion in this very silly film. *Sleepless* is the sort of celluloid fantasy in which careers are conceived wholly in decorative-lifestyle terms. The director Nora Ephron, like Woody Allen, obviously views architecture as an attractive occupation, one that leaves its practitioners with plenty of time for fretting about their love lives over midday lattés and that underwrites the stylishly appointed Houseboat Beautiful in which architect and son reside. *Housesitter* (1992) stars Steve Martin as a Boston architect who is mopily courting his proper girlfriend—played by Dana Delany in tartan skirts and starched shirts—but by the end of the film is happily cohabiting with a bohemian drifter, played by Goldie Hawn in spandex leggings and off-the-shoulder sweaters. This girlfriend switch is accomplished via plot machinations too contrived for easy description, but which pivot around a piece of architecture presented (as in *Blandings*) as the fulfillment of the national domestic dream: a clapboard neotraditional retread located in a woodsy New England suburb with picket-fence charm to burn.

One Fine Day (1996), the only film on my list with a female architect, puts Michelle Pfeiffer, as an associate in a big Manhattan firm, through some flustery, woman-in-distress paces as she juggles career and parenthood. As in *Sleepless in Seattle*, architecture has no organic relation to the plot of this inconsequential film; it merely signals "career woman" and allows the set decorator some extra fun. But to the extent that it shows its heroine at work, *One Fine Day* offers a telling misinterpretation of architectural culture: the office shown here looks not like a design firm but rather like the kind of granite-lined extravagance by which corporations trumpet their membership in the global business oligarchy, and its hierarchy is so rigid, with the partners working in vast secluded grandeur, that it suggests a latter-day court of the Sun King. The late-eighties comedy *Three Men and a Baby* (1987) puts Tom Selleck, as an associate in a big Manhattan firm, through some paces of his own as he juggles work and parenthood. Another silly film, *Three Men* is distinguished from most recent movies about architects by the outrageous—one could even say courageous—tacky taste of the three men's Central Park West condo, an eclectic bachelor's paradise of fey murals, postmodern doodads, Tiffany lamps, cactus plants, club chairs, pool table, and juke box.

The last comedy on my list owes its inclusion to what some readers might see as misplaced zeal for the subject. *The Brady Bunch Movie* (1995) is an example of a peculiar show business trend: the creative necrophilia that prompts moviemakers to pump plot steroids into ostensibly beloved TV shows and inflate them into feature films. But the concept of this painless and often funny movie actually works. Although the action (I use the term loosely) has been updated to the nineties, the Brady clan is frozen in their seventies heyday—the blonde girls, brunette boys, and their ageless, just-pals Mom and Dad are still living in their split-level with the vertical siding and earth-toned decor; they've still got shag haircuts and shag rugs; the kitchen is spic-and-span; and the L.A. sky is a Kodak moment. In the case of Mike Brady, paterfamilias of the bunch and professional architect, this plot conceit condemns him to period design purgatory and provides the movie with its chief visual joke: no matter what the commission, he designs exactly the same seventies ranchburger.

The River Wild and *Losing Isaiah*, both from the mid-1990s, have an unusual symmetry: each film features a powerful female character whose husband is an architect, and in each the husband is played by the same actor. In *The River Wild* (1994), David Strathairn plays a workaholic Boston architect married to an earth mother outdoorswoman, played with athletic gusto (and great muscular definition) by Meryl Streep; in *Losing Isaiah* (1995), Strathairn plays a hard-working Chicago architect married to an earth mother social worker, played by another strong blonde actress, Jessica Lange. In *Losing Isaiah* Strathairn has little to do. He is mainly on hand, as Lange's mostly loyal spouse, to support her struggle to adopt a black, crack-addicted baby. But his presence, as professional and breadwinner, underscores the movie's comparison between the spheres of comfortable, largely white privilege and bleak, mostly black poverty.

In *The River Wild*, however, the architect-husband is called upon to do a great deal. He is required to leave the frenzied but familiar setting of his office, where life is filled with horrendous but predictable pressure, and journey to the forbiddingly immeasurable landscape of a great northwestern national park, there to accompany his wife—once a champion rafter—and son on a trip down a dangerous winding river. But the worst danger they encounter comes not in the natural form of treacherous rapids but in the human form of a psychotic drifter, played by Kevin Bacon. No architecture in sight in this spirited and well-made adventure—and yet the architect's professional identity registers in telling details: for example, in how he fussily cleans and straightens his delicate wire-rimmed eyeglasses and in various ways exhibits the finicky discomfort of the displaced urbanite. But this emphasizes one of the dramatic lines of the script: the trial-by-wilderness of the architect—a consummate indoorsman—as he gradually loses his drafting-room pallor and reconnects with his manly instinctual self.

CELLULOID SILLINESS

From the postwar neocolonial that is the Blandings' exurban fantasy to the stylistic melange that is the dream house in *Indecent Proposal*; from the cantilevered-slab high-rise that represents high design in *The Fountainhead* to the code-flouting deathtrap that is *The Towering Inferno*; from Kirk Douglas passing love notes to Kim Novak across his drafting table to Wesley Snipes having sex with Annabella Sciorra across *his* drafting table; from the messianic imagery of *The Fountainhead* and *Fearless* to the Christ-like poses struck by Brian Dennehy in *The Belly of an Architect*; from Albert Finney in his Mercedes sports coupe in *Two for the Road* to Richard Gere in *his* Mercedes sports coupe in *Intersection*; from the ship-shape houseboat of the insomniac Seattle architect to the *outré* condo shared by the *Three Men and a Baby*; from the architect being cuckolded by the businessman who makes the *Indecent Proposal* to the big-bellied architect being cuckolded by a younger designer with a flatter stomach—what a hothouse is the world of film architects! Confronted with these fevered melodramas and *à la mode* comedies, architects in the audience might want to smile wanly, or maybe to giggle, to watch these movies for the unintentional humor provided by the tin-ear "architectural" dialog, the dated designs and *Architectural Digest* sets, and the over-the-top representations of professional life.

It is almost too easy to poke fun at the art-history-made-easy references with which diverse screenwriters attempt to account for their protagonists' professional identities. Particularly promiscuous use is made of the rhetoric and touchstones of modernism. The characters in *The Fountainhead*, for example, do not so much converse as declaim at one another: in this architectural universe, dialog has given way to sloganeering. But one can only wonder at what Louis Sullivan's reaction might have been had he heard the famous phrase from his *Kindergarten Chats* echoed in the deathbed lament of Roark's Sullivanesque mentor: "Skyscrapers! the greatest structure invented by man, yet they made them look like Greek temples, Gothic cathedrals....I told them! I told them that *the form of a building must follow its function*."

The screenplay of *Strangers When We Meet*, in contrast, is believable and sometimes perceptive when its architect-hero is talking with his wife, or his lover, or his client. But when architects meet with other architects, the speech becomes absurdly pretentious. One night over dinner, for example, the hero's erstwhile employer, the head of a big L.A. firm, tries to woo him back with this excessive compliment: "That schematic you did had more imagination than anything the Bauhaus ever came up with!" Even so featherweight a film as *Three Men and a Baby* cannot resist the allure of utopian lingo. "I design cities of the future," says the architect played by Selleck. "I ought to be able to diaper a baby." A throwaway puff of dialog, to be sure; but slyer interpretations are possible. Observing that the architect character cannot actually, at the moment, diaper a baby, the mordant viewer might construe the line as a devious—albeit unintentional—dig at the urbanistic ambitions of architects.

Indecent Proposal recycles one of the famously gnomic and inspirational architectural musings of the century: giving a slide lecture to a class of rapt students, the architect played by Harrelson quotes from Louis Kahn's "what a brick wants to be" homily. Generous viewers might see this "quotation" as evidence that the filmmakers undertook to research their subject. But the pasting of Kahn's words into the script feels forced, as awkward and self-conscious as *The Fountainhead*'s cribbing from Sullivan. And it feels slapdash too, given that the slides flashing by as the architect speaks show such nonexamples of brick construction as the Parthenon, Chartres cathedral, and Le Corbusier's chapel at Ronchamp.

Credulity is strained not only by pseudo-artsy dialog but by the aggressive posturing and bad behavior that in some of these movies pass for professional conduct. It is perhaps imprudent to single out any scene in *The Fountainhead* as particularly wrongheaded, since the entire movie can be watched, by the mirthfully inclined, as a warning of what can happen when High Seriousness trips the wire into High Parody. But one sequence is especially startling. At a project meeting, a group of clients and "collaborating" architects study a model of Howard Roark's latest *chef d'oeuvre*, a towers-in-the-park scheme for low-cost housing. The designers, kowtowing to the client, fail to comprehend the full-blown genius of Roark's building and declare their intentions "to give it a human touch" by adding "a few balconies" and "some kind of trimming over the entrance." This queasy scene peaks when one of the architects picks up a pointer and deliberately smashes Roark's pristine model. And this boorish act of design violence merely foreshadows the story's most famous, or infamous, act of artistic destruction: Roark's dynamiting of the housing project in response to the "human touches" inflicted upon *his* brainchild.

The central point of *The Fountainhead*, of course, is the supreme importance of the individual ego; both book and movie are paeans to the "I" against the "We." Several of these movies have what might be called "Fountainhead" moments. In *Intersection*, the Vancouver architect played by Richard Gere reinforces his high-design *bona fides* by throwing, in reaction to client demands, a wounded-*artiste* mini-tantrum on the construction site of a downtown commercial building.[1] His business-minded partner, played by Martin Landau, tries to calm him, reminding him that clients and their miserable existence are old facts of architectural life. "Even Michelangelo had to please the pope," he says. To which the architect-hero replies, in an observation that is undeniable but irrelevant, "The pope didn't ask for parking spaces." But the most flagrant ego-eruption happens in *Jungle Fever*, early on, when the African-American architect played by Snipes is denied by the firm's white owners the partnership he feels he deserves. His disappointment climaxes in a thumpingly histrionic display of temper, during which he careens through the office pointing at photos of projects on the walls and insisting upon his authorial status with shouts of "Mine! Mine!" Architecture is not, to say the least, a field that suffers from a shortage of ego, and this is perhaps the kind of cathartic conniption that many an under-recognized and overworked associate has fantasized. Still, such intemperate outbreaks bear little likeness to the usually quite suave and studied public self-presentations of architects.

Model-mauling and spleen-venting are not the only misreadings of design sociology committed by the movies. Arguably the most outlandish misapprehension is contained in *Indecent Proposal.* I refer to the catalytic decision of the drama: the futile attempt by the architect and his wife to win, in the corporate casinos of Fremont Street, the $50,000 they need to avoid foreclosure on their dream house. Although the architect's personal background is left vague—probably to encourage the greatest degree of audience identification—he is described in one scene as having the sort of credentials that prepare one for membership in the profession's elite: "first in his class" in architecture school and "recipient of the Prix de Rome." And indeed, without stumbling too blindly through the ill-marked precincts of the American class structure, one can make a good case that architecture is a profession dominated, historically and now, by the values and mentality of the upper middle class; and one can make the further case that the attitudes of this class toward the gambling mecca in the desert tend to range from snobbish dismissal ("not my kind of place") to intellectual connoisseurship (the Yale studio that resulted in *Learning from Las Vegas*) to *philosophe*-hipster appreciation (much reading of the Vegas-mad Jean Baudrillard, et al.). One could, I suspect, spend many years in architecture and never encounter a single architect for whom a Vegas windfall presents itself as an operative solution to a cashflow problem. But the filmmakers are clearly unaware that the architect in this story would venture to Las Vegas not to shoot the moon at roulette, but rather, in the tradition of one of the authors of *Learning from Las Vegas*, himself a recipient of the Prix de Rome, to *learn*.

DREAM REALITY

One could continue to spotlight such foolishness, lingering on the demographic gaffes and cultural *faux pas*, at the ways in which the movie portraits of architects are smudged, out of focus, artlessly composed, and carelessly cropped. But to do so would be to overlook a more interesting and illuminating aspect of these films. To catalog the obvious inaccuracies would be to miss the possibly discomfiting verisimilitudes, for in these films the everyday reality of life has made way for the superior reality of the dream. If the movies fail to achieve a facsimile of actual professional circumstances, they manage to picture something more potent: to capture the mystique of architecture, that heady mix of high-minded purpose and glamorous lifestyle, of the social weight of business and the romantic aura of art.

That architecture has a mystique seems inarguably obvious. Anyone who spends time in the field can easily observe that architecture possesses that ill-defined and diaphanous quality known as "social cachet," which makes people assume that architecture is an "interesting" thing to do and architects interesting people to know, and that the field commands what the French sociologist Pierre Bourdieu termed "cultural capital," a particular kind of power dependent upon specialized knowledge, institutional affiliations, educational credentials, and personal charisma.[2]

The edges of professional reality—the tensions between artistic ambition and professional service, the difficulty of establishing and maintaining a vital practice, the fierce competition at every level for the best positions and prize projects, the struggle for recognition, the inevitability of compromise, the frustration that stalks so many careers, the low salaries and chronic insecurity that make all the rest even harder to bear—are hard-lined and clear-cut. The contours of the mystique are comparatively soft-focus, teasingly indefinite, suggesting limitless possibility—and of course they shift from one generation to another. Earlier in the century the idealistic student or frustrated practitioner might have felt inspired, even ennobled, by the concept of architecture as heroic undertaking, by the image of the masterbuilder whose works enhance civilization and whose achievement was attended perhaps by an austere sort of prestige that did not much interfere with the pursuit of masterbuilding. More recently the designer might be said to pursue a different set of goals, heroic idealism having mutated into the type of artistic ambition that seeks not to save the world but to critique it, that sees the artist as outsider and transgressor, and whose fulfillment is accompanied by the kind of fame that necessitates, in this celebrity-saturated era, nonstop activity and public presence. On another level, the mystique of architecture in its various permutations has usually made room for the more worldly perquisites of artistic life such as freedom from bourgeois constraints—which can range from marital fidelity to workplace etiquette—and the wherewithal to fashion and maintain the kind of artsy-luxe, camera-ready domestic settings worthy of a creative personality.

That the dream-meisters of Hollywood, and even the more serious devotees of cinema art, should choose to disregard the exigent and adult realities of practice and fasten instead upon this seductive and adolescent mystique is hardly astonishing. One could even say that architecture, without this glamorous aura, would be an unlikely subject or setting for a motion picture. The highs and lows that mark the typically intellectual and sedentary lives of designers—the creative breakthrough at the board or on the screen, the tussles with contractors and clients—do not percolate with dramatic intensity, and they lack the obvious political and social resonances, not to mention the life-and-death dealings, of courtroom battles, medical heroics, police sleuthwork, or even mobster musclefests. But the architect's mystique does offer filmmakers the chance to present wish-fulfillment fantasies in which charismatic and free-spirited personalities occupy a rarefied zone of high artistic creativity and enviable creature comfort.

ARCHITECT AGONISTES

Central to the mystique of architecture—in life and in the movies—is the idea of the architect as a person of marked creativity, creativity so strong it can seem a primal or religious force, allowing the architect to envision what does not yet exist, and so fundamental to his identity that others cannot help but acknowledge it, with various degrees of admiration, awe, envy, and fear.[3] Central to the popularization of this mystique—architect as artistic messiah—is *The Fountainhead.* Ayn Rand's novel-cum-treatise has proven remarkably durable: a fountainhead that will not be stoppered. The story continues to fascinate, although now, more than half a century since the book's publication and the film's release, the fascination is triple-distilled: not so much with the story itself, or even with its astonishing success, but rather with its persistence as a cultural presence.

And persist it does. A journey to the World Wide Web makes that apparent, for if you type in the keywords "Ayn Rand," you find yourself plunged into the vast, branching cybercatacombs of Randiana; an Infoseek search one afternoon retrieved the astounding bounty of 42,884,048 hits.[4] A good deal of the buzzing in this digital hive concerns the ideas that Rand labeled "Objectivism," which entail the glorification of individualism, denunciation of collectivism, and, following from these, passionate advocacy of *laissez-faire* capitalism.[5] En masse these Internet postings suggest an impressively extensive network, with much information on the Ayn Rand Institute in Southern California and on how to start your own club or campus chapter, lists of suggested reading, an entry form for *The Fountainhead* Essay Contest for high schoolers, and tributes from enraptured readers of *The Fountainhead.*

I mention all this because the temptation to dismiss *The Fountainhead* as a mossy midcentury relic, a literary potboiler by an untalented zealot, is very strong, especially among the academic and cultural elites, including architects. In Boston in 1992 I attended an odd, fitful public discussion, a panel on *The Fountainhead* in which a group of eminent and emeriti architects and historians, including Vincent Scully, pondered the book and its influence. The tone of the evening was intelligent, informed, inevitably somewhat ironic. The speakers puzzled over the enormous success of a cultural artifact that seemed to them so obviously third-rate, so exaggerated in its effects, so demonstrably unrealistic in its portrait of architecture. But they seemed exasperated, too, at the very fact of the discussion, as if they wished, once and for all, through some combination of piercing critique and devastating dismissal, to put the matter to rest, to file the story in some attic trunk or basement archive along with other unmourned mementos of middlebrow culture. Their exasperation seems to me highly understandable. I read the book in my twenties, much too late in life to surrender to its Manichean dualities, its chest-thumping histrionics, its vision of sex as a matter of cruel denial and even crueler partaking. This sprawling tale of the twenties and thirties seemed an overripe example of an earlier style of American patriotism, an idiosyncratic reaction on the part of a Russian Jewish émigré to the bootstrap rhetoric of prewar socialism—a literary soapbox upon which Ayn Rand, born Aline Rosenbaum in czarist St. Petersburg, could argue her pro-capitalist theories.

Its paean to free markets notwithstanding, *The Fountainhead* is a vividly imagined and painstaking detailed panorama of an early-twentieth-century architectural world. The story chronicles the struggles of Howard Roark, architect of genius, supreme individualist indifferent to the ideas or opinions of others, against a host of cultural and political forces that would have him compromise and conform. Ranged against Roark are a Hearst-like publishing tycoon; a megalomaniacal architecture critic and self-proclaimed spokesman for the common man (modeled partly on Lewis Mumford); and almost the entire architectural establishment, collectively portrayed as weak-willed, obsequious to clients, lacking ideas and convictions, and thus bobbing pathetically on the waves of fashion and success. But ultimately these forces prove to be not great mountainous obstacles but mere hilly impediments to Roark's triumph: testing grounds, in a sense, for his genius.

Rand's story did much to popularize the figure of the twentieth-century architectural genius and the mystique of the embattled master builder, but it cannot claim to have invented either the figure or the mystique. Although the author began her project with no special passion or knowledge about architecture—she chose the field because it straddled art and commerce and thus implied the wide applicability of her political theories—the choice was clever. For a storyteller and would-be philosopher who views the world as a battlefield upon which opposing ideologies compete, and all human endeavor as furthering one or another ideology, the architectural culture of the day, with its revolutionary rhetoric, its sense of mission, its teleological view of progress, must have seemed made to order—a fertile field for a writer wishing to seed a story of the conflict between a forward-looking genius and the entrenched reactionaries of his time. The ideas that inspired and informed architects in the decades between the world wars—architecture as a vital activity upon which the very salvation of civilization might depend; the need to create a new architecture for the new century and its unprecedented technology; the belief that this architecture would embody truths unavailable to older styles and represent a possibly final stage of architectural progress—are all stitched into the vast fabric of *The Fountainhead.* Also woven into the crazy quilt of the novel are similarities to the remarkable life of Frank Lloyd Wright. Rand always denied that her hero was modeled upon Wright, but the denial seems disingenuous. Although Rand researched her book by working as a clerk in the New York office of Ely Jacques Kahn, during the years of her writing Wright was the most famous architect in the country, fully ensconced upon the triumphant last stage of his singular career and his reign as the great American architectural patriarch. His genius was widely proclaimed, not least by the genius himself.[6] In *The Fountainhead* these powerful tendencies of the time—the revolutionary fervor, the genius worship—are, to be sure, wildly distorted. But the very distortions, like the jagged views reflected by a cracked mirror, contain disconcerting shards of truth.

And what of the movie? Warner Brothers lavished upon the production the resources usually allocated to serious dramas based upon bestsellers: although miscast and past his peak, Gary Cooper was, in the late 1940s, a screen icon identified with the portrayals of such legendary Americans as Sergeant York and Lou Gehrig; the director, King Vidor, had been a respected filmmaker since the silent era; the sets (by Edward Carrere) were extravagant and bizarre, the script was by Rand herself.[7] Nonetheless, the movie was neither a popular nor critical success; even those involved in its making, including Rand, were dissatisfied. And with reason: the compression of the 754-page novel into a 114-minute film squeezed out not only the political and architectural philosophizing but also much of the character development. What remains on-screen is a brooding, noir-like melodrama in which the leading players, jaws clenched and brows furrowed, move stagily through settings that range from robber-baronial excess to sub-Miesian simplicity, arguing vaguely about architecture while playing an odd switch-partners sexual game.

Also remaining is the dramatization of Roark's superiority—the exaltation of the architect as a privileged visionary, a messianic figure. With much of the plot pruned away, both script and direction, words and images, are devoted to the glorification of Howard Roark. The film begins with a series of vignettes in which Roark is discouraged from pursuing his vision by teachers, friends, colleagues. Being a genius, however, he has no choice. Although he could achieve worldly success by designing what one character calls the "great big marble bromides" that constitute fashionable architecture, Roark cannot help creating austere, minimalist, "modern" structures. And he cannot help creating masterpieces; indeed, one of the more extraordinary assumptions of *The Fountainhead* is that genius does not require the lengthy, often agonizing realization of potential but simply exists, fully formed, in certain prodigies and all their works. In scene after scene, Roark moves among the other characters, ramrod straight, coolly imperturbable, effortlessly superior, like a secular savior bearing the blueprints for the New Jerusalem. Cooper's strong physical presence—his lean body and simple handsomeness—emphasizes this superiority. Dressed in a plain suit or, more often, in physique-flattering shirtsleeves, Cooper/Roark is too confident and good-looking even to need the crutch of costume; this is in pointed contrast to his adversaries—to the publisher Gail Wynand (Raymond Massey), who dons a yachtsman's jacket and cap when sailing, and to the critic Ellsworth Toohey (Robert Douglas), who is encumbered by a fussy formal suit that appears to date from the teens and accentuates the writer's grandiose oddity.

The film retains as well the novel's vision of architecture as an utterly autonomous art. *The Fountainhead* confronts moviegoers with an unrelenting, almost merciless vision of artistic confidence. Roark is superior not only to the publisher and critic who attempt to damage his career but also to the clients who seek his designs. "I don't build in order to have clients," he declares. "I have clients in order to build." In the story's famous climactic action, Roark raises the stakes even higher, arrogating to himself the godlike powers of creation and destruction: when his housing project design is altered by others, he dynamites the building, leveling it to the ground. Speaking in his own defense at the trial that follows, Roark articulates his credo and wins his freedom with this dumbfounding speech: "The creator stands on his own judgment. The parasite follows the opinions of others.... The creator's concern is the conquest of nature. The parasite's concern is the conquest of man.... I designed Cortlandt. I made it possible. I destroyed it. I agreed to design it for the purpose of seeing it built as I wish." The finale of the movie completes the canonization. Roark stands atop the steel frame of his latest, greatest project, "the world's tallest building." He is alone, arms akimbo, the bandana around his neck ruffling in the wind. We watch from the point of view of his adoring new bride, who rides the open-sided construction elevator higher and higher, past all the other buildings in the city; as she ascends, the figure of Roark grows taller and taller, finally filling the screen, framed only by the sky: a colossus in khakis.

Strangers When We Meet bears little superficial resemblance to *The Fountainhead*. Photographed in high-contrast black and white, the latter is set in an urbane prewar Manhattan, where every interior offers vistas of jostling skyscrapers, newsboys hawk the latest edition to throngs of distracted passers-by, and dinner is served at eight to jacketed men and bejewelled women. *Strangers* locates the architect in Los Angeles, circa 1960. Here the *Sturm und Drang* of visionary design is bleached out by the California sun, muted by the prosperity of an easygoing place, where comfortable homes open onto year-round patios, where barbecues begin and end with pitchers of martinis, where every driveway sports a recent model from Detroit.

The architect-hero played by Kirk Douglas is a sole practitioner named Larry Coe. He lives with his pretty wife and young sons in the kind of sprawling, one-story house that *Sunset* magazine used to illustrate the postwar good life in the Golden State. Unlike the great arcs of plot in which the characters of *The Fountainhead* are swept up, the drama of *Strangers* is simple: Larry is restless. His marriage is comfortable but not passionate; his practice pays the bills but offers little artistic challenge. In the opening scenes, this midlife vacuum is filled by a dream commission—a house in the Bel Air hills for a rich writer—and a daydream blonde. For the rest of the film, Larry juggles work and women. Will he choose his dark slender wife or fair zaftig lover? Will he seize the creative moment and design a residential masterpiece?

It is in response to this last question that *Strangers* makes its contribution to the mystique of the architect as creative messiah. In Douglas's focused performance, Coe is intelligent and attractive, affable but not weak, ambitious but not pretentious, charming but not slick—a very un-Roarkian figure. And yet subtly but surely, Larry is shown to be special. In the placid, pre-sixties America pictured here, the America of the organization man and the lonely crowd, the architect-hero is animated by his powerful sense of vocation and his instinctive independence. In contrast to the other breadwinners who slouch through the film—in contrast, say, to the husband of his paramour, who droops home after work and is all but absorbed into the nubby depths of his wing chair—Larry is inspired by passion for his work. He possesses the discipline not only to be self-employed but also to work late into the night in his home studio, filling the ashtray with half-smoked cigarettes and the wastebasket with half-rendered plans. "I've got things I want to *state* as an architect," he says early on to his wife. "If I don't get them out, I'll burst."

But *Strangers* is not content simply to show the architect fulfilled by work; the film portrays him also as a charismatic personality whose creativity exerts a powerful, life-transforming influence on others. This ability is dramatized through Larry's relationship with his client, Roger Altar, the wealthy author. As played by Ernie Kovacs, Roger is a period hipster, a Rat-Pack, make-mine-a-double kind of guy; he is also a financially successful author who writes to please his publisher, not himself, and who produces potboilers he disdains, rather than the serious fiction he fears to attempt. In a series of scenes tracing their volatile relationship, the writer is by turns admiring and defensive, alternately attracted and threatened by the architect's example of devotion to craft. "Are you one of those temperamental artists?" Roger asks Larry at their first meeting, over breakfast in a downtown businessman's joint. "If you want to call it that. . . . Designing a house for somebody is a very personal thing," Larry replies evasively. Later, at his bachelor-lair apartment, over drinks poured by his baby-doll girlfriend, Roger frets over the progress of the design. "I showed your sketches to some of my friends," he says. "They said I'd have to be *nuts* to live in a house like that." Moved to anger, Larry is ready to roll up the drawings and pack it in, but he stops and looks hard at Roger. "We both start with the same thing: a blank sheet of paper," he says slowly. "But every time I play it safe I come up empty.... You can't try to please them all. What would happen if you broke loose? To hell with the critics!" To hell and back, as it happens; by the end of the picture, the writer has both a new home and a renewed artistic life. Not only has Larry designed for Roger a hilltop villa that pleases them both and is Larry's artistic "breakthrough," but also, in a marathon surge of creative juices, Roger has produced a critically celebrated novel.

The theme of architect-as-messiah rumbles like a rich deadly meal through *The Belly of an Architect*, too. One of many themes, in fact; as fans of the idiosyncratic work of director Peter Greenaway know, this movie, like most in his *oeuvre*, lays out a banquet of motifs. About Greenaway, the English film historians Jonathan Hacker and David Price have written, "He is a feast for any semiologist who might like to decode and deconstruct films."[8] Decoding and deconstructing *The Belly of an Architect* might keep a roomful of semiologists feasting for years. In a description Greenaway seems to relish, the film critic Pauline Kael has called the writer-director a "cultural omnivore who eats with his mouth open."[9] And *Belly* is easily one of his more omnivorous works, gnawing away on diverse themes and variations, often presented in opposition: virility and impotence, artistic productivity and creative sterility, mechanical reproduction and human childbirth, architecture and nature, sex and death, America and Europe, Enlightenment rationality and modern totalitarianism, panoptic spaces and private quarters.

These intellectually *au courant* subjects are presented in highly didactic style. The action is ritualized and the camera is static, aloof from the actors, discouraging any sentimental identification with the characters. But few of these, except the lead, would inspire much of that anyway. *Belly* records the decline and fall of an American architect, Stourley Kracklite, who has been invited to Rome by an ill-defined Italian cultural consortium to design an exhibition of the work of Boullée. As the film opens, the architect and his wife are making love on the train speeding them to Rome. The drama unfolds over the next nine months, during which the architect's wife carries to term the child conceived on the train, and during which the architect discovers that his Italian hosts are embezzling funds from the exhibition and plotting to remove him from the project, that his wife is betraying him with one of the scheming Italians, and that he is dying of stomach cancer.

In *The Belly of an Architect*, the messiah trope is both generalized and personal: suffused throughout the film and attached to the character of Kracklite. *Belly* is soaked to its skin with an atmosphere of art-for-art's sake. The world presented here begins and ends with architecture, with the monuments of the vanished ancient empire, of the Church, of fascism, all heavy with history and meaning. Kracklite and his wife are taken to dinner the night they arrive at a restaurant near the Pantheon. "Good architecture should always be applauded," says one of the Italians, upon which the dozen or so diners, whose expressions betray only the barest hint that they are doing something inherently ridiculous, give the ancient stone temple a rousing ovation. (Scenes like this go far to explain why the characters in Greenaway's films seem like pawns of the director's game and so rarely spring to complex life.)

When his Roman sojourn turns sour, which is almost right away, Kracklite seeks solace in artistic gods, figures whom he idolizes but with whom he also identifies. He develops a morbid identification with Caesar Augustus, first emperor and one of the great architectural patrons of Rome. Learning that Augustus was possibly poisoned by his wife, Livia, Kracklite starts to suspect that his own wife, Louisa, is poisoning him, and begins to suffer chronic stomach ache and indigestion. One afternoon he visits the ruined mausoleum of Augustus—a place of keen interest to Mussolini as well, who once planned to hold rallies on the site—and that night, working late and alone, he takes a postcard, a photograph of a marble statue of Augustus, and photocopies the image, enlarging it to human scale and placing the image of Augustus's muscular torso over his own round belly: the architect who would be emperor. But the chief architectural deity (and object of grandiose identification) in Kracklite's personal pantheon is Boullée. The American architect is obsessed with the eighteenth-century French master—an artist with his own strong sense of the sublimity of art, and one who also preferred Roman architecture over Greek—and, as his marriage curdles and work fails and health worsens, Kracklite pours his thoughts not into a journal but into a series of postcards to the French architect. These postcards are a form of personal journal, for writing to the long-dead Boullée is Kracklite's way of addressing himself, and the degree to which he cannot tell himself apart from his hero underscores his mental disintegration. And finally, at the very end of this film set in the seat of western Christendom, in a scene that suggests that Greenaway has the courage of his convictions and then some, the messiah imagery becomes almost crudely obvious. As the Boullée exhibition opens, and as Louisa gives birth to their child, Kracklite ascends to the upper floors of the exhibition space and, spreading his arms like Christ upon the cross, flings himself out the window and falls to his death.

MEN OF STEEL

The mystique of the movie architect is manifest not merely in studio but in bed as well; on celluloid, at least, artistic power is linked intimately with sexual potency. The movies would not be the movies, after all, were they not fixated upon what a character in one of Preston Sturges's comedies calls "Topic A." Daring achievements at the drafting board are one thing, but a kiss is still a kiss.

The Fountainhead is galvanized—almost short-circuited—by an erotic current. Working in those long-gone days of production codes, when movie kisses were timed (seven seconds maximum) and the screen bedrooms of even married couples were furnished with twin beds, the makers of *The Fountainhead* display a palpable fondness for the architectural set pieces and construction paraphernalia, the high-rise buildings and power tools, that can be pressed into symbolic service. The central romantic drama of the film is the sexual duel between Howard Roark and the story's equally uncompromising heroine, the unhappy heiress Dominique Francon, played with an angular frenzy and Midwestern accent by the young Patricia Neal. The early stages of their affair are rife with strategic sublimation. While staying at her family's estate in Connecticut, Dominique first

Howard Roark (Gary Cooper) drills while Dominique Francon (Patricia Neal) looks on amorously in *The Fountainhead* (1949).

glimpses Roark in an appropriately rugged setting: the stone quarry owned by her family where the architect, his career stalled, is working as a day laborer. Striding through the quarry in a billowy dress—looking rather like a model in a *Vogue* shoot—Dominique spots Roark, and she (and the camera) linger on his muscular, sweaty forearms as he steadies his power drill as it penetrates the earth. Later that day, Dominique paces around the neorococo rooms of her mansion, shuddering as she hears the distant blasting from the quarry. Soon she finesses an introduction, and she and Roark are exchanging cryptic remarks about marble, about "pressure" and its "consequences," which, says Roark, include "infiltration." Thus is set up the infamous encounter in which these consequences are realized, when Roark breaks through the French doors of Dominique's bedroom and rapes her. Contemporary filmmakers would, of course, do full justice to the sexual content and psychopathology of this "love scene" (which the prefeminist Rand described as "rape by engraved invitation")[10]; here the camera backs discreetly away as Patricia Neal struggles prettily and Gary Cooper envelops her in his tall body.

The power drill he operates, the high-rising buildings he designs—these are the unsubtle props with which the movie suggests not only Roark's extra-duty virility but also its inextricable connection to his professional identity. Roark drills into the quarry walls, wresting from the earth its raw material; Dominique, Roark's *überfraulein* soulmate, watches and falls passionately in love. Roark conceives the structures in which the stone will be used, and Dominique rides an open elevator, in an ecstasy of anticipation, to join her new husband atop the steel frame of his towering creation. In *The Fountainhead*, artistic creativity and sexual power are practically the same thing: great lovers make great buildings.

With *Strangers When We Meet,* we are returned to the less rarefied milieu of a sea-level subdivision where characters do not hurtle through their lives as if propelled by superhuman drives and desires. The men and women who inhabit *Strangers'* tidy, suburbanizing Los Angeles are recognizable human beings. But here too the architect-hero is shown to possess not only design talent but high sexual desirability, and here too architecture and sex are shown to be inseparably entangled.

Strangers offers the architect two cures for the doldrums in which he languishes, and he grasps them both. One is the commission from the writer. The other, more potent elixir strolls into Larry's life in high heels and red sweater, dangly earrings and upswept hair. She is Maggie Gault, new to the neighborhood, played by the breathy-voiced Kim Novak; she and Larry meet through their young sons, who are friends. Like many illicit lovers, Larry and Maggie begin their affair under the enabling delusion that they too are "friends." The start of their liaison, in terms of its connection to architecture, is telling: their first "just friends" date occurs one morning when Larry sees Maggie at the school bus stop and invites her to Bel Air to help him measure the site of the writer's future house. Scrambling around the scrubby hill, Larry instructs Maggie where to walk with her end of a tape measure, and Maggie totters obligingly in her heels, happy to be outside in the hot sun with this handsome man, helping him with his interesting work. Thus is one of the more mundane chores in the architectural repertoire transformed into the first fluttery stages of a seduction. Which is precisely the point: Larry and Maggie's affair is conducted in parallel to Larry's architectural work. The ripening of their relationship can even be compared to the stages of a design project. There is the predesign phase, the morning on the hill where they take not just the measure of the site but, like all potential lovers, the measure of each other. Next is the schematic phase, where they drive up the coast to Malibu for a clandestine rendezvous at a beach shack called the Albatross. Maggie is nervous, Larry direct. "I want to make love to you," he says. The success of this first encounter is conveyed by the film's most flagrant sex-and-architecture montage, a kind of visual wink: the scene fades as Larry and Maggie kiss in the dark Malibu night, and then jumps quickly to the next morning at the construction site, where the bulldozers are busily moving the earth and hoses are spraying the ground.

Next is the design development, during which afternoons at the Albatross become a regular event. Scenes of Larry at his drafting table, sketching in a frenzy of inspiration, alternate with vignettes of Larry and Maggie scampering on the beach, of Larry caressing Maggie's back, her black dress unzipped. Then, as the exciting potential of design gives way to the fixed decisions of construction, the lovers realize they must confront the consequences of their affair: is it a frisky fling or a sturdier part of their lives, necessitating divorce and other messiness? The final scenes emphasize the symmetry of work and love. The denouement of the affair occurs at the new house; walking from room to room, like a bride and groom come home, the lovers know that the end of the project is the end of the affair. But the movie hints that while an episode is over, a pattern may have begun. As Maggie drives away, she exchanges a quick but marked glance with the worker operating the gate. As for Larry, who knows? He plans to move with his family to Hawaii to accept the job of designing a new city, offered by the colleague who compared his work favorably with the entire legacy of the Bauhaus. Will Larry stick close to home or will he require, to design a city, the kind of extracurricular stimulation that made his pencil move so well on the design of the house? In either case, *Strangers* has left little doubt about the link between creativity and virility, between his labors as an architect and his performance as a lover.

Most of the movies I watched elaborate, to varying degrees, this link between high creativity and high libido: the idea that the power to create the great structures of the earth is accompanied by or even dependent upon the power to create in more fundamental ways. Like *Strangers When We Meet*, *Intersection* sets up a romantic triangle, with the alpha-male architect played by Gere as the object of desire for two women: his beautiful, repressed wife and his beautiful, libidinous girlfriend. Unlike *Strangers*, this film is explicit about the hero's amatory prowess: in the upfront nineties, suggestive montage has made way for sex-manual *mise-en-scène*. *Intersection* begins with a fast series of gauzy shots of the architect and his girlfriend making passionate love. In the same scene, moreover, it illustrates the all but seamless ties between art and *amour*: afterward, as his lover sleeps, the architect works on a model of his latest project. Thus is he established as the kind of nonstop professional who takes his work with him *wherever* he goes and whose postcoital afterglow finds its best release in building design. "What are you working on?" the girlfriend purrs from the bed. "The fenestration," the architect replies, staring intently at the model: fornication is clearly good preparation for fenestration. Architecture and sex have their moment together in *Indecent Proposal*, too. In one of the film's domestic tableaux, the architect played by Harrelson sits on the floor of the bathroom, while the wife played by Moore lies on the floor with her head in his lap; with his right hand the architect sketches on trace paper taped to the wall, while his left hand is lost in the folds of his wife's shirt. That this arrangement might prove a distraction to design seems not to have occurred to the fabricators of this movie. The designer's gaze remains fixed upon his drawing, his wife's *deshabille* an encouragement to creativity: from her breast to his right brain.

In a couple of these movies, the sexiness of the architect is communicated through a sex-in-the-studio scene. In *Jungle Fever*, the affair between the married black architect and his white secretary begins one night when both work late. The studio is dark except for their Luxo-lit corner, the view of Manhattan is glittery and dramatic; their gazes lock and soon they are entwined upon the drafting table. Never mind that the entire scene hinges on various improbabilities: that the secretary would be working late (she would have been on the rush-hour subway to Bensonhurst) and that an architect would have sex on top of his drawings (he would at least have worried about protection for his work). Improbable or not, the telegenic potential of studio sex was irresistible to Spike Lee, and the scene is artfully shot and sexually charged. In *The Towering Inferno* the segue from design to desire is worked literally into the plan of the architect's office. The movie establishes early on that the architect played by Paul Newman is a man among men. As the film opens, he is flying over San Francisco in a helicopter (entering the city from the heavens: a minor messiah moment). He wears those mid-seventies sartorial signals of rangy, free-spirited manhood: aviator glasses and safari jacket. He is returning from an extended retreat in some manhood-testing western wilderness. "They say he used to wrestle grizzlies in Montana," says one female character. Clued in to his high-testosterone idea of recreation, we are not surprised to see what awaits the architect-hero in his office, located in the soon-to-be-infernal tower. Beyond the triple-height work space is a bedroom suite and within the bedroom, in a negligée, is his eager girlfriend, played by Faye Dunaway. This sequence—swooping helicopter to midday rendezvous—can be pooh-poohed as one of those Playboy-mansion fantasies in which the movies like to indulge; but it can also be viewed, especially the studio-seraglio setup, as another example of how the movies emphasize the connections between the architect's professional and personal dimensions.

In some films, the superior masculinity of the architect-hero—highly sexed, free-spirited, inner-directed—is brought into ruddy relief by the presence of less-gifted males. In *Two for the Road* this study in flattering comparison is comically exaggerated. As the architect, Finney is witty and rakish; as his wife, Hepburn is smart and elegant; their relationship is portrayed as a love affair with a marriage license, equal parts love and lust, witty talk and sexy fun. They are among life's lucky few, but, to drive home the point, in the middle of the picture, another couple joins them on one of their summer trips through France. As played by William Daniels, who went on to play a series of killjoys, from dour John Adams in *1776* to the splenetic doctor in the TV show *St. Elsewhere*, the husband proves to be a textbook collection of fidgets, one of those road worriers whose ability to wreck a trip—dithering endlessly about the schedule, the luggage, the mileage, the receipt and how to split it—is unerring. And just to turn the screw even tighter, the filmmakers have given him the sort of occupation that, especially in the sixties, suggested nothing so much as head-banging, team-playing boredom: he is an *efficiency* expert. (Talk about the anti-architect!) *Fearless*, too, exploits professional stereotypes in order to cast a glow around its hero. The architect played by Jeff Bridges, who has survived a plane crash, spends much of the movie absorbing the psychological blows of survivor guilt and free-floating terror; having undergone a terrifying, to-the-brink-and-back experience, he is struggling manfully to come to grips with it. In this effort he is the reluctant target of various oversolicitous postdisaster professionals. Among the least sensitive are his lawyer (played by Tom Hulce), whose behavior suggests a catalog of shyster tics; confronted with the architect's spiritual agony, he blinks and proceeds to calculate the biggest possible settlement from the airline. Only slightly better is the psychiatrist (played by John Turturro) hired by the airline to counsel the survivors, an earnest clinician who cherishes what seems to be a naïve faith in the efficacy of talk therapy. Both the snaky lawyer, for whom the only real damage is a compensable damage, and the teddy-bear doctor, who knows everything about "post-traumatic stress disorder" except what it feels like to have it, serve to magnify, through negative comparison, the depth and complexity of the architect-hero.

FAREWELL, UTOPIA

The mystique I have been describing—the image of the architect as artistic messiah and superpotent creator—can be more or less placed in time. The movie architects who embody this dream-reality most fully date from the midcentury and just after: Howard Roark, of course; but also Larry Coe in *Strangers When We Meet*; even the architect played by Finney in *Two for the Road*, with his uncomplicated sense of the cultural importance of his work. The designer-as-savior figure shows up here and there, in later films. It appears in *Fearless*, when the architect becomes known as the "good samaritan" after helping other passengers escape the crashed plane, and when, back in San Francisco, convinced he is invincible, he turns daily life into a test of this power by walking through traffic, eating foods to which he is allergic, driving his car into a wall. It steals quietly into *Intersection*, whose architect is conceived in the high modernist mold and displays little postmodern defensive distance from this heroic ideal. But these are exceptions. As early as the seventies, the movie image of the architect as heroic artist began to show signs of tarnishing: it began to devolve, on the one hand, into eye-candy displays of dishy lifestyles, and, on the other, to darken into the more troubling vision of the architect as a modern Icarus, the artist-hero who reached too high, the savior without portfolio.

This last and more interesting transformation can be observed in three dissimilar films. Despite its reflexive presentation of the architect as grizzly-wrestling tower builder, *The Towering Inferno* is shot through with deep suspicion about modern architecture and its achievements. The movie is highly ambivalent about its main prop, the Portman-style high-rise with its cluster of curtain-walled shafts, its "sky" elevator and plaza with *de rigueur* fountain. On the one hand, the tower is touted as a magnificent feat, its 138 floors accommodating offices that satisfy every need (including the architect's studio with adjacent love-nest), *pieds-à-terre* for the rich, and a ficus-filled penthouse-nightclub from which revelers can look down on the lesser towers (and humbler citizens) of San Francisco. On the other hand, the whole point of the movie is to watch this heaven-reaching artifact of architectural hubris become an inferno—an architect-designed hell. Although the movie stops short of blaming the architect (played by Paul Newman, after all) and locates the cause of the fire in the dastardly practices of a building contractor (played by Richard Chamberlain, a dimmer star), the screenplay is extremely disapproving of the building itself and of the very *concept* of the high rise. In fact, *Inferno*, which could be subtitled "The Tall Building Regulatorily Reconsidered," painstakingly dramatizes the heroics of the San Francisco Fire Department, to which, moreover, it is dedicated. The architect somewhat redeems the honor of his profession by participating in several derring-do rescue operations, but at the end he is chastened by the fire chief. "We were lucky tonight—body count's less than two hundred," says the tired firefighter, played by McQueen. "You know, one of these days they're gonna kill ten thousand in one of these firetraps. I'm gonna keep eating smoke and bringing out bodies, 'til somebody asks us how to build 'em." Taking his medicine like a man, the architect says, "Okay, I'm asking." The chief smiles ruefully: "You know where to reach me, architect." And as the movie ends Newman's character slumps on the low steps of the plaza, ambulances swarming, body bags piling up, his safari jacket dirty, his great creation a smoking ruin: the architect has plummeted a hard long way from the sky-framed Howard Roark, standing tall on *his* world's tallest building.

In *The Belly of an Architect*, architecture and architects suffer even greater indignities. Having offered up the vision of architecture as the most monumental of the arts, deserving of reverence, and having established the heroic ambitions and mighty desires of its hero, the film then charts his downward trajectory. The architect's last effective act occurs, as it happens, in the first minutes of the movie, in the opening scene in which Kracklite and his wife make love on the train and conceive a child. As the sad story progresses, Kracklite endures multiple humiliations and losses. He is cuckolded by his pregnant wife who, while castigating her husband for his girth and gluttony, begins an open liaison with the slender, good-looking Italian architect who is directing the Boullée exhibition. At one point Kracklite inflicts upon himself the humiliation of watching the lovers through a keyhole, and sees them not only making love but using one of the models from his Boullée exhibition (the spiral tower) as a prop in a lewd sex pantomime. He is betrayed by his Italian colleagues, who since his arrival have been plotting to remove him from the exhibition and surveilling his every action, monitoring his movements as if he were an overfed American rat running through their Roman maze. And he is told by a doctor that he has a fatal cancer in his stomach.

From the very start of the film, his potency as an architect is questioned. Kracklite is described scornfully by his wife as having built "six and a half buildings, just like Boullée," and we learn that one of the buildings was their own house, which Louisa's father funded. "Two marble cubes and a brick sphere on stilts," says Louisa. "Boullée would have loved it." His fixation on the French architect, the film hints, is self-serving—an excuse by which an architect with a rich father-in-law but without ideas can justify his own lack of production. But Greenaway does not allow Kracklite to imagine that the power of his legacy will rival that of his idol. Again, Louisa supplies the *coup de grâce*: "Do you think anyone will mount an exhibition of *your* work two hundred years after you're dead?" she teases. The content of Boullée's legacy is criticized as well, when one of the Italians raises the uncomfortable issue of Boullée's appeal to the Nazis, noting how his architecture, unbuilt in its day, inspired the short-lived monuments of Albert Speer. Indeed, the placing of Boullée upon an artistic pedestal is telling: the architectural spirit who hovers over this film, whose work is being honored with an exhibition, is an architect whose built legacy comprises half a dozen buildings, whose fame rests upon the design of buildings not only unbuilt but probably unbuildable. Soon after arriving in Rome, Kracklite becomes impotent, and the film suggests that architecture, too, is impotent, unable to achieve its earth-shaking ambitions. Hadrian's villa and the tomb of Augustus, the paper architecture of the last kings and the first republicans of France, the Newton cenotaph and the Reich chancellery: the architecture of this film is the architecture of loss, decay, death, the hubris of power, the folly of ambition. To those who have been swallowed up in this belly, the creations of architects are not so much visions of a new world as way stations to the kingdom of death.

Both the architect and the mystique of the profession, endure still more humiliation in *Indecent Proposal*. Here the architect is not dying or even sick but rather beset with a condition that, in the slot-machine mentality of this movie, is worse than death: he is broke, one of those losers who blows into Vegas with high hopes and slinks out of town forty-eight hours later, his last hundred sucked effortlessly into the immense invisible tills of the gambling conglomerates. Adrian Lyne, whose directing style favors the quick knockout over fancy footwork, wastes little time in getting to the heart of the tawdry plot, the billionaire's indecent proposal, a million bucks for a night with another man's wife. The proposal may be indecent but it is irresistible too; the architect, David, and his wife, Diana, agree to this Faustian scheme "for the sake his career," for the dream house on the beach, and because the prospect of life without money is too hellish to imagine. "It's just my body," Diana actually says. "It's not my *mind*." The billionaire, who has been given the suggestive name John Gage, and who is played by Robert Redford with an air of remote embarrassment, flies the wife to his yacht, where he is courtly and tender, and where, as it were, he consummates the deal. That the businessman-lover has no regrets about the outcome of his latest venture becomes evident back in Los Angeles, where he begins courting Diana. Thus is the lopsided triangle arranged: the down-on-his-luck architect, the top-of-the world billionaire, the woman they both want.

The architect can offer his wife what he has been offering for years—love, commitment, a "lover and best friend" kind of marriage defined by a funky little bungalow filled with artsy bric-a-brac, lots of spontaneous kitchen-floor sex, walks on the pier where they exchange soulful looks. And of course he can offer as well his sense of vocation, his passion for his work, his ambition as an artist. Not bad, maybe, until the all-conquering business hero appears. As the film makes clear, the billionaire can offer the wife admittance to what is here envisioned as earthly paradise, that ethereal zone where money is vague in origin but endless in supply, where quotidian cares vanish, where life is viewed from the roomy backseat of your sedan or the deck of your boat or the terrace of your Brentwood estate.

Whom will the architect's wife choose? Her struggling talented husband of many years? Or the smooth sugar daddy who knows that she is worth a million? In the counting-house cosmology of this movie, only a dreamer or an artist would even ask the question. Halfway through the story Diana has left her husband for her lover: traded her L.A.-on-a-budget garb—overalls, slouchy hats, long straight hair—for the high-maintenance getup—structured dresses, tortured coiffure—that signals a certain self-imposed concubinage; and moved from the starter-house bungalow to the Versailles-scaled villa. Meanwhile her dejected husband has moved his few possessions into a dingy studio, where he sleeps on the couch with his retriever; defeated in love, he is even trounced in work, for the billionaire has bought the mortgage on his half-finished house, "because it was a good deal."

What has happened, of course, is that the architect, the form-making artist whose biggest asset turned out to be his wife's shapely form, has been thoroughly routed by the businessman: the man with the creative gift has been brought low by the man with the Midas touch. At the end the wife returns to the architect, but only because the billionaire wishes to end their union. In a world where the Vegas casinos are a kind of secular mecca, the money man holds all the cards that count. From confident midcentury masterbuilder to edgy *fin-de-millennium* stylemeister—what a stretch of cultural distance has been covered since *The Fountainhead*, in which the man of business, the publisher whose office contains clocks that tell the hour in every time zone, comes to revere the architect, to see him as a touchstone, his better self, a man whose integrity revives his own sense of decency and shame. Or even since *Strangers When We Meet*, in which the wealthy writer is reinvigorated by his relationship with the architect, with a set of values at whose center is something other than money. Movies have always best reflected the dream life of architects, and the nervous characterizations of recent years mirror the unease that now accompanies the designing life.

NOTES

1. *Intersection* is one of the few movies that has sought to substantiate, in any meaningful way, its hero's talent. The hero has been given the portfolio, so to speak, of Canadian architect Arthur Erickson. At the least, one of his latest buildings is shown to be Erickson's Museum of Anthropology in British Columbia. Not a bad choice, although one wonders if chronology were an issue: the museum was completed in 1977, suggesting that the makers of this 1994 film conceived of the architect as something of a late-modern classicist. More likely, the building was geographically convenient and, with its concrete forms and large volumes, looked "architectural."
2. For a discussion of Pierre Bourdieu's concept of "cultural capital" applied to architecture, see Garry Stevens, *The Favored Circle: The Social Foundations of Architectural Distinction* (Cambridge, MA: MIT Press, 1999).
3. I use the masculine pronoun here and elsewhere, partly because most of the movies being discussed feature male not female architects, and partly because the use of a more inclusive construction would gloss over what seems to me

an important issue: not only has architecture been male dominated, but the role of design messiah in particular has been reserved for men. And while many women are now in the field, it remains true that the stars, the king-makers and powerbrokers, are almost all men.

4. I conducted the computer search mentioned on January 4, 1999. Even accounting for the digital detritus that clogs the Internet, the number is impressive.

5. Alan Greenspan, current chairman of the Federal Reserve Board, has been loosely associated with Ayn Rand and her Objectivist circles; see Barbara Branden, *The Passion of Ayn Rand* (Garden City, NY: Doubleday & Company, 1986).

6. For a discussion of *The Fountainhead* and the way it both uses aspects of architecture culture and in turn influences that culture, see Andrew Saint, *The Image of the Architect* (New Haven: Yale University Press, 1983), ch. 1. For a more pointed analysis of Rand and Wright, one critical of Saint's book, see Neil Levine, *The Architecture of Frank Lloyd Wright* (Princeton: Princeton University Press, 1996), 419, 501 fn.

7. For a discussion of the sets, see Donald Albrecht, *Designing Dreams: Modern Architecture in the Movies* (New York: Harper & Row, 1986), 167–74.

8. Jonathan Hacker and David Price, *Take Ten: Contemporary British Film Directors* (Oxford: Clarendon Press, 1991), 189. I suspect the authors meant to write that Greenaway's *films* are a feast; however, given the director's gustatory obsessions, including cannibalism, their word choice, intentional or not, is weirdly apt.

9. Hacker and Price, *Take Ten*, 213.

10. Branden, *The Passion of Ayn Rand*, 134, fn.

WHO BUILT MR. BLANDINGS' DREAM HOUSE?

PHILIP NOBEL

BEFORE IT SLIDES into satire, *Mr. Blandings Builds His Dream House*, the 1948 comedy hit starring Cary Grant and Myrna Loy, makes a calculated appeal to the patriotism of its postwar American audience. The film opens with an adoring skyline pan, and these words, interrupted by brassy fanfare: "Manhattan! New York! USA!" The narration continues—"Manhattan! Drifting modern giant of concrete and steel, reaching to the heavens!"—illustrated by raking worm's-eye shots of the RCA Building and Wall Street, and by sidewalk scenes that echo the city as it was frozen by E. B. White in his essay "Here Is New York," written the same year. It is Manhattan as a crystallization of the American spirit, unbroken, unrivaled, overshadowed by nothing but the bomb. The movie also carries within it other less obvious souvenirs of World War II: the pent-up demand for mobility that expresses itself in the Blandings' flight to the country, the pent-up optimism of that same move, and the pent-up talents of one of the movie's principal players, the Blandings' architect, Mr. Simms.

World War II had important repercussions on the professional identity of American architects, and the ineffectual Mr. Simms, as sent up in the film, is the perfect symbol of this transformation. While the wartime mobilization gave architects a unique chance to display their expertise to the government and the public, it also raised the possibility that their services would be overlooked, that

engineers, contractors, other designers and government agencies—especially the military itself—would be called upon instead, circumscribing what architects saw as their rightful areas of influence. The war forced the profession to focus on devising new roles for the architect, but it also threatened to further architecture's degree of marginalization relative to others in the building industry. When the government, in the end, did not seek out their services, architects began a new phase of soul-searching identity crisis that continued well into the postwar period. This is where we find Mr. Simms: earnest but cowed, unable to weigh in on technical issues, seemingly second to everyone on the job site. After a scene in which the Blandings hijack the schematic design of their new home, wrestling with Simms for control of the drafting board, the architect is reduced to an all-but-outdated legal necessity: the guy who stamps the drawings. His only real service is to render reflections of the Blandings' own starry-eyed dreams.

In the original novel by Eric Hodgins, published in 1946, Simms lands the Blandings job only after an even more hapless architect, a Mr. Funkhauser, lately of Brooklyn but affecting New England roots, leads the family far astray with his groundless visions for their home. His planned renovation of the crumbling farm house they purchase results only in his "covering reams of sketch tissue with the graceful swashes of a 6-B pencil."[1] For the Blandings, in both the film and the prose versions of their ordeal, progress results only from the capable ministrations of an engineer, a contractor, a well-digger, a backhoe operator, and a dozen other characters who, while fleecing the family mercilessly, nonetheless comport themselves with a dignity and resolve that reflects a mastery of their trades and highlights the limitations of the architects with whom they must work. Even the Blandings' lawyer is a hero. As Funkhauser gets out of control, Mrs. Blandings shares her reservations with her husband: "I only mean that Mr. Funkhauser is so enthusiastic about everything that I sometimes think he gets carried away, and I'd like to have some other sort of person take a look at the

OPPOSITE: **Publicity image for *Mr. Blandings Builds His Dream House* (1948), with Cary Grant and Myrna Loy.**

old house before we get too far along, just to make certain that it's going to keep on standing up, and things like that—an engineer, or somebody." Mr. Blandings calls in an engineer who condemns the old house on sight. Funkhauser, "still dreaming towers and battlements, spires and turrets, onto a lousy old wreck of a farmhouse," is fired "with a thunderclap suddenness"—the only decisive action ever taken by Mr. Blandings.[2]

Where in this story is the confident, competent architect? A year after *Mr. Blandings* was first screened, an opposing image of the architect was presented in the film version of Ayn Rand's *The Fountainhead.* But the heroic adventures of Howard Roark, first described in Rand's 1943 novel but set in the period between the wars, reflect a hubris that few architects—even Frank Lloyd Wright, the loose model for Roark—would carry through World War II into the 1950s. Like most of their real-life peers at the time, Simms and Funkhauser were likely emerging from nearly a decade of hardship and confusion: overlooked by their government, bested by rival professions, scarcely relevant to the nation they would have liked to have served in its time of need. By way of a giant digression into the fate of nonfictional architects during World War II, the story that follows attempts to illustrate the climate that might have led Hodgins, himself a lapsed engineer, to caricature architects with his scatterbrained Funkhauser and his browbeaten Simms. We know more about the wartime activities of at least one other architect in film—Kirk Douglas's character Larry Coe dodges questions about combat in the 1960 drama *Strangers When We Meet*—but Funkhauser and Simms—the one flighty, the other futile—are ideal stand-ins to represent the condition of American architects immediately after World War II. Had Hodgins set his narrative a few years earlier, in the period described below, we would have seen these architects enduring experiences scarcely less humiliating than those they helped bring upon their clients, Mr. and Mrs. Blandings, as they pursued their simple plan to build a new home for themselves away from the bustle of the city.

ARCHITECTS MUST BE USED

For a profession recovering slowly from the Depression and the decade-long dearth of private-sector building, World War II appeared as only a bittersweet salvation. War-related construction offered the potential for employment and patriotic engagement, but at the price of increasing the profession's already heavy reliance on government patronage. After an uneasy relationship with New Deal building programs, American architects did not welcome this development. In many ways the government's insensitivity to architects in the 1930s—which included the establishment of in-office design divisions for the overwhelming majority of the bureaus affiliated with the Public Works Administration—was exemplified by the publication, in 1939, of a large survey of projects done under PWA auspices. This book, *Public Buildings*, omitted the name of every architect involved, whether salaried employee or independent consultant.[3] In the pages of *Pencil Points*, the self-styled "journal for the drafting room" that dedicated itself to promoting architectural employment, there was an immediate and angry response. One letter published in the magazine made the connection between this instance of government neglect and the profession's Funkhauseresque over-emphasis on its artistic side: "Our insane desire to excel in the art of designing at the expense of all other considerations has already brought the architectural profession to a sort of *cul de sac*. We have for so many years carried our heads in the clouds that the ground on which we stand has been seriously undermined by the commercial and political world to the point where our foothold is now in an approximate state of collapse."[4]

This comment highlights some key factors that affected the profession on the eve of American involvement in World War II. Perceived competition from the savvier design professions—particularly the expanding field of industrial design—moved architects to re-examine their business practices and public relations, while the concern for the profession's poor standing with government strengthened interest in the lobbying potential of the American Institute of Architects (AIA). Still, while there was an increasing desire to be respected as a technical profession, which would, ironically, justify the anonymity decried in the responses to *Public Buildings*, there was also the continuing need to be identified and appreciated as creative artists capable of a uniquely broad vision. In a 1941 editorial entitled "Architects Must Be Used," Kenneth Reid, the editor of *Pencil Points*, argued that the architect's unique synthesis of technical ability and creative vision should be recognized by the government as an asset to the war effort: "We must carry on the fight with redoubled pressure upon the responsible authorities in government until they are made to recognize that the architect is not a mere prettifier but a planner and a coordinator, endowed more often than not with the quality of creative imagination which seems lacking in so many administrative centers today."[5]

The widespread fear that architectural services would be seen as a luxury incompatible with an economy mobilizing for total war was responsible for a tension that is palpable beneath the calls-to-action that appeared frequently in the architectural press from the time of the first hostilities in Europe. While the rhetoric of architects at the onset of the war is unflagging in its patriotism, it often served double duty as a reminder to the government and the public that architecture could be more than just an art. With purely aesthetic expertise now a liability, the profession attempted to recast its image: the lone gentleman practitioner, expert in design and arbiter of taste, would be replaced by what was frequently referred to as the "technical planning professional," a team player who would fit more easily into the apparatus of wartime bureaucracy. In the spring of 1941, an English architect invited to speak at a meeting of the AIA in Washington, D.C., clearly defined this course of action: "The problems presented to us are chiefly of a technical nature. The architect's position in our period consequently depends upon his capacity to be a technician, and to convince authorities and public alike that he is a good technician. Emotional inspiration has to be limited to the most discreet expression."[6] In a 1942 letter to *Pencil Points*, Royal Barry Wills, the author of a primer on the business of architecture, similarly urged architects to transform themselves from long-haired aesthetes to bureau-ready technicians. Wills wrote that "many of our old ideas, and certainly most of the ideas of the hide-bound members of the profession, will have to be thrown into the wastebasket in order [for the profession] to survive."[7] He illustrated his point with a sketched cartoon: a crew-cut architect is shown wielding a T-square and rolling up one sleeve. Behind him, a hat, spats, and striped pants spill out of the trash. The caption reads: "Let's throw the silk hat and the gardenia in the wastebasket and beat the hell out of everybody!"

The war provided both the necessity and the mechanism for this professional makeover. For architects to compete with other design professionals and building interests for government work, it was crucial to convince the War Department that they, too, could be entrusted with complex technical assignments. To this end, architecture was portrayed as an expert profession that could be called upon to consult on a wide range of war construction projects, from the efficient design of factories and workers' housing, to the effective provision of Air Raid Precautions (ARP) and camouflage. Indeed, the story of the profession during the war years can be seen as a collective effort to compile a portfolio of potential areas of architectural involvement, often departing from traditional architectural services, and to aggressively promote the products of this hastily constructed fiefdom to the government and the public.

THE RIGHT PEOPLE FOR THE RIGHT JOB

Representing architecture as a technical planning profession was a predictably hard sell at a time when architects were still mostly trained according to the compositional precepts of the École des Beaux-Arts. To facilitate the wartime repositioning, a whole new paradigm of professional service was needed. The expansion of American interest in modern architecture in the 1940s coincided with this need to redefine the architect's professional identity, but this development should be viewed more as a case of convergent evolution than a widespread conversion to the formal or ideological bases of the modern movement itself.

It seems clear now that the embrace of modern architecture in the United States was not a cataclysmic event, as the polemical modernist histories portrayed it, but was a more incremental assimilation of new forms and attitudes into a stubbornly inertial American context. Throughout the 1930s, modern and other tendencies typically coexisted in a noncommittal way; in the professional magazines, "modernistic" houses were often illustrated without special emphasis next to examples of various revival styles. Such treatment suggests that each style was seen to have a specific value that could be drawn upon by an ideologically neutral architect to diversify his offerings and satisfy a broader range of clients. What debate modern architecture did spark in the 1930s had not yet effected serious, professionwide change by the time of the war. However, when the approaching hostilities in Europe began to displace the recognized masters of modern architecture to American universities, the professional debate intensified and refocused on the battleground of the schools.

An early and important critique of this emigration was voiced in 1937 by Charles Killam, then professor emeritus of architecture at Harvard University, at an address to the Association of Collegiate Schools of Architecture. Given only a month after Walter Gropius arrived at Harvard, Killam attacked the new chairman, stating that "[the school's] function is to train architects, not painters, sculptors, or commercial designers for machine-made products. An architect can find out enough about the possibilities of materials by watching skilled workmen instead of amateurish fumbling with his own hands."[8] Killam also challenged the economic viability of teaching modern design, in the process revealing the depth of its embrace by students: "Students spend all of their time doing [modern storefronts, gas stations, houses] disregarding the fact that they have got to earn a living by designing buildings for owners who, in most cases, do not want modern designs. We know this by observing what is being built in the United States, not what is being talked about."[9] And in denouncing what he called "super-designers"—architects versed in design at all scales, from products to regional plans—Killam rejected the expanded role of the architect that Gropius promoted and that the adaptation to the war would soon make an ideal. Two years later, in a piece entitled "Is Architecture Going to the Bauhaus?" *Pencil Points's* resident satirist Eugene Raskin echoed Killam's sentiments but cast them in the context of the competitive challenges to the profession. In the voice of the Great Architect, his regular interlocutor, Raskin wrote: "While we architects lose ourselves in complex theorizing and the cutting up of paper dolls, industrial designers are taking our work out from under our noses. They realize, just as we do, that people use not only buildings, but furniture, autos, ships, trains, planes, clothes, canned food, fountain pens—and so on through the whole list of material goods. And instead of sitting around discussing it, they are out designing all these things, pioneering ahead of us, and making us look rapidly obsolete."[10]

Against such resistance, it is unlikely that the infusion of European teachers alone would have been enough to bring the greater part of American architecture into the orbit of the modern movement. Despite the benefits of a disproportionately large exposure in the press, the impact of the Europeans was limited by the fact that they were only educating a tiny percentage of new architects each year, and, although they may have captured the imagination of younger architects and students at more traditional schools, the older, practicing core of the profession was mostly threatened, annoyed, or indifferent. The decisive moment for the acceptance of modern architecture came when its attributes were seen to support the professional repositioning that became necessary at the onset of the war. Because of modern architecture's air of rational efficiency—embracing engineering achievements, celebrating functionalism, and stressing experimentation with contemporary materials and techniques—it became a natural means to encourage the shift from an aesthetic understanding of architecture to one that was founded on efficient methods and appropriate techniques. The Swiss émigré William Lescaze, in a guest editorial in *Pencil Points*, advocated modern architecture for these reasons:

> Let us be frank. In many places—official and political circles, War and Navy circles, in the mind of a large part of the public—the function and the services of the architect are not understood. They still think that one shouldn't bother calling an architect in unless it's a matter of looks, of decoration; unless it's a building of marble and granite. And now they say that since we need useful structures, we can't really afford to have architects. I say we can't afford not to enlist all of our experts. We can't afford not to insure that in each field, in each area, *the right people be put to do the right job.* As a matter of fact, some architects have not waited until 1940 to re-discover and re-state what their true functions, their real services

are. During the last twenty years, these men have perfected a technique—a method that is ready now to serve their fellow men intelligently and economically. That method is modern architecture.[11]

Of course, the unspoken fear suggested by Lescaze's italics was that even if architects retooled for the war effort, engineers and industrial designers—among others—would supplant them. To a large extent this turned out to be the case. Already by the summer of 1941 it was possible to report that "jobs have been snatched away from the Architect's own drafting-board by enemies with no more than a loud voice. The rival Engineers have team-chanted 'We Are Efficient' until they believe it themselves. The Industrial Designers have sometimes brandished the work of architectural men they employ, to win jobs and confidence away from Architects."[12] In this atmosphere, architects sometimes stretched the description of their own abilities into caricature. In a 1941 radio interview, a prominent California architect suggested that "the architect, like the scientist, is a specialist in planning. That is why, as our defense program gathers more definite form, I foresee the architect playing an increasingly important role in defense."[13]

The situation of the profession in the early stages of the war led to architects favoring a more technical image, which may have brought a large, heretofore untouched mass of the profession closer to modern architecture. This expedient approach was then reinforced by experience during the war itself, both at home, working under the limitations of the materials priorities system, and closer to combat. By making other types of architecture impossible, the war effectively enforced a *de facto* modernism in all construction: buildings were built without ornament, simple volumes and finishes were favored, and inventive structural systems were explored. Architects who could find work, whether civilian or military, were forced to make do with limited resources, tight budgets, and impossible schedules. This privileged the habits of thought and methods of modern architecture, and it virtually mandated functional design. Because younger architects were generally more sympathetic to experimentation, and less hidebound by tradition, a sort of generational/educational gap in wartime usefulness developed in the profession. This situation was suggested by Thomas Creighton toward the end of the war in terms that would have applied perfectly to our own Messrs. Funkhauser and Simms:

> There was no more tragic example of war casualty than the architect who had a nice little suburban practice in colonial houses, Georgian schools, and modernistic storefronts. He had to close up shop, of course, and he got a job with one of the architect-engineer combinations that had a war contract. Poor soul, he sat there in a daze while a group of youngsters fresh out of school dashed off details of roof overhangs, simplified wood sash, truss connections. It wasn't a matter of age; the value of the man lay in his training and background. If he had been schooled to think freshly, be imaginative and technically quick-witted, he was usable. If his technical mentality had been channeled into traditional grooves from which it couldn't raise itself, he had to be discarded as actually detrimental to the war effort.[14]

Unfortunately, even the "youngsters fresh out of school" were not always prepared to serve in the armed forces in any capacity that took advantage of their professional training. In March 1945, an architect serving as a lieutenant in the Coast Guard Reserves reflected on his experience in the war and indicted the architecture schools for their failure to prepare graduates to make meaningful contributions to the war effort: "While older men had acquired sufficient experience to be of real value in the [military] construction program, the newcomers in the profession found their education by itself of little value to a nation at war. The pitiful fact is that [the student] has given little evidence of adaptability in work. He is surrounded by an aura of aestheticism."[15] Still, it is likely that it was the older, practicing core of the profession—those "aged plus or minus forty [who were] made to feel that their usefulness to their country [was] less than that of an eighteen-year-old apprentice in a flying school"—who went through the worst transition pains during World War II.[16] In many ways the concern for the neglect of the profession was limited to an effort by this group of middle-aged men—too old to fight but too young to comfortably sit idle—to endow themselves with some of the attributes of a technical sensibility.

PENCIL POINTS GOES TO WASHINGTON

During World War II, the greatest forces behind the profession's efforts to remake itself were its periodicals, and among these *Pencil Points* stands out as one of the architect's most dedicated and vociferous advocates. Under the direction of Kenneth Reid, editor from 1926 through 1946, *Pencil Points* assumed a hands-on role in preparing architects for the war. Reid, an architect by training, had served in World War I as a lieutenant at a navy yard in Portsmouth, New Hampshire, an experience that may have made him especially sensitive to the plight of architects in the military. Between the January 1940 editorial that proposed a campaign to prove that "the architect is practical," and the impassioned post-Pearl Harbor supplement that promised to fight to find applications for the "special technical abilities of the architectural man as long as we draw breath," Reid's editorial page featured more than a dozen essays justifying a role for architects in the preparations for war. At the same time, the magazine itself underwent a transformation that mirrored the changes it was advocating for the profession. Its namesake sketches became fewer, and then, after a nostalgic series on prewar Brittany in the fall of 1940, disappeared altogether; its long-running "Monograph Series" on colonial architecture was replaced, at the beginning of 1941, with the "Preparedness Series" that featured a new wartime building type each month; the "Threshing Floor" letters department was slowly taken over and then replaced by a regular Washington correspondent; and, in March 1942, the magazine entered a period of limbo under the name *New Pencil Points* that lasted until it emerged from the war in 1945 as *Progressive Architecture.*

After the United States officially entered the war, and the long years of relatively slow defense preparations gave way to the frenzied pace of the Victory Construction Program, as the government's official building effort was known, it became apparent that *Pencil Points*' rhetorical efforts to increase the employment of architects in the war effort would not bear fruit. In February 1942, the magazine launched a program to take a census of the profession, and to send a representative to Washington to lobby firsthand to find jobs for architects. The next month, with some fanfare, the editors reported that they had already received "the records of over 3,500 men, with more coming in every day"—evidence, they claimed, "of the existence at this time of a substantial reservoir of high-class personnel with mental habits of planning and coordination and a broad background of familiarity with technical processes."[17] At the same time, they announced the selection of Willis Vogel, an Ohio AIA officer, to be the Washington representative, now referred to by the Orwellian title Technical Personnel Advisor.

The result of this effort was to reveal the extent of the government's resistance to employing architects during the war. By June, the grand campaign had only placed about two hundred people, and Willis Vogel, writing periodically from Washington, was constantly downgrading his expectations. In July, he was withdrawn from Washington after the AIA pledged to continue his direct advocacy. By that time, after more than two years of persuasive writing, Kenneth Reid had finally conceded that "definite opposition to architects as personnel has been encountered in our dealings with government bureaus, and particularly with the War and Navy Departments."[18] Indeed, it seems that the dark days of 1942—after Pearl Harbor but before the Battle of Midway and the first Allied rallies in North Africa—were reflected in a growing pessimism in *Pencil Points* regarding the future of the profession. In this spirit, the magazine reprinted a "burning editorial" from *Smudges*, an Australian student journal, entitled "Death of the Architect." It expressed what the editors may have felt was too alarming a message to deliver directly: "The young men of architecture know that the profession is, for good or bad, gone for good. It died because in peace it could not produce good architecture; in war it could not provide worthy national service. The typical client is blamed for the former, the Government for the latter. It is of little importance what the difficulties were; the test was whether the profession could surmount them. Everybody knows it could not."[19]

BIAS IN GOVERNMENT

In one important way, the problems faced by architects were directly caused by the government. The contract structure for procuring war work was designed in a way that seemed to willfully preclude the participation of architects, both in firms and as individuals. During the defense period, which was characterized by the kind of administrative disorganization that favored larger companies and firms with well-established Washington contacts, army contracts were given out by the Quartermaster General's office directly to large contractors on a fixed-fee basis. These contractors could then, at their discretion, hire architects or engineers as each job demanded. In February 1941, Ely Jacques Kahn expressed what must have been a majority opinion among architects when he attacked this system: "We realize that there is already much irritation simply because many works initiated by the government have been turned over to contractors to design, manage, and build. If the architect appeared at all it was by grace of the contractor! Is this accidental or have the powers that be decided that executive strength is more potently applied this way than through the normal practice of having an architect run the enterprise and use the contractor where he best fits?"[20] That summer, at their convention in California's Yosemite Valley, the AIA passed a resolution protesting these "encroachments" where "various agencies have assumed the professional functions of the architect."[21]

Because of accounting problems with this first type of contract, it was replaced, in December 1941, by what came to be known as the Architect-Engineer-Manager (AEM) contract. Under the new system, which was administered by the Army Corps of Engineers, the government restored somewhat the traditional relationships between architects, engineers, and contractors, but at a new scale that reflected the scope of wartime construction. The principal contractor in an AEM contract provided "all architect-engineering services incident to design, inspection and supervision of the project," and subcontracted for the services directly related to construction.[22] But because the government, to avoid bureaucratic bottlenecks, had relieved itself of some of the responsibilities expected of a client, the AEM would also be responsible for project supervision and management at a scale that was impossible for all but a few of the largest design-build firms in the country. Six of these huge firms eventually shared nineteen multiproject AEM contracts that totaled almost half a billion dollars. Furthermore, these contracts were usually given out as a set of smaller contracts, so the prime contractor would need a managerial staff that dwarfed its relatively unimportant design department.

As a result, even the largest architecture firms were edged out by industrial giants such as the Austin Company, Engineers and Builders, which built several bomber plants, including an innovative windowless facility in Fort Worth. This plant, which required the development of a highly insulated wall section, was a product of a close working relationship between the Austin Company and large manufacturers like Owens-Corning, Truscon Steel, and the United States Gypsum Company. Despite the fact that it was designed without prominent involvement by architects, the plant was published extensively in the architectural press, and it became an icon representing the building industry's contribution to the war effort. Ironically, advertisers then chose it as an image with which to market their products to architects in the trade publications.

Responding to the AEM structure, solo architects and smaller firms began to associate with engineers to form cooperatives that would have the required scale and depth. This tactic was suggested by Willis Vogel in one of his 1942 progress reports from Washington: "It should be noted that stress is being laid on the use of organizations which include all the technical planning professions and not groups that consist only of architects. While the architect is primarily a planner, an executive, and an inventive designer, he must now assume a cooperative role with the various branches of engineering [to form] a complete organization to handle an entire project."[23] One of the largest of these associations was Construction Planners Inc., a cooperative effort of the State Association of California Architects. The corporation was structured as an open association to which any registered architect, landscape architect, or civil, structural, or mechanical engineer could apply for membership. Its main goal was to form "a responsible party to which the government [could] confidently allocate defense projects of any kind for rapid handling with undivided responsibility."[24] Other attempts to consolidate with engineers created teams that were smaller in scale, and more coherent as firms. To compete for a commission to design barracks and officers' buildings for the army on leased British bases in the Caribbean, the New York firms of Voorhees, Walker, Foley and

Smith, architects, and Parsons and Brinckerhoff, engineers, joined forces and incorporated briefly in 1941 as Caribbean Architects-Engineers. Following a similar but less representative model, Skidmore, Owings & Merrill achieved its trademark breadth of service during the war as a result of large-scale government projects that required it to absorb an entire construction company and become "a kind of stock company."[25] More than any other form of architectural practice during the war years, these associations were successful in supplying design services to the government throughout the country, and directly inspired the large, integrated design firms that became more prevalent after the war.

ABSENCE MADE VISIBLE

Far from filling the leadership roles that they had envisioned for themselves, and facing the prospect of appearing embarrassingly superfluous to the construction industry, architects identified alternatives to traditional practice that would give them visibility during the war. Chief among these was civil defense. From November 1940, when Serge Chermayeff began writing regularly on Air Raid Precautions (ARP) for *Pencil Points*, and culminating with *Architectural Forum's* comprehensive civil defense issue in January 1942, there was a steady effort to portray the architect as an expert in this crucial area—following the successful model of English architects, who had achieved prominence in their country's more intense civil defense efforts. In the context of the blurring of professional roles that was then being promoted by the government, the image of the architect as an expert in civil defense became an important component of the new portfolio of architectural services.

In the atmosphere of public fear and perceived government inaction, architects saw their growing expertise in ARP as an opportunity to impress the public with their patriotism and technical competence. In the case of camouflage, the artistic abilities of architects could also be exploited and, in a sense, justified by their application to an essential wartime activity. Accordingly, on both coasts—where the fear of bombing had dramatically increased after Pearl Harbor—there were organized efforts to corner the market on civil defense. In

California, the state architecture association established an ARP advisory board within two weeks of the bombing of Pearl Harbor. This board actively promoted public awareness of civil defense procedures and techniques through bulletins and radio programs. That the board's public relations function was equal to its role as a public service was frankly explained by its director: "Every possible effort is being made to bring the name of the architect before the public. Through the efforts of the public relations counsel many columns of publicity have been obtained in the press and in all cases the word 'architect' has been emphasized."[26]

The schools also played an important role in establishing the profession's right to civil defense work. Columbia offered courses in "protective obscurement" and bombproof design; Yale compiled a defense bibliography and offered, as early as the 1939–40 school year, a complete cycle of defense-related design studios; and Pratt students researched and compiled the first architect-produced camouflage manual of the war. Of course, architects' claims to hegemony in civil defense work did not go unchallenged. There was widespread public belief that civil engineers were best suited to deal with the technical complexities of defending against aerial bombardment. Addressing this issue, Chermayeff fell back on the old canard of the architect's unique vision, arguing that, although engineers had made valuable contributions and would continue to do so, architects were better suited because "the whole pattern [of civil defense preparations] requires synthesizing minds to bear upon it, in order to give point and value to each contributive element including that of the specialist engineer."[27] After the war, the rivalry between architecture and engineering would continue to be an important point of conflict and a major source of anxiety about the marginalization of architecture as a profession. Then, too, the architect's synthetic vision would often be promoted as a desirable, distinguishing quality.

Amid the posturing and speculation about what architects might do, it is often hard to get a clear idea of what they actually did during the war. In some ways, the picture of architects' involvement in World War II can be characterized as an absence made visible by the flurry of invective that decried it. The representatives of the profession tried to mask the fact that many of their co-practitioners were simply waiting out the war, looking forward to the postwar building boom that was already being discussed as early as 1937. In stark contrast to the rhetoric of the architectural press, there is scant mention of architect's contributions elsewhere. Consider, for example, that in the official army history of the Corps of Engineers in World War II, published after information about the Manhattan Project was declassified, SOM's celebrated designs for the Manhattan Project town of Oak Ridge, Tennessee was reduced to a mention of the abandoned farmhouse that they used for an office and a passing reference to the Cemesto panels that clad one of their buildings. A brief but glowing account of the rapid design of the Pentagon Building by George Bergstrom, then president of the AIA, was likely included only because it was so close to home. The fact that so little was recorded in Army records—or in the memoirs of the chairman of the War Production Board, the man ultimately responsible for the conversion of industries in this country—belies the image of the architect as a visionary technical professional somehow capable of winning the war from his studio. That image, a funhouse inversion of the experience of the majority of the profession, nonetheless became a staple of wartime advertisers who preyed on architects' doubts by selling them the myth of their indispensability. A 1942 advertisement for Celotex Sound Conditioning reads: "Architect Anderson hasn't shot down any Japs, but he's a hero to plenty of war workers. He eliminated 'sabotage by noise' from a great new war industries building." More typical was a series of spots promoting the Dixon company's Eldorado pencils: "Pencils are projectiles, too!"

One architecture firm that could claim to be indispensable to the war effort was Albert Kahn Associated Engineers and Architects Inc. Prepared by a long and innovative career in which he virtually reinvented the American industrial building—his early projects included Ford's revolutionary River Rouge plant—Kahn's organization of six-hundred-plus employees literally set the pace for the design and construction of production facilities in World War II; in 1939, the Glenn L. Martin airplane works in Baltimore was completed and in operation within three months of the first phone call. Not surprisingly, he became a hero to the rest of the profession during the early years of the war. On the occasion of an AIA tribute to

Kahn just months before his death in 1942, a citation was read that made explicit the manner in which his work was valued by the profession's official lobby: "Exponent of organized efficiency, of disciplined energy, of broad visioned planning, he has notably contributed to the expansion of architectural practice. Master of concrete and steel, master of space and time, he stands today at the forefront of our profession in meeting the colossal demands of government in its hour of need."[28] Kahn's response included the line: "Let us not fail in proving our worth to the community and to our Government in the present crisis." On another occasion, the AIA used Kahn's prestige to attack the large nonarchitectural design-build firms. In February 1942, just as the Austin Company's Fort Worth bomber plant was receiving the most attention, the AIA released a statement by Kahn questioning the wisdom of designing such windowless factory buildings. Specifically, Kahn cast doubt on their effectiveness for blackout purposes, and called into question their usefulness after the war. Kahn's statement was a veiled warning to government of the pitfalls that awaited projects built without the benefit of an architect's superior synthetic foresight.

HOUSING, ANYONE?

Beyond the special case of Albert Kahn, a more general exception to architects' wartime experience was in housing, which became the one area in which the government favored architects. The official guidelines for the "Division of Responsibilities and Work Among the Planning Professions," released in 1941, mandated a leadership role for architects, stating that in normal conditions the architect should be the "coordinating authority" in team contracts. In part because of this favored status, and the huge number of housing projects undertaken during the war, even younger, independent architects with small practices could sometimes find war housing work. Hugh Stubbins' 1942 defense housing project at Windsor Locks, Connecticut, is an example of one such opportunity; it was by far his largest project in a practice then only two years old. Completed three years after his stint as Walter Gropius's assistant at Harvard, it is an interesting case study in the pragmatic merger of modern ideals and military requirements. Less compromise is seen in Gropius's own project, Aluminum City Terrace, designed with Marcel Breuer to house workers at an Alcoa plant near Pittsburgh. The spare, unfinished wooden exteriors of the two-story bar buildings spurred a local uproar, in which the buildings were referred to as "rabbit hutches" and "chicken coops."[29] In 1944, two years after its completion, *Architectural Forum* was moved to defend this conspicuous architectural contribution to the housing emergency. After taking a detailed survey of the residents, and comparing Aluminum City favorably to the adjacent "smoky little factory town," the editors concluded somewhat disingenuously that "89 percent have decided that they like it."[30]

Other housing projects by then-prominent architects include Richard Neutra's celebrated Channel Heights development in San Pedro, California, and Carver Court, designed by the newly formed firm of Howe, Stonorov, and Kahn in Coatesville, Pennsylvania. Louis Kahn, of course, was little known outside of Philadelphia at this time, but George Howe's involvement helped to bring attention to this innovative project, which addressed the growing presence of the automobile by creating sheltered parking under its stilt-supported units. In 1942, during the construction of Carver Court, Howe was appointed Supervising Architect of the Public Buildings Administration, the highest position for an architect in government. In this role, despite its limited power, Howe was a strong advocate for architects, stressing greater involvement in the war effort and preparing official Washington for the general acceptance of modern architecture. Nonetheless, like Gropius and Breuer at Aluminum City, aspects of Howe's projects that were perceived as too modern met with resistance. At Pine Ford Acres, a defense housing project of 1942 by Howe and Kahn in Middletown, Pennsylvania, the flat roofs had to be pitched to silence local critics. Other experiments in housing were better received, such as William Wurster's Valencia Gardens in San Francisco or Baldwin Hills Village in Los Angeles, both of which were begun under federal low-cost housing programs during the late 1930s but used as workers' housing upon their completion during the war.

With the exception of Pine Ford Acres and Baldwin Hills, the projects discussed above became well-known, and remain so today, because of their inclusion in the Museum of Modern Art's *Built in USA: 1932–1944* exhibition. This was one of a number of shows the museum mounted to bring attention to work done by architects during the war, including several devoted to mass housing. In the popular catalog for *Built in USA*, which had sixteen-thousand copies in circulation by the end of 1945, Elizabeth Mock, acting curator of the Department of Architecture, lamented that "many people still prefer to entrust serious building problems to engineers, and the architect is still regarded as the man who supplies the trimmings." Elaborating, she placed the exhibition squarely in the context of the wartime repositioning of the architect's role: "Any architect who applied for work in connection to the gigantic military construction program at the start of the war was apt to be told, 'Oh, no, nothing for architects. We're just building here, you know. Nothing fancy.' The fallacy of that argument is proved by the success of the few jobs which were given to competent architects."[31]

While housing for defense workers accounted for much of the work done by architects in private practice during the war—as much as one-third of all independent commissions in California—it allowed very little opportunity to change the prevailing attitudes challenged by Mock and so many others. Architects still had to go outside of housing, and sometimes architecture itself, to contribute to the war effort in a more direct way. An excellent example of this is the career of Robert Evans Alexander, one of the architects who contributed to Baldwin Hills Village. Alexander left that project in 1942 to work in Lockheed's Production Control Division as an industrial engineer charged with managing the operation of aircraft factories. In a sense, this course epitomized the transformation of the architect into a "technical planning professional" and vindicated Kenneth Reid's editorial visions of a wider application for the architect's special skills. Nonetheless, in an appreciation of Alexander written by Larry Perkins in *Pencil Points*, his work at Lockheed required careful explanation: "What more logical place could there be for a mind trained to plan, visualize, and act than in improving methods and doing things? This job [Alexander] holds is a distinct contribution to a profession which is fighting out from behind the impractical dreamer reputation; for, make no mistake, this is no 'Architectural Engineer' or practical man. In the old sense he would be considered a plain, straight designer and a red hot one at that."[32]

Perkins also suggested that Alexander's involvement in Lakewood Village, another Los Angeles-area housing project, gave him the expertise in mass production that allowed him to be effective at Lockheed. Undoubtedly many architects gained such expertise during the war, when the scheduling and scope of housing projects put a new emphasis on planning and production. But these quiet innovations were unlikely to impress a government that was at that moment marshaling the largest outpouring of innovative industrial production in history. In addition, the techniques of economical mass-housing were not the sole domain of architects—prefabrication was largely an independent initiative by manufacturers that many architects saw as a future threat—and were in part the product of innovations by industrialists such as Henry Kaiser, the important West Coast shipbuilder. Moreover, after the war, Kaiser—like the Levitts in the East—adapted his wartime experience in workers' housing and effectively edged the privately practicing architect out of the huge low- and medium-cost postwar housing market in California. Smaller, designer-led efforts in prefabricated housing, such as Buckminster Fuller's Dymaxion House and Konrad Wachsmann and Walter Gropius's General Panel System, never came close to challenging these large developers for market share, or influencing the course of the notoriously inertial American housing industry. Still, the wartime conditions brought both projects closer to realization than might have been possible at any other time.

Instead of casting the architect as a home-bound war hero, the scale of architectural involvement in housing may have strengthened the government's enduring suspicion that architecture was only relevant when construction had to be modified to accommodate aesthetic sensibilities. This government attitude is exemplified by the experience of architects who served in the Seabees, the Navy's construction battalion. To facilitate their island-hopping strategy, the navy created the Seabees as an all-purpose building corps trained in the rapid construction of the airfields and port facilities that were the backbone of the war in the Pacific. The personnel for the Seabees, which was rapidly formed in December 1941, were typically "veterans of the last war eager to get their licks in—blacksmiths, crane operators, plumbers, oilers, electricians, welders."[33] Instead of being given the technical tasks that these builders were retrained to handle, the thousand-odd architects in the Seabees were responsible for designing the buildings important for troop morale; in the islands of the Pacific, they built "palm-festooned churches," "swank officers clubs," and mess halls in which "bamboo was used pleasingly to trim the interiors."[34] If we were to backtrack five years from the construction of Mr. Blandings' dream house, we might find his contractor and tradesmen paving the way to victory in the Pacific while his architects busied their fingers writing letters to magazines and the AIA.

In a nation at war, a presence at the front was an essential means of justifying and publicizing a profession's contribution to the war effort. After the war, the role played in the Seabees by the mostly middle-aged men from the construction trades was widely acknowledged. In the same way, the achievements of the Corps of Engineers added luster to the image of that profession; the Corps expanded the accepted roles of engineering in exactly the way that architects wished their own roles to be changed. In December 1941, when the Corps was given responsibility for all wartime building by the army, it claimed "no special competence in the housing and building fields."[35] However, after controlling the huge wartime building program, the Corps, and by extension individual engineers, could easily claim competence in these areas. With the help of the Corps of Engineers, there was full employment of the engineering world in all areas of the industrial mobilization. What is remarkable is that although huge engineer-builders dominated construction, there was also room for smaller engineering practices to make valuable contributions. One example of this scale of private participation was the development of the Corbetta Beehive Magazine by the small, New York-based Corbetta Construction Company. After the war, the army credited the Corbetta brothers' innovative spherical powder magazines with huge savings of time and materials during the course of the war.

The success of such small-scale engineering initiatives highlights the limited wartime utility of privately practicing architects, who were, in effect, shut out of the wartime formation of the military-industrial complex. Indeed, developments in American architecture after the war were in part reactions to the marginalization that took place during the war years and carried over, as new roles were solidified, into the 1950s. George Howe, in his capacity as Supervising Architect, neatly summarized architects' concerns for the future of their profession:

> The relation of the architect to government is a question that interests him particularly at this moment. The reason is obvious. During the planning and construction for war government has made him feel that his profession is of secondary importance if not largely superfluous. If, as seems possible, the government at all levels is to exercise a preponderant influence in planning and construction for peace, the architect cannot help wondering whether he is to be relegated to a secondary place in peace as well as war.[36]

AFTER THE WAR

In January 1946, *Progressive Architecture*, *Pencil Points*'s postwar incarnation, published a special issue assessing the war's effects on architecture, centered on a long article by Thomas Creighton. (The following month, Creighton became an editor at the magazine, and exactly a year later he replaced Reid as senior editor when Reid left to establish a practice as an architectural public relations consultant.) After a month-by-month reading of the wartime issues of the three national architecture magazines—*Architectural Record*, *Architectural Forum*, and *Pencil Points* in its many forms—Creighton wrote "Pearl Harbor to Nagasaki, A Review of Architectural Progress During the War." It was an optimistic report, ostensibly for the returning G.I., as Creighton suggested in the introduction: "It is possible that you haven't seen any of the architectural magazines for the years 1942, 1943, 1944, or 1945. Perhaps you were in the service doing nonarchitectural work. Perhaps your practice folded up and you went into one of the many kinds of defense jobs."[37] In this spirit, "Pearl Harbor to Nagasaki" offered a selection of notable buildings, a catalog of new techniques, and, predictably, an introduction to the difficulties faced by architects on the home front. In one section, "Since You Went Away There Has Been Progress, Against the Odds, in Building for the Armed Services," Creighton summarized the government's reluctance to hire architects. Relying on the familiar concept of the architect's broad vision, he stressed that architects were necessary during the war—but were also resisted—because of "the lack of creative imagination inherent in the regular Army and Navy training," and he applauded those architects who were able to push their visions through despite resistance from "engineers in uniform." As examples, he showed SOM's Main Reception Building at the Great Lakes Naval Training Station in Illinois—"One of the first war buildings which succeeded in proving wrong the official attitude of disinterest in good design"—and Gardner Dailey's Maritime Training School, two projects by then well known because of their inclusion in the Museum of Modern Art's *Built in USA* exhibition.[38]

In writing "Pearl Harbor to Nagasaki," Creighton suggested that the themes that governed so much of the architectural discourse during the war would continue to affect practice in the immediate postwar period. Rather than being assuaged by the abundance and opportunity of the postwar building boom, which began after the last material controls were rescinded in 1947—just about the time the Blandings would have broken ground—architects were still extremely concerned with fixing a new professional identity and they confronted the problem in the terms of their marginalization during the war. In a sense, architects' relationships to the other professions, their self-presentation to clients and the public, and their approach to meeting the demands of new techniques all mimicked tropes that evolved in response to their experiences during World War II. From this observation, it is possible to suggest some ways in which the professional strategies that developed as reactions to the war ramified in the very different world afterwards. Consider the fundamental issue of the architect's dual roles: in the 1950s, the tastemaker or artistic model of practice that had been abandoned by necessity in the lean war years returned with renewed relevance and coexisted with the more sober architect-as-technician formula that had taken hold during the war. But both of these broad models of architectural practice still sought to distinguish the architect from the engineer or bureaucrat by stressing the lasting benefits of design—as a consumable commodity for the artist, and an economic expedient for the technician—and by continually pointing out the need for the architect's unique synthetic vision. What follows are some speculations on the ways in which the profession's responses to adversity in World War II may have woven themselves into the new complexity of architectural culture in the postwar years.

OLD RIVALRIES AND NEW TECHNIQUES

At the end of the war, there was a *detente* in some of the more extreme wartime positions. For example, the rivalry with industrial designers, which had became so shrill, seems to have mellowed considerably as early as October 1945. That month, in a move that would have been inconceivable only a year earlier, *Progressive Architecture* devoted twelve pages and much praise to an office building designed by an industrial designer. Nine months later, in one of his last editorials, Reid included in a reference to the architectural profession, "all serious, able and conscientious building designers of no matter what official title."[39] And at the end of 1946, *Progressive Architecture* published a glowing photo essay on a new Boeing B-29 plant designed by the Austin Company, which had been vilified during the war for their very similar building in Fort Worth. Still, interprofessional tensions persisted, and were sometimes aggravated by new factors, such as the challenges and opportunities presented by materials and techniques developed during the war.

The war spawned such diverse inventions as fluorescent lights, structural wooden laminates, light steel construction, and plastics. In an effort to keep architects abreast of these developments, even before they were available for use, *Pencil Points* published notices of military material breakthroughs almost every month. In January 1943, they summarized progress to date in a special issue, "Materials for Tomorrow." *Architectural Forum* followed in March 1944, with "Materials for 194X." Beginning in 1945, *Pencil Points* made promoting the mastery of new materials its most visible editorial priority. In January of that year, the magazine published an encyclopedic account of products developed during the war, from Armorply (a stainless steel and plywood hybrid) to Zonolite fireproofing plasters. In July 1945, *Pencil Points* inaugurated "Materials and Methods," a monthly technical section that often accounted for half of the editorial content of each issue. The enormous interest in this subject was reflected in letters printed the following month. Writers praising the new focus included Nathaniel Owings, Ely Jacques Kahn, William Wurster, and Pietro Belluschi. Walter Martens, an architect in West Virginia, wrote that the new section was necessary because "the average architect has spent some three or more rather inactive years, has gotten behind in his files, his drawings, his contacts."[40] Beyond basic professional responsibility and the need for "orientation," the profound interest in keeping up with materials and methods was driven by the rivalries that blossomed during the war. Architects worried that if they ceded the high ground of technological expertise to engineers, industrial designers, or the manufacturers themselves, it would lead to further limitations on their role in building. The editors of *Progressive Architecture* rose to this fight as they did to the related ones during the war, declaring, in January 1947, that "now is more than ever the time for architects to assert themselves as the factor that controls the use of materials."[41]

Asserting control in this area and others proved to be very difficult. The profusion of new materials and techniques, and the grand new scale of building more common after the war, further upset the traditional relationships between architects, engineers, and manufacturers. At the same time, the flood of new building types, and their increasing structural, mechanical, and financial complexity, created openings for other professions to intervene between the architect and his client, which now, more than before the war, was likely to be a corporation with rigidly defined needs rather than a more pliable individual like our Mr. Blandings. Facing this new complexity was a daily experience for architects specifying materials for their buildings. Although there was of course enthusiasm for the new possibilities these created—Louis Kahn suggested that architects indulge in "experiments in form" to find the beauty promised by such wartime products as metal sprays, texture guns, and asbestos—there was a certain anxiety, too, as technological complexity increased.[42] One measure of the size of the task facing architects was the growth of the

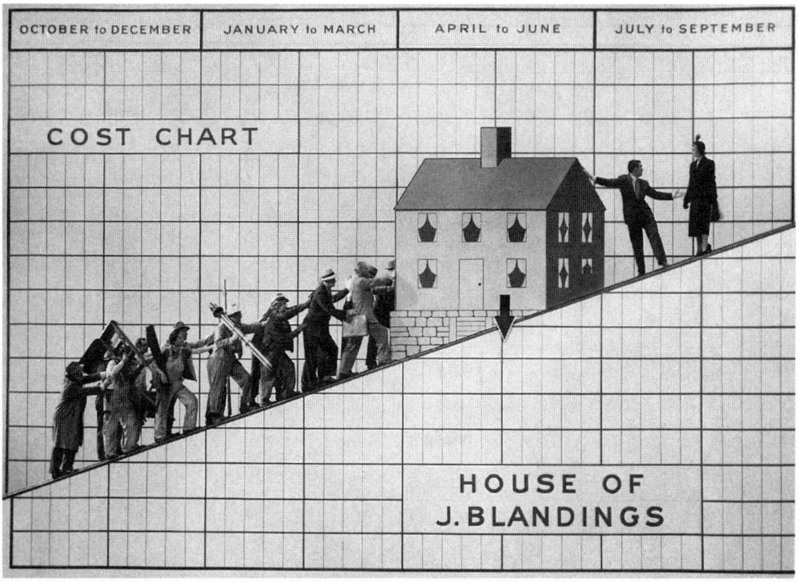

Part of the publicity package for *Mr. Blandings*, this chart shows various construction professionals, including the architect, pushing up the cost of the Blandings' house. No longer the man-in-charge, the architect has been subsumed by the "building industry," leaving the Blandings to rely on only themselves.

Sweet's catalog of architectural products. At the 1954 AIA convention in Boston, architect Ben Small compared his father's catalog, "an emaciated one-volume affair," with his own, "comprised of 1,387 catalogs, issued by 1,167 firms, spread over 11,988 pages, describing 555 broad designations of building products."[43] Toward the end of the decade, Hugh Stubbins reflected on the way in which architects' autonomy had become a casualty of the newly complicated "building industry" a term, incidentally, which was on the ascendant after the war, reflecting an expanded roster of rival professions:

> In 1900, one man could know practically everything required for architectural practice. Today, one man can be thoroughly proficient in only a limited area, and consulting engineering services are essential. The complexity of modern life, the tempo of exploration, and the compilation of facts, theories and knowledge make it nearly

> impossible for one man, one architect, ever to know all he should know about design and building—to say nothing of the disciplines that impinge on the creation of the total physical environment. More and more other fields—real estate, finance, engineering, and business promotion are initiating and developing our physical surroundings.[44]

NAVIGATING POSTWAR COMPLEXITY

The interplay between novel postwar conditions—new techniques, new building types, new roles for the architect—and the war-tested professional responses can be seen in the design of one of the first skyscrapers to be completed after the war: Harrison and Abramowitz's Alcoa Building, built in Pittsburgh in 1952. Alcoa, which had promoted possible future architectural uses for sheet aluminum throughout the war, commissioned Wallace Harrison and Max Abramowitz to design an aluminum curtain-wall for the building. This new system was in turn marketed to architects in a series of how-to pullouts, complete with measured construction details, that appeared in the architectural press. The Alcoa Building is also notable as an early example of the limitations imposed by certain building types. Unlike the more complete design of Gordon Bunshaft's Lever House of 1951, where the technological innovations in the curtain wall were matched by bold urbanism, the Alcoa Building might be seen to inaugurate the era of skin-and-lobby architectural involvement in skyscraper design. Because of the increasingly strict demands of the structural and mechanical systems, and the mysterious financial regimens necessary to make the building pay, tall commercial buildings offered little space for a comprehensive architectural solution. To remain viable, then, many architects cast themselves as technical specialists or team managers, just as they sought to do under similar conditions during the war. For some, of course, the affluence of the 1950s created another option. Architects interested in emphasizing design could now market themselves again as tastemakers, experts in creating imagery for the new institutions of the postwar world. The success of Harrison and Abramowitz can be attributed in part to their mastery of these two modes, managing the work of others at the United Nations headquarters and conspicuously designing when called for at Lincoln Center or the Albany Mall. In the Alcoa Building, they approached the wartime ideal of the synthesizing architect; they demonstrated technical expertise in the development of the aluminum system, preserved aesthetic credentials in its patterned resolution, and managed a team of associated architects. The plan of the building, however, dramatizes their role as a sort of aesthetic consultant: like the aluminum skin, the detached entrance hall is an architect-designed element of fantasy, while, across a small gap, the rest of the building is redolent of the crude exigencies of loading docks, elevator cores, duct shafts, and leasable floor areas.

Other new building opportunities tended to cast architects in narrower roles. The State Department's foreign embassy building program, begun in earnest in 1954, employed architects primarily for their image-making abilities, thus confining them to the same role that they often played in government projects during the war. After satisfying the security and protocol demands of the program, carefully insured by a rigid sequential review process, the architects were given a relatively free hand to design. Still, though novel development of the complex program is evident in some of the buildings, it is clear that architects were empowered primarily to fabricate suitable imagery—usually pan-cultural exotic in the Third World, pseudo-monumental in the West. Thus the embassy building program, which was one of the most visible examples of government patronage in the 1950s, may have reflected and perpetuated trends that stereotyped the architect in exactly the ways they had resisted during the war. Indeed, just as in the war, the ability of architects to do anything beyond theatrical scene-setting seems to have been in doubt in the federal government. For example, in 1947 the AIA was approached to consult with government agencies on a federal building program, the design of Veteran's Administration hospitals. Echoing wartime fears, the AIA warned that "if the results are not outstanding, we may find ourselves set back a generation, and the government bureaus convinced that to get a job done they must design it themselves."[45] By 1954, this worry seems to have developed into a fear that the profession would be limited by persistent government distrust. In a session entitled "The Impact of Government on Architecture" at that year's AIA convention, a Washington economist warned that "In an era when government is acquiring a 'pervasive' influence in the shaping of architecture, architects must be on guard lest the inherent conservatism of government confine their profession by rigid dogmas."[46]

ARCHITECTURE AS AN ART

Such war-aggravated uncertainties naturally encouraged a new emphasis on assessing the place of architects and architecture. Building on momentum gained during the war when it was a staple topic, self-conscious evaluation became a signal feature of the late 1940s and the 1950s. Typical of the efforts to assess the profession in the wake of World War II was the conference held at Princeton University on March 5 and 6, 1947. At this conference, entitled "Planning Man's Physical Environment," a comprehensive cross section of the profession gathered to map a future for architecture after the uncertain experiences of the war. All camps were represented, from AIA traditionalists to modern icons and theorists, including Frank Lloyd Wright and Siegfried Giedion. The director of the conference, Arthur Holden, acknowledged that this "broader course reduced the likelihood of specific accomplishment" but defended it on the grounds that a large, frequently dissenting group would more readily discover and understand "those diverse forces which are likely to influence man's environment in the future."[47] Accordingly, there was little openly agreed-to or resolved at the conference, save those ideas motivated by the lurking common concern for maintaining architecture's viability.

Speakers at Princeton suggested subtle ways to buttress the architect's position in the cycle of building, relying on strategies developed during the war. As chairman of a session on "The Physical Possibilities and Limitations of Design," John Burchard, then serving as a government consultant on prefabrication and modular standards, suggested that architects increase their involvement in these pursuits as a way to reclaim more complete control over building design: "Today, the architect is too much the designer at the end and not at the beginning."[48] By putting the "architecture" into the off-the-shelf componentry that many then saw as the inevitable future medium of American construction, architects might be assured a continuing role in design. Later, at a session called "Architecture Transcending Utility" the opposing (or complementary) strategy was suggested. In remarks that at once recalled wartime attitudes and defined a way for the profession to go beyond them, Theodore Greene, a Yale philosophy professor, stressed the primacy of architecture over "mere engineering": "Architecture must transcend engineering because the human activities which it houses are not merely physical and utilitarian in the narrow sense, but also, and significantly, cultural and spiritual. To recognize and promote [these qualities] is the distinctive task of architecture as an art."[49]

Greene's comments neatly define an important area of reaction in the 1950s. The emphasis on "architecture as an art" became a feature of postwar architecture that was rooted in a negation of the profession's actions during the war. In part, it was an effort to put back on the "silk hat and gardenia" that Royal Barry Wills symbolically discarded in 1942, to regain the expansive practice that existed before the Depression, wartime modesty, and government neglect relegated architects to more limited roles. In the newly affluent and optimistic America of the 1950s, there were also clear economic motivations for reviving this type of practice. By stressing architecture's relative proximity to the fine arts, architects could at once distinguish themselves from the other building professions and assign themselves certain values presumed to be attractive to their upper-middle-class patrons.[50] Cast as artists, they were also less immediately accountable for maintaining currency with the various technologies that they could no longer hope to master. In a sense, the architects who adopted this strategy forfeited claim to some traditionally held areas of influence in order to exaggerate others that were seen to be more distinctive, thereby creating a clearer, more marketable role to present to their chosen clientele. Pursuing a course in which it was essential to be perceived as a member of an elite group, they also distanced themselves from the body of practicing architects.

The major American proponent of the new architecture-as-an-art was, of course, Philip Johnson. Beginning with his and Henry-Russell Hitchcock's aestheticization of modern European architecture in the *International Style* exhibition of 1932 at the Museum of Modern Art, and continuing through his influential tenure as *éminence grisé* at MoMA, Johnson had a singularly powerful hand in directing American architecture toward self-consciously aesthetic design. Vincent Scully's often-repeated account of his own awakening to Johnson's message attests both to Johnson's influence and to the novelty and mock heresy of his position:

> [1949] is the date when Philip Johnson began to give his splendid talks which those of us who first heard them regarded almost as the pronouncements of the Devil. He stood up on the platform at Yale University, and he said to a shocked hush across the room, "I would rather sleep in the nave of Chartres Cathedral with the nearest john two blocks down the street than I would in a Harvard house with back-to-back bathrooms!" This terrible and even rather frightening pronouncement was the one after which, for the first time, I remember students saying to me, "He's talking about architecture as an art!" And suddenly I realized that that is what it was all the time.[51]

The combination of Johnson's erudition and celebrated wit won him the hearts and minds of many students, especially those at Harvard and Yale in the late 1940s and early 1950s. These students—some Johnson's Harvard classmates during his belated education there—affected what Peter Blake has called Johnson's "naughtiness," his aristocratic disdain for the trappings of the business of architecture, and modeled that sass into a new mode of practice. Such Harvard-bred reactionaries as Victor Lundy, John Johansen, and Paul Rudolph chose this studied irreverence and artistic intensity as elements of a professional strategy that resisted marginalization, preempting it, in a sense, with specialization. Outside of Johnson's sphere, the disciples of Wright, notably John Lautner and Paolo Soleri, emulated their master's more rural eccentricity to similar ends.

THE PERSISTENCE OF VISION

Ironically, while the "artistic" practice favored by many younger architects might be seen as a romantic return to a prewar model, the more conservative wing of the profession generally proposed a continuation of the newer models developed during the war. In *The Architect at Mid-Century*, the AIA's monumental two-volume appraisal of the state of architecture after the war, the architect was promoted as a master of synthesis in both management and design—a bold, technically literate leader of the group, not an artist catering to individual tastes—a formulation that descends directly from the bureau-ready "technical planning professional" who appeared during the war. In the foreword, Ralph Walker, AIA president when the study was commissioned in 1950, described the ideal of the "master-designer," opposing it to the "mere artist concept":

> There is everywhere in evidence a need for the over-all designer who takes the many parts and successfully molds them into an efficient whole. But there is a danger that the architect may attempt to revert to the mere artist concept, letting others do the coordinating and eventually losing control of the way the building itself is constructed. The complications of modern life make it very difficult for any concept of the master-builder to develop. There is, however, a great need for the master-designer fully conversant with construction requirements who can take leadership not only in production of architectural and engineering design but also in guiding the actual building in the field. In America there has developed a recognition by the building industry as a whole that the architect should take this position of leadership.[52]

The bulk of *The Architect at Mid-Century* broadly described the current state of practice with an eye toward repelling perceived incursions by engineers, consultants, and the "package builder." While it is clear that the editors wanted to avoid the appearance of being openly partisan—they saw their study joining the scientific surveys already undertaken by many other professions after the war—the impartial analysis is often disrupted. Concerning the architect's relationship to the engineer, still portrayed elsewhere as the greatest rival to the architect, the editors allowed themselves only this telling harangue, buried in a footnote: "The occasional absence of [complete cooperation between architects and engineers] has at times led to disagreements, suspicion, and even antagonism, which provoked a segment in each profession to desire the absorption of the other or to assume the other's function."[53] The necessity of continuing good relations may have softened the official view toward engineers; the editors warmed to the task of demeaning those professions whose points of intersection with architecture were less exact, poorly understood, and therefore more threatening: "Another type of consulting service has appeared in recent years, furnished by individuals who profess special knowledge of a particular type of building such as schools, hospitals, and churches. Many of these new consultants, though not architects, exceed their legitimate counsel and endeavor to usurp architectural functions which the architect cannot properly relinquish."[54] The most vitriolic language in *The Architect at Mid-Century* was reserved for the so-called "package services," those speculative builders who offered customers in-house architects to expedite the design and construction of their products, usually small houses in new suburban subdivisions. A full page of dense legalistic justification was followed by this warning to the consumer: "Package Service is thus a vending operation devoid of professional standards and subject only to the rule of 'let the buyer beware.' As such, its very use of the term 'service' is paradoxical and misleading. In light of all its hazards, few owners, embarking on a major building enterprise, can afford to adopt a system which so clearly involves so many shortsighted gambles."[55]

There is a clear connection between this warning and the one issued by the AIA in Albert Kahn's name in 1942. In each, in order to define the unique scope of architectural production, the architect is cast as a master of synthesis whose vision is ignored at the client's peril. Similarly, it is possible to see the Princeton conference and *The Architect at Mid-Century* as part of a larger culture of analysis and critique that could be considered one of the most important legacies of the uneasy passage of architect through the war. It is significant that shortly after the war, in November 1946, *Progressive Architecture* published its first tentative "experiment" in architectural criticism.

In an explanatory editorial, Thomas Creighton and Kenneth Reid suggested that "professional criticism" was the proper peacetime function for a magazine bent on reforming the profession it served.[56] Later, *Architectural Forum* began publishing its first criticisms of built work, ostensibly in support of its stated mission, "to bring architecture into focus as the primary force in building an American civilization."[57] Speculating further, one can look at popular books such as *Building USA*, published in 1957 by the editors of *Architectural Forum*, where the most bitter language of the war years reappeared to popularize the idea that "the Architect is, in the end, the one figure who can really create architecture in America, by organizing and synthesizing the various building forces for his client."[58] Chapters on all aspects of American building such as the corporate client, new materials, and the relative merits of architecture and engineering were also punctuated by overtly mythologizing passages and chapter headings, reminiscent of the false grandeur of *The Fountainhead.* One read, "He Carries the Ancient Moral Commission." "The '60s: A P/A Symposium on the State of Architecture," edited by Creighton, offers another late echo of architectural insecurities clearly voiced in the war. Over three months in the early spring of 1961, *Progressive Architecture* published the responses of fifty architects asked to reflect on the status of architectural theory, practice, and technology. Far from reaching the redemptive resolution that seems to have been his goal—the production of a consensus future course for architecture and architects—Creighton declared the results evidence of structural failure in the profession and coined the term Chaoticism to describe its increasingly confused output.

MR. BLANDINGS GETS HIS DREAM HOUSE

The combination of the war and the subsequent affluence, neglect by the government and the sometimes contentious turf battles that ran through the 1950s, contributed to the persistence of the dual images of the tastemaker and the technician, one veering toward art and the other toward engineering, which became loosely standardized as broad strategies to resist ongoing threats to the autonomy of the profession. Their common hope, that the architect would establish himself in the building industry as the focus of creative vision, was used to stave off the identity crisis faced by architects when areas of intervention were closed to them during the war. As the useful caricatures of Simms and Funkhauser reveal so plainly, after the war architects were still very much at sea. No artistic affectation or technical veneer could hide the fact that they had abruptly entered the modern age cleaving to professional models that had served them well for centuries, but would no longer. They were battered by events, out of their depth in a new world of materials, outclassed by professions that had used the war as a time to grow, not gripe. In the end, thanks to his engineers and contractors, Mr. Blandings got his dream house. What did his architects get?

NOTES

I would like to thank Joan Ockman, who guided much of this research over many years.

1. Eric Hodgins, *Mr. Blandings Builds His Dream House* (New York: Simon and Schuster, 1946), 59.
2. Ibid., 59, 68.
3. C. W. Short and R. Stanley-Brown, *Public Buildings: A Survey of Architecture* (Washington, DC: U.S. Government Printing Office, 1939).
4. "The Threshing Floor," *Pencil Points* (April 1940): 19.
5. Kenneth Reid, "Architects Must Be Used," *Pencil Points* (May 1941).
6. Michael Rosenauer, "The Architect's Position in the Present Period of Emergency," *The Octagon* (May 1941): 12.
7. Royal Barry Wills, letter to the editor, *New Pencil Points* (June 1942): 8.
8. Charles Killam, "School Training for Architecture," *Pencil Points* (July 1937): 442.
9. Ibid., 443.
10. Eugene Raskin, "Is Architecture Going to the Bauhaus?" *Pencil Points* (April 1939): 237.
11. William Lescaze, "How Can I Be Useful?" *Pencil Points* (September 1940): n.p.
12. Charles Magruder, "Architects and a New Era," *Pencil Points* (June 1941): n.p.
13. "Architects in National Defense: A Radio Broadcast by Ernest E, Weihe, AIA," *Architect and Engineer* (May 1941): n.p.
14. Thomas H. Creighton, *Planning to Build* (Garden City, NY: Doubleday, Doran and Co., 1945): 76.

15. Lieutenant Lawrence A. Benenson, "Have the Schools Met Their Responsibility?" *Architect and Engineer* (March 1945): 19–20.
16. William Lescaze, *On Being an Architect* (New York: G. P. Putnam's Sons, 1942): 255.
17. "Washington Progress," *Pencil Points* (March 1942): 122.
18. "Editorial Comment," *Pencil Points* (May 1942): 244.
19. R. Penleigh Boyd, "Death of the Architect," *Pencil Points* (April 1942): 182.
20. Ely Jacques Kahn, "Talk If You Must But Act!" *Pencil Points* (February 1941).
21. "Notice of Amendments-Resolutions Adopted by the Seventy-Third Convention of the American Institute of Architects," *The Octagon* (June 1941): 26.
22. Lenore Fine and Jesse A. Remington, *The Corps of Engineers: Construction in the United States,* from the series *The United States Army in World War II* (Washington, DC: U.S. Army, 1972): 566.
23. Willis A. Vogel, "Our Campaign Progresses," *Pencil Points* (May 1942): 267.
24. Walter R. Hagedohm, "Can the Planning Professions Cooperate?" *Pencil Points* (March 1942): 168.
25. Nathaniel Owings, *The Spaces in Between* (Boston: Houghton Mifflin, 1973), 88.
26. Samuel E. Lunden, "The Architect in the War Program," *Pencil Points* (April 1943): 24.
27. Serge Chermayeff, "Architects vs. Engineers," *Pencil Points* (March 1942): 10.
28. "Tribute to Albert Kahn," *The Octagon* (July 1942): 32.
29. "Aluminum City Terrace Housing," *Architectural Forum* (July 1944): 67.
30. Ibid., 65.
31. Elizabeth Mock, ed., *Built in USA: 1932–1944* (New York: Museum of Modern Art, 1945), 9.
32. Larry Perkins, "Perspectives," *Pencil Points* (September 1944): 61.
33. "The Seabees: The Navy's Fighting Builders," *Architectural Forum* (February 1944): 50.
34. Ibid., 58.
35. Fine and Remington, *The Corps of Engineers*, 440.
36. George Howe, "The Relation of the Architect to Government," *Weekly Bulletin of the Michigan Society of Architects* (31 July 1945): 1.
37. Thomas Creighton, "Pearl Harbor to Nagasaki," *Progressive Architecture* (January 1946): 42.
38. Ibid., 60.
39. "Make That Housing Good!" *Progressive Architecture* (June 1949): 55.
40. "Readers Say," *Pencil Points* (August 1945): 87.
41. "Architects and Manufacturers," *Progressive Architecture* (January 1947): 1.
42. Louis Kahn, "On Monumentality" in Paul Zucker, ed., *New Architecture and City Planning* (New York: Philosophical Library, 1944), 583.
43. *Architectural Record* (August 1954): 294.
44. Hugh Stubbins, "The Challenge to Architectural Education," *Journal of Architectural Education* 2 (autumn 1958): 15–6.
45. *Architectural Forum* (April 1947): 16.
46. *Architectural Record* (August 1954): 292.

47. "Planning Man's Physical Environment," Princeton University, 1947, 1.

48. Ibid., 6.

49. Ibid., 10.

50. See Robert Woods Kennedy, *The House and the Art of Its Design* (New York: Reinhold, 1953): 18–21. Using an admittedly flip and subjective chart to determine the possible client base for modern architecture, the author concludes that only 5 percent of the population—the "innovating" part of the upper-middle class—would consider employing a modern architect.

51. Vincent Scully, "Doldrums in the Suburbs," *Journal of the Society of Architectural Historians* 24 (March 1965): 36–47. See also Johnson's "Seven Crutches of Modern Architecture," *Perspecta* 3 (1955): 40–4.

52. Turpin Bannister, ed., *The Architect at Mid-Century: Evolution and Achievement*, vol. I, and *Conversations Across the Nation*, vol. II (New York: Reinhold, 1954): xiv.

53. Bannister, *The Architect at Mid-Century*. vol. I, 64, n. 11.

54. Ibid., 39–40.

55. Ibid., 23.

56. "Architectural Criticism," *Progressive Architecture* (November 1946): 55.

57. Richard Miller, "Disenchantment and Criticism: The State of Modern Architecture" *Journal of Architectural Education* (1959): 12.

58. *Architectural Forum, Building USA: The Men and Methods That Influence Building in America Today* (New York: McGraw Hill, 1957), 141.

Cinematographer Albert Maysles with camera looking toward the Getty Research Institute at the Getty Center.

BUILDING *a* FILM:
MAKING *Concert of Wills*

BOB EISENHARDT

BACK IN 1985, when the Getty Trust was envisioning what would become, a dozen years later, the Getty Center in Los Angeles, they made a bold decision to document the entire design and building process on film. For Maysles Films this decision began an endeavor that paralleled the architectural creation and shared some of the same creative struggles in an often analogous process. As co-filmmaker and editor of the resulting film I am admittedly not its most objective critic. Nevertheless, there can be little doubt that *Concert of Wills: Making the Getty,* which was shown first at the opening of the center in December 1997 and released nationally in 1998, is a unique production, unlike any other film about architecture.

In truth, relatively few documentary films about architecture are made at all. Though architecture is the most intimate of the arts—we sleep in it, eat in it, work and play in it—there seems to be little audience interest in films about it. Those that do get produced tend to be surveys or profiles of an important architect and his work (the protagonist almost inevitably being male). Sometimes these films make it to public television. The Getty project offered an opportunity to make a different kind of film, one in which the focus was on the actual process of making architecture. From the outset, our primary goal was to make the audience feel a part of the ongoing struggle to create the center.

This approach was particularly appealing to me, because I had trained and practiced as an architect before turning to filmmaking. Unencumbered by plumbing details and ventilation systems, with film I felt I could communicate ideas and emotions in a more direct, effective way. In practice, I found the development of a building program remarkably similar to the manipulation of images to tell a story. This is especially true in the editing of a documentary film, where the process is one of identifying the parameters of existing material, developing an underlying concept, and shaping each element to contribute to a central idea.

Prior to the Getty project I had been able to make only one other film about architecture. In 1983, I produced and directed *Spaces: The Architecture of Paul Rudolph*. It was well received (it earned an Oscar nomination and won an Emmy), but its scope was limited. Only thirty minutes long, made on a small budget raised from the National Endowment for the Arts and the New York State Council on the Arts, it showed Rudolph in the final design stages of the Emory University Chapel, followed by the presentation of those designs to the client in Atlanta. The film also traced, mostly in Rudolph's own words, the progression of his work and some of the controversy it generated. Admittedly, the film fell into the hagiographic survey/profile category.

When the Getty's trustees approached Maysles Films with the idea of creating a visual document of the design process, they were undecided about what kind of film, or even how many films, they wanted. What they did know was that they wanted to create an archive of the entire design and construction process, and that they wanted to do so honestly and inconspicuously. This meshed well with Maysles' *cinema verité* approach to filmmaking, developed by the brothers David and Albert Maysles in a series of important nonfiction films, including *Salesman* (1969), *Grey Gardens* (1975), and *Gimme Shelter* (1970), which followed the Rolling Stones on a tour that ended in the Altamont concert murder. The Maysles helped propagate what they called "direct cinema," a risky approach that consumes considerable time and resources, and may well not succeed in finding a story to tell. This is performed with the smallest possible crew, ideally two persons (a cinematographer and a sound recorder), to facilitate mobility and minimize intrusiveness. It is the role of the film editor to shape the incredible mass of raw material gathered by this crew (almost two hundred hours by the end of this project) into a viable film.

In fact, Maysles was not involved in the Getty project from its inception. When we began work, in 1985, planning and preparation for the center had already been under way for some time. The Getty Center was made possible when, upon the death of J. Paul Getty in 1976, the bulk of his estate—some $700 million—was left to the trust he had founded. In 1983, the endowment grew to $1.7 billion following the takeover of Getty Oil by Texaco, and the Getty set about its broad mandate "to oversee a museum, a library, and the diffusion of general and artistic knowledge." Under the leadership of Harold Williams, a chairman of the Securities and Exchange Commission during the Carter Administration, the trust envisioned not just a museum but an institution that would combine formal galleries with facilities for education, conservation, and scholarship. A search was undertaken for a suitable site to accommodate such a campus, resulting in the purchase of an astonishing hilltop location in Los Angeles with commanding views stretching from the San Gabriel mountains to the Pacific Ocean. This magnificent site would prove to be both the governing design factor and the source of unending complications for everyone involved.

The Getty had also selected an architect before we began filming. In an arduous selection process, they had formed an advisory committee, assembled a list of thirty-three architects, chosen seven of these as semifinalists, and whittled that list down to three: James Sterling, Fumihiko Maki, and Richard Meier. All three had experience designing museums, but the Getty board awarded the "Commission of the Century" to Meier. When Williams was asked, some thirteen years later, why Meier had been chosen, he made special note of Meier's promised commitment of time. In fact, for much of the following thirteen years Meier would live in a house on the site.

Both the selection of the site and the architect would have been informative had we captured them on film; questions about these two fundamental choices colored the entire project. In the end, we were forced to rely on interviews and on other scenes in which these decisions were referenced to convey the Getty's rationale for both choices.

Architect Richard Meier with Maysles and producer Susan Froemke in the entrance hall of the J. Paul Getty Museum at the Getty Center.

If the "direct cinema" approach demanded that we work without preconceived notions of where the project was leading, we were not alone. In an unusual move, the Getty had hired Meier before settling on an architectural program. Because the Getty was still defining what it wanted from the project, it had determined neither how much space to devote to its various needs nor how those spaces should be disposed in relation to one another. It was Williams's intention that Meier develop the program and the design concurrently while interacting with Getty staffers. Though we did not necessarily understand it at the time, the consequence of the Getty's decision to proceed on such an uncharted course was the very "concert of wills" that gave the film its title and generated its various dramas.

One of those dramas was quickly proving to be the difficulties posed by the site. Homeowners from the wealthy neighboring communities of Bel Air and Brentwood demanded stringent conditions be placed on any development, finally imposing more than 170 conditions on the Getty, including height restrictions and a prohibition against white or reflective exterior surfaces. On camera, Meier playfully chided the locals' concerns about the high visibility of the project: "'If you're going to build, build it in a way we can't see it.' Well, that's not so easy!" Another restriction stated that no earth could be removed from the site: "Every spoonful of dirt that you take out of one area you have to find a home for in another," explained construction superintendent Ron Bayek—a gigantic logistical problem.

The restrictions on the exterior cladding also proved a stumbling block for Meier, who believes strongly in the use of white surfaces, inside and out, to allow the forms of his buildings to be perceived clearly. On camera, Meier explained that "white is not the absence of color, but the abundance of color." Whereas the use of a light surface on the exterior was a problem for the neighboring communities, the white walls of Meier's painting galleries drew fire from within the Getty itself. John Walsh, director of the museum, believed that the Getty's collection of fifteenth- to eighteenth-century art called for dark, textured backgrounds in galleries more traditional in character—not Meier's modern, open spaces.

In September 1986, Meier was filmed proposing the master plan. The scheme located the six major buildings on two ridges that stretched out across the site like arms. Between the two ridges would be a central garden designed to tie them together. These ideas revealed themselves in a series of meetings that Maysles Films was invited to California to shoot. This became the method. When the Getty felt there was an event or meeting that was appropriate to film, Maysles would be invited to attend. This was unusual for Maysles, as we normally feel unrestricted access to a film's subjects is essential. Although it gave the Getty considerable control over what was filmed, it also made logistical and economic sense for our New York-based team. During the early stages of the project, filming took place only two or

Harold M. Williams, former president of the J. Paul Getty Trust, and artist Robert Irwin at the Getty Center.

three times a year. As time passed, it became apparent that the project was taking much longer then anyone had anticipated. Construction began on a "fast track" in 1990, long before drawings were complete. While trying to hold down costs and keep the project on schedule, and while attempting to find a compromise between Walsh's and Meier's gallery aesthetics, the Getty trustees decided that Meier's concept for the central gardens was falling short of expectations.

If these various conflicts now seem clear and relevant to the final result, that was not how they appeared in 1988, when we first reviewed our material. More than three years of shooting had produced about thirty hours of raw footage, much of it meetings, most of it very technical and detailed, with the minutiae and relevant information given seemingly equal weight. After producer Susan Froemke and I viewed the footage, I began making "selects," pulling out the best footage and reducing it by about 50 percent to bring the most significant material forward. We then began to discuss what parts of that action could be developed into story lines. This process would continue throughout the project.

In 1992 the Getty hired Robert Irwin, a conceptual artist, to work on the design of the central gardens. A few months later the Maysles team was on hand for a presentation of Irwin's preliminary scheme, a meeting that famously escalated into an argument between Meier and Irwin. It became apparent that no collaboration between the two would be possible when Meier associate Harry Wolf asserted that the Meier scheme better suited the site, and Irwin curtly responded, "Bullshit."

For us the meeting was also a watershed. Some Getty staffers believed the argument never would have happened if the camera had not been present, but it seems quite clear from the footage that the camera had little influence over what transpired. As with the material included in the film, the material we cut showed the participants to be quite unaware of the camera's presence. Nevertheless, a concerned Getty felt that ours might be the wrong type of film and began to actively search for a replacement to Maysles. They also assured us that the footage of that meeting would never appear in a film. It was a year before the Getty decided to continue with Maysles and we were invited back to continue shooting.

On the issue of the central gardens, the Getty decided to proceed with the Irwin scheme instead of Meier's solution. The continuing debate over the colors of the painting galleries was also resolved when Thierry Despont, an architect who had been recreating period rooms for the display of the decorative arts collection, was commissioned to rework Meier's interior designs. Meier's loss of control in these areas, and the subsequent conflicts, compromises, and frustrations this loss of control entailed, unfolded as the film's most dramatic story line.

Ironically, *Spaces: The Architecture of Paul Rudolph* told a similar story. The film followed Rudolph to Emory University, where he presented a design for an altar that would serve as the centerpiece of the school's new chapel. The client rejected the proposal, leaving Rudolph to wave an exasperated arm in disgust: "Let them finish it!" Rudolph returned later for a ceremony in front of the substitute design, swallowing his pride in a telling demonstration of the compromises inherent in the making of architecture for an institutional client.

Maysles continued to film whenever the Getty felt that something important was happening, and pushed for access to what we considered ongoing story lines. In 1995 the Getty asked us if we could make a twenty-odd-minute film from the material on hand to show in the auditorium of the new center. After filming for ten years and having now compiled more than one hundred hours of "selects," we began to assess if indeed there was a film to be found somewhere in that footage. As we suspected, we found that we had most of the elements needed to tell a story. Certain threads emerged. The effects of the land-use restrictions, the choice of the building's exterior cladding material, the debate over the gallery interiors, and the struggle over the central gardens all seemed like issues that described the process. We felt we had a story that could be told, but that it would take at least ninety minutes to do so. The Getty was comfortable with our proposal, and we were given the go-ahead.

As with the selection of Meier as architect, Getty's choice of Maysles brought with it a distinct aesthetic perspective. Though the film was essentially *verité* in approach, the scope of the project—the number of players involved, the intricacy of the subject, and, particularly, the factor of time—demanded a creative mingling of filmmaking styles. Informal interviews—Froemke dubbed them "updates"—became useful, natural, and eventually welcome opportunities for all of the participants to air their sides of the story. This technique also became a way to clarify technical issues for our audience. Architecture is always complex, and this was an exceptionally complex piece of architecture.

In August 1997, as the center was nearing completion, we presented a rough cut of *Concert of Wills* to the Getty. We felt it was a frank and honest account of their twelve-year struggle but knew it would be controversial. The notorious Meier-Irwin garden meeting was included. Many of the film's participants were present at the screening and, at the very least, were faced with the uncomfortable prospect of watching themselves age a dozen years in a hundred minutes.

The end of the film was greeted by an uncomfortable silence. This was followed by the airing of concerns that the film failed to make clear the basic goals that Williams had established for the center

Meier, Maysles, and Froemke at the Getty Center.

and that complaints by the architect were excessive and redundant. For the next two months we struggled to redress these anxieties. Every area that raised a red flag was carefully examined, and much was re-edited. However, it became apparent that some of the requested changes would damage the integrity of the project. The film was presented again, controversial aspects intact, and the Getty bravely accepted it.

The film is currently being prepared for national broadcast on the Public Broadcasting System (PBS), which demands that the film conform to a standard time slot (ninety minutes) almost twelve minutes shorter than the version released to theaters nationally in 1998. The first few minutes came off like those few extra pounds you finally admit you must lose before summer arrives and the beach beckons. The process then became more difficult, the amputations more painful. Perhaps therein lies the great lesson of the Getty Center: in the end, we are all forced to compromise.

PART TWO

BEHIND *the* SCENES

CEDRIC GIBBONS: ARCHITECT *of* HOLLYWOOD'S GOLDEN AGE

CHRISTINA WILSON

OF ALL THE artists who created screen settings during cinema's Golden Age, none was more famous than Cedric Gibbons. As head of Metro-Goldwyn-Mayer's art department, he gained unparalleled recognition as one of the film industry's most influential designers. Gibbons set Hollywood's artistic standards with elegant settings that attracted audiences to MGM films, garnered critical acclaim, and popularized ideas about architecture and interior design. Between 1930 and 1957 Gibbons received eleven Academy Awards—and was nominated an additional twenty-nine times—for his achievements in art direction, an indication of the high status he enjoyed in Hollywood throughout his career. Ironically, the Oscar itself is his most recognizable production: Gibbons designed the streamlined statuette in 1928.

The films Gibbons designed varied significantly in genre, style, and scope, from contemporary dramas and period pieces to musicals and war pictures. Although his repertoire was immense, Gibbons was particularly renowned for introducing modern design to Hollywood films, as exemplified by such ensemble dramas as *Grand Hotel* (1932) and *The Women* (1939). These films, made during the dark years of the Great Depression, encapsulate what made MGM's films so suc-

OPPOSITE: **Cedric Gibbons photographed with the Oscar statuette.**

cessful and what propelled Gibbons' career. The studio's combination of stars, sentimental stories, and elegant settings created escapist dream worlds for audiences that desperately needed them. The consistent box office success of these films made MGM among the most successful of Hollywood's studios amid the financial storms of the 1930s, and Gibbons benefited as a result of the company's stability. The architectural environments that he created at MGM during this period served as the paradigms of progressive set design during the Golden Age of American cinema, the most celebrated phase of Hollywood history and Gibbons' career.

Little is known of Gibbons' early years—largely because he was reluctant to discuss his personal history. The son of a builder, he was raised in an Irish Catholic neighborhood in Brooklyn. His artistic career began at the Art Students League of New York, where he studied art, particularly life drawing, between 1915 and 1918. In 1918, he joined Goldwyn Pictures, a small studio founded two years earlier in New York. From its 1916 inception, the fledging studio boasted films that aspired to high art. To reinforce the point, founder Samuel Goldwyn appropriated one of the stone lions guarding the recently completed New York Public Library, located across the street from the company's Forty-second Street offices, as the house symbol. Goldwyn hired Hugo Ballin, an academic painter, to design sets and to create pictorial compositions for the movie screen; Ballin would serve as Gibbons' artistic mentor from the moment the young artist joined the studio, just two months before his twenty-eighth birthday. After a brief stint in the navy during World War I, Gibbons moved with Goldwyn Pictures to California in January 1919 and soon started designing his own sets. Although many of these films have been lost, photographs suggest Gibbons' earliest cinematic aesthetic was typical for the time: interiors filled with patterned wallpaper, dark furniture, elaborate woodwork, and an array of heavy fabrics and rich textures.

Gibbons' career changed dramatically in 1924 when theater magnate Marcus Loew purchased Goldwyn Pictures and merged it with Metro Pictures and the Louis B. Mayer Production Company, forming Metro-Goldwyn-Mayer. Both Louis B. Mayer and Irving Thalberg, the heads of the new studio's California operations, were impressed with Gibbons and his ability to produce attractive sets within one of Goldwyn's most efficiently run departments. Gibbons was one of only two department heads to be retained when most of the employees from both Metro and Goldwyn were purged from the new conglomerate. The earliest records from MGM, which date from the summer of 1924, list Gibbons as head of the art department and indicate that he was one of the first department heads to be appointed. Gibbons quickly demonstrated his value by designing sets for several films, from the colossal stages for the epic *Ben Hur* (1925) to the elegant drawing rooms of the Greta Garbo vehicles *Flesh and the Devil* (1927) and *The Mysterious Lady* (1928).

From the beginning, Gibbons ran MGM's art department as if it were a large architectural office. By the late 1930s, he supervised a staff that ranged between fifty and eighty highly trained specialists including architects, decorators, and sketch artists as well as renderers, draftsmen, carpenters, painters, secretaries, and clerks. The department had divisions responsible for props, miniatures, and models, made and upholstered its own furniture, and manufactured drapes, wall hangings, and rugs exclusively for its film settings. These furnishings, as well as the disassembled sets, were stored in warehouses on the MGM lot.

The department's large size during this period reflected the needs imposed by the studio's annual output of more than fifty pictures, each of which required between fifteen and forty sets. In order to produce so many films each year, MGM typically had several pictures in production simultaneously. The result of this enormous output was that Gibbons was responsible for the creation of hundreds of sets every year. To ensure that each film received adequate artistic attention, Gibbons divided the work up among his staff by breaking down the production process into a series of systematic steps. Although this meant that much of the work was done by subordinates, Gibbons remained an active and integral part of the design process. Indeed, a studio's head art director was widely recognized during these years as far more than a designer. He was an astute businessman capable of producing sets and all their furnishings within a fixed budget, as well as an artist adept at implementing architectural principles with a high degree of photographic integrity so that those sets would be visually appealing on the screen. Like a successful architect, Gibbons deftly managed often conflicted relationships between client (producer and director) and his own craftsmen while assuring a high quality of design.

At MGM, Gibbons was often the first department head to receive a script, leaving it to him to take the initial steps toward giving a film visual form. There was generally scant written guidance: early scripts contained little if any detail about setting and provided only minimal information about locale and atmosphere. After reviewing the script, Gibbons normally created a number of what he called "roughout" sketches that would determine the general configurations for the sets' plans and the camera angles from which they would be shot: what he called "practical considerations." Once the details of the plan were resolved, the design process would commence.

The roughouts provided the first tangible information about the film's physical form for the producer, who met with Gibbons in a series of conferences to discuss general ideas for the settings. During these meetings, Gibbons also submitted estimates for the number of sets needed, their cost, and the stage space required for them. In addition, Gibbons met with the film's director, who contributed ideas and explained his own requirements. Gibbons described his meetings with directors as "long huddles."[1] Gibbons then assigned the film to a unit art director, a designer who oversaw the day-to-day work on a film and would report back on its progress to him. During the 1920s, the art department had just two or three other art directors on staff. By the 1930s, Hollywood's largest studios, including MGM, employed an average of ten unit art directors, one in charge of each film under production.

Gibbons, who created an elaborate architecture and design research library at MGM, frequently used films in the present to introduce "the most modern forms of architecture," which he lauded for their "considerable freshness in their visual impact."[2] Gibbons' use of the term *modern* suggests not the dogmatic high modernism promoted by the Bauhaus and other ideologically inclined European architects, but the variety of styles and pseudostyles devolved from it—moderne, streamline, and the like. Indeed, it has often been suggested that

Entrance foyer to the home of Diana Medford (Joan Crawford, dancing at right) in a scene from *Our Dancing Daughters* (1928).

Gibbons picked up his knowledge of modern design while attending the Paris Exposition des Arts Décoratifs in 1925—the fair whose name inspired the term *art deco*. MGM records, however, clearly indicate that Gibbons did not actually attend the fair—he was busy supervising set production for *Ben Hur*, *The Big Parade*, and several other films. Nevertheless, he would certainly have been aware of the influential Paris event. As the *New York Times* reported in 1926, the fair's design aesthetic of bold, abstracted forms and exquisite craftsmanship was "steaming toward us on every boat from France."[3] Gibbons first experimented with these design trends in the film *After Midnight* (1927), where he created the interior of a clothing shop with triangular wall sconces and glass-block shelving, an environment typical of the department stores where most Americans got their first glimpses of the modern movement.

The sets Gibbons created for the silent *Our Dancing Daughters* (1928) secured his reputation as one of Hollywood's most forward-looking designers. Gibbons designed a modern house of bold, abstracted backgrounds for the fun-loving Diana Medford (Joan Crawford), which he claimed suited her "vivid, restless personality." The house's entrance foyer features vast, unadorned walls dramatically offset by a long staircase articulated with a sharp zigzag pattern, crisp geometry, and machinelike precision. Arches flank both sides of the room with wide, deeply recessed moldings, a form of exaggerated ornamentation that enhanced the set's presentation on film. Triangular wall sconces, blocky chairs, and a hexagonal table complete the room's ensemble of modern architectural forms. The sets for *Our Dancing Daughters* were a revelation to the moviegoing public. In *Collier's*, Betty Thornley Stuart described how they caused a stir amongst critics and filmgoers alike by introducing previously unknown modern forms to a mass audience. Stuart concluded that the film would place the art director's craft on a plane of greater importance both in Hollywood and on Main Street.[4]

Though Gibbons' earliest modern settings were created for silent films, he quickly adapted the style for sound pictures. *Grand Hotel* (1932), made just three years after MGM released its first sound film, achieved a new level of dramatic depth by combining a dialog-driven plot with settings that achieved the spatial qualities of three-dimensional architecture. Gibbons' design for this film suggests what art director William Cameron Menzies would later describe as the "ideal" movie set for sound films: an ingenious combination of art, architecture, dramatic knowledge, engineering, and craftsmanship conveyed with simplicity and restraint.[5]

As the film's title suggests, the sets for *Grand Hotel* serve as a key element in the plot. The film's opening shots showcase the hotel's gracious lobby, immediately establishing the importance of the architectural space as an active component in the story. While guests move through the hotel's ground floor, bird's-eye camera placements reveal a vast central space surrounded by open balconies that serves as the building's nucleus. Unlike Gibbons' settings for silent films, which often appeared two-dimensional—like theatrical backdrops—his settings for *Grand Hotel* achieved a complex three-dimensional space that provides a compelling visual framework for the film's intermingling characters.

Set reference still of the lobby for Edmund Goulding's *Grand Hotel* (1932).

The impressive spatial grandeur conveyed in the film's opening shots is juxtaposed with more intimate views of the lobby, where the characters' paths begin to cross. After establishing the configuration of the hotel's central space, the camera zooms in on the reception desk, the lobby's focal point. Here, the curvilinear forms of the lobby's overall massing are reproduced in the building's decorative details, from the circular desk and shining metal railings to the rounded patterns in its tiled floor. Dark shafts that frame sections of the walls and metallic mullions that divide the large windows offset the lobby's circular forms with strong vertical lines. The convincing architectural space in *Grand Hotel* accommodates both the realism of dialog and the ever-shifting gaze of the moving camera. As the characters move from the central lobby to other parts of the building, the camera follows them through what film critic Edmund Cousins described as a "honeycomb set," a series of interlocking spaces that create the illusion of an entire building, although in actuality it was composed of several unconnected sets constructed on sound stages.

The resulting environment was so convincing that filmgoers could easily be transported to the splendid luxury presented before them. In an environment filled with so many creature comforts, a Depression-weary audience could lose track of the dark day-to-day circumstances awaiting them outside the theater. Yet, the characters in *Grand Hotel* find little happiness in this posh pleasure palace. All struggle with financial troubles and self-doubt, leaving the audience free to empathize with characters for whom well-appointed interiors provide little relief.

Grand Hotel's plot is driven by the dramatic device of drawing characters from a variety of social and economic backgrounds—who would otherwise not associate with one another—within a place that serves as a catalyst for their relationships. Throughout the film, director Edmund Goulding uses the hotel's architectural forms to frame the characters in compelling visual compositions. Early in the film, the streetwise stenographer Flaemmchen (Joan Crawford) looks for the room where she has been summoned to do some typing. Her search parallels that of the terminally ill Kringelein (Lionel Barrymore), who has come to Berlin's finest hotel to spend his savings and die. As they both move through the hotel lobby, into an elevator, and then along one of the hotel's upper balconies, the camera follows them as they separately admire the building's splendor. Although Flaemmchen and Kringelein have come to the hotel for vastly different reasons, the building's circular design soon brings them together. Images like these are frequently combined with views of the hotel's grand central lobby. As Flaemmchen awaits her secretarial appointment by gazing down at the lobby, she is joined by the Baron von Geigern (John Barrymore), whose aristocratic title and dapper persona conceal his identity as a jewel thief. As in many instances in the film, the hotel continually provides the essential context for the shared experiences of the characters as they become acquainted and the plot unfolds.

The careful attention to detail Gibbons lavished on the hotel's public rooms also appears in its most private areas. Kringelein's room conveys an atmosphere of luxury where the sickly clerk has come to spend the last days of his life. The room is shot from high above, making Kringelein appear small, uncertain, and even helpless in a grand space that he has claimed for himself, but to which he is not accustomed.

In *Grand Hotel*, Gibbons used one building to serve as both the catalyst and the backdrop for the film's story. In *The Women* (1939), he employed a far broader sampling of interiors to represent a wide range of late 1930s design trends. Whether the film showcases a cozy living room or a trendy beauty salon, all of these environments serve as vehicles for a plot that unfolds with the fiery dialog of catty women, the ultimate amalgamation of sound and setting on the 1930s movie screen. These settings, particularly domestic interiors, combine traditional forms and modern elements in a manner that received praise from contemporary critics and maintained Gibbons' reputation as the Hollywood art director who, as one critic wrote, "reigned supreme" in all matters artistic at MGM.[6]

The film opens in the upscale grandeur of Sydney's Salon, where ladies of ample means while away their days with mudbaths and manicures. The salon lobby establishes the film's fanciful tone in a space combining a framework of modernist forms with a touch of whimsy. This grand room is dominated by a staircase that descends from a volumetric cantilevered balcony fashioned out of taut, planar materials rendered in white. These architectural elements stand alone as separate plastic shapes joined together with wide curves, from the sweeping stairs to the swollen, spiraling legs of a glass-top table. Mounted on a flared and fluted pedestal, a larger-than-life woman's hand holding a clear orb provides an almost surreal aspect to this dreamy space. The salon also contains several of Gibbons' signature details, including an abstracted sculptural figure below the balcony that serves as a visual focal point, and rounded niches filled with shelves of perfume and cosmetics. The painted backdrop of a beach with multicolored umbrellas, blue sky, and puffy clouds adds an even more fantastic air to this place of luxury.

The salon's reception room also contains a series of Gibbons' elegant design touches. The walls, covered with a textured, striped wallpaper, are articulated with tall, fluted shafts and mirrors, framing devices Gibbons frequently used to add depth to flat surfaces.

Scene in the reception room of Sydney's Salon from *The Women* (1939).

Throughout the film, women in stylish hats and mink stoles fill the set and chatter with delight as they wait for their beauty treatments. This breezy fantasy world sets the stage for a film about pampered wives with nothing better to do than lunch and gossip between hair appointments, a pleasure-filled fantasy for Depression-weary moviegoers.

The seductive appeal of Sydney's creature comforts is also present in the film's picture-perfect domestic interiors. These spaces received notable attention from critics of the period who praised Hollywood's art directors for their creation of ideal domestic environments on the screen. Such "real" interiors quickly became models that (female) moviegoers could attempt to approximate in their own homes. The country house of *The Women*'s Mary Haines (Norma Shearer) revels in a display of cozy domesticity, an environment *House Beautiful* described as "Hollywood Provincial," and recommended as a suitable modern prototype because it "makes such a friendly home." The set's comforting domestic forms were also reflected in the personality of the occupant, a devoted wife and mother who wanted nothing more than marital bliss. The living room was a showplace of colonial revival design, a large and inviting space filled with elements praised by *House Beautiful* as essentials to a proper home environment and the "American ideal of good living."[7]

House Beautiful particularly admired Gibbons' handling of furniture. Sofas and chairs arranged at right angles and pulled together by a low coffee table made good use of space while creating private niches for conversation, essential elements in the "grammar of good American decorating." In *The Women*, several intimate conversations occur within this room's ensembles of furniture. As Mary's gossipy friends invade her home, the film's paradigm of good against evil emerges. Peggy (Joan Fontaine), devoted to all things domestic, coos about how much she admires her hostess. Sylvia (Rosalind Russell), on the other hand, curls up on the couch like a snake and can hardly wait to reveal her discovery of Stephen Haines's infidelities.

This room assumes an added dimension when an unexpected call from Stephen Haines interrupts the gathering. When he cancels plans with Mary at the last minute, a recurring pattern in recent months, Mary begins to wonder if there is more going on than extra work at the office. In the same room, Sylvia had just finished sneering that Mary is "living in a fool's paradise," while repeatedly dropping hints about Stephen "stepping out" on her. As Mary pauses, surrounded by a seemingly happy home with comfortable furniture, ancestral portraits, and niches filled with antique porcelains, the comforting elements of the colonial revival suddenly seem threatened just as Mary begins to suspect that her domestic ideals are in crisis.

Mary leaves the security of her country house to confront her domestic dilemma in the family's New York apartment, a stylized ensemble of period forms in a modern setting: an arched cupboard filled with figurines and an eighteenth-century French dresser coexist with glass-topped tables and sofas and chairs covered with shimmery, quilted fabric. Statues placed judiciously throughout the room provide vertical focal points that contrast with the furniture's horizontality. Two stylized Bakelite sculptures mounted on the mantel subtly accent an otherwise blank space. The spareness and simplicity of the room are indicative of Gibbons' propensity to decorate with carefully chosen details while avoiding overcrowding.

If Gibbons frequently blended traditional forms with a modern aesthetic during the late 1930s, he also continued to showcase what Paramount art director Hans Dreier referred to as "Modern with a capital M" in MGM films. In *The Women*, the best example of this is Black's Department Store, which provides the context for Crystal Allen (Joan Crawford), the savvy shop girl who has lured Stephen Haines away from the trappings of cozy domesticity. Here the sharp, contemporary lines of commercial design contrast sharply with the traditional forms in the Haineses' homes, a juxtaposition between the glitzy commerciality of downtown and the comforting ambiance of old money. Black's perfume department, like the rest of the store, features stylized towers articulated with thin shafts, curving lines, and sparkling beads complete with glass shelves displaying perfume and cosmetics. When Sylvia and Edith (Phyllis Povah) go to Black's to see the woman who has nabbed Stephen Haines, they are surrounded by these moderne towers as they size up the home wrecker. The store's displays and glass shelves create an abstract pattern of verticals and horizontals, dramatically offsetting Sylvia and Edith's tailored clothes, frilly hats, and catty demeanor.

For her part, Crystal is deeply annoyed when her *sanctum sanctorum*—an exotic bathroom with a clear glass tub and mirrors galore to nourish her narcissism—is disturbed, particularly by her stepdaughter, who struggles to be polite. When Crystal resolves to "have it out" with little Mary, the child explains that her father is fed up with her and declares, "I think this bathroom is perfectly ridiculous!" Sly Sylvia also invades this room, helping herself to Crystal's chocolates as she discovers a mysterious man calling on the bathroom's private phone. Whether Crystal confronts little Mary or evades Sylvia's intrusion, the setting serves as a continual reminder of her hard edges and provides the essential physical context for the conversations that propel the plot to its conclusion.

Gibbons' set for the ladies' cloakroom at the Casino Roof Club lends a distinctly modern backdrop to the film's final showdown. Several low, curve-backed chairs arranged around the perimeter of

Set reference still of the ladies' cloakroom at the Casino Roof Club from *The Women*.

the set create a large space in the center of the room articulated by three shallow, curving steps. The room's careful arrangement and spare furnishings allow it to serve as a kind of fashion ramp. Women in an array of evening gowns—the fanciful creations of Adrian, MGM's costume designer—parade through the space as Mary waits anxiously for Sylvia and Crystal to appear. After Mary tricks Sylvia into revealing Crystal's infidelities, the vixens get their due as Mary exposes their deviousness and then triumphantly rushes into Stephen's arms, a perfect happy finish to the film's whirlwind of vicarious pleasures. Although *The Women* ends with elegantly dressed ladies clawing at each other like cats in a scene almost slapstick in its silliness, Gibbons' set gives even the film's most ridiculous moments a convincing sense of place.

The year of 1939, often cited as among the richest in cinematic history, saw the apex of Gibbons' cinematic achievements. His sets for *The Women*, which ranged from cozy domestic environments to luxurious modernistic spaces, represent the pinnacle of his creative endeavors for the screen. Although Gibbons continued working at MGM throughout the next decade, his settings from the 1940s and later do not possess the aesthetic flourish of his earlier work.

With America's entry into World War II, the strict rationing imposed on consumers was also felt at Hollywood's studios, where new building materials and set dressings became increasingly scarce. Gibbons' settings from this period, including *Cabin in the Sky* (1943) and *Thirty Seconds Over Tokyo* (1944), are considerably leaner in their visual character from films made just a few years earlier, a telling illustration of the limitations necessitated by wartime rationing. Whereas movies made during the 1920s and 1930s highlighted architecture, clothing, and other vicarious pleasures, war films emphasized sacrifice and duty to country. Not surprisingly, movie sets from the early 1940s generally displayed a limited range of architectural expression.

By the mid-1940s, the vigor that characterized Gibbons' earlier career also started to fade as his health began a slow but steady decline. Heart problems caused a series of disabling strokes that prohibited him from working with the restless energy of his earlier years. Gibbons' deteriorating health paralleled the decline of MGM, which, like the other Hollywood studios, began to unravel after World War II. The all-powerful studio system, within which Gibbons had forged his career, began a downward spiral during the 1940s and 1950s from which it never recovered. In 1950 the Society of Motion Picture Art Directors presented Gibbons with an award recognizing his contribution to the art of filmmaking. While the award honored his achievements, it also signaled the ending of his career, implying that his glory days of designing for the screen were over.

Gibbons' entry into the film industry in 1918 coincided with Hollywood's recruitment of professional artists and architects to give the movies legitimacy by linking them to the fine arts. Gibbons developed his craft throughout the 1920s with sets that served as the basis for pictorial composition on the silent screen. When sound came to the movies in the 1930s, Gibbons infused sets with a spatial dimension that accommodated the added realism of dialog. By the end of the decade, Gibbons had perfected his craft just as the medium itself was reaching aesthetic maturity. Gibbons used the new art of film to inform and transform the ancient art of architecture while creating an atmosphere of elegance, sophistication, and high style. His motion picture settings constitute an essential component of the films produced during Hollywood's Golden Age, a period when stylish films gave audiences the ultimate in artistic visual experience.

NOTES

1. Morton Eustis, "Designing for the Movies: [Cedric] Gibbons of MGM," *Theatre Arts* 21 (October 1937): 797.
2. Cedric Gibbons, "Motion Picture Sets," in *The Theatre and Motion Pictures: A Selection of Articles from the New 14th Edition of the Encyclopedia Britannica* (New York: Encyclopedia Britannica, 1929), 27.
3. "French Furniture," *New York Times* (25 October 1925).
4. Betty Thornley Stuart, "Movie Set-Up," *Collier's* 92 (30 September 1933), 36.
5. William Cameron Menzies, "Pictorial Beauty in the Photoplay," in *Cinematographic Annual* (Hollywood: American Society of Cinematographers, 1930): 175.
6. Ralph Flint, "Cedric Gibbons," *Creative Art* 11.2 (October 1932): 117.
7. "Why the Movies Are Influencing American Taste," *House Beautiful* 84 (July/August 1942), 37.

Ken Adam, 1962 drawing for the War Room set of *Dr. Strangelove: Or How I Learned to Stop Worrying and Love the Bomb* (1964).

DR. CALIGARI'S CABINETS:
The SET DESIGN *of* KEN ADAM

DONALD ALBRECHT

BORN IN 1921 to a prosperous Jewish family in Weimar Berlin, Klaus Adam grew up in the shadow of Adolf Hitler. His youthful reality haunted by the Nazis' swift rise to power, Adam found an outlet for his imagination in the fictional world of the movies. No film made a stronger impression than Robert Wiene's 1921 expressionist masterpiece *The Cabinet of Dr. Caligari*, which Adam can still recall seeing for the first time. With its sinister, distorted decor and demonic, all-powerful villain, the film has exerted a powerful influence throughout Adam's five-decade career as a production designer for film.

Adam's paired interests in film and design are hereditary. In 1928 his father, Fritz Adam, hired Ludwig Mies van der Rohe to design a new building for the family dry-goods store in downtown Berlin (it was never built). A film buff, Fritz also directed some of the family fortune into a consortium that financed the production of motion pictures. The Adams' wealth and position, however, provided little protection from the Nazis, and in 1934 they were forced to flee Berlin for London. Two years later Fritz Adam died a broken man. Klaus (now Ken) Adam continued his studies in Britain, attending schools in Edinburgh and London before taking a job at an architecture firm and studying design at London University's Bartlett School of Architecture. After war broke out, he enlisted in the Royal Air Force, distinguishing himself as a fighter pilot. Adam began his film career in 1947 as a draftsman, rising quickly to assistant art director, art director, and finally, in 1956, to the position of production designer on Jacques Tourneur's classic shocker *Night of the Demon* (released in 1957).

While perfecting his craft as a production designer, Adam conjured a celluloid universe in which he could exorcise the evil spirits of his youth. (Perhaps attacking his oppressed German homeland in World War II triggered this release.) Expressionist flourishes permeate *Addams Family Values* (1993) and *The Madness of King George* (1994), the master-of-paranoia's most recent Oscar-winning design, but his work on such movies as *Dr. Strangelove: Or How I Learned to Stop Worrying and Love the Bomb* (1964), *Chitty Chitty Bang Bang* (1968), and the seven James Bond thrillers for which he is best known illustrates his well-earned reputation as the Frank Lloyd Wright of decor noir. Cool and depersonalized, Adam's looming forms and menacing perspectives conflate the war room and the board room to evoke a post-atomic landscape of limitless power. They are intimidating spaces where Orwellian organizations with ominous names like Spectre, Power, and the Pentagon mastermind global conspiracies of Cold War violence and death.

To depict a society that glamorizes death as stylish sport, Adam transformed military hardware into Warhol-like icons of mass destruction. The giant map in the War Room of *Dr. Strangelove,* for example, acted as a superpower scoreboard, rendering mankind's extinction as more show than substance; a graphic spectacle detached from the reality of human suffering. The gridded canvasses of Piet Mondrian inspired Adam's design of the pyramid control room of Hugo Drax, the billionaire industrialist in the Bond epic *Moonraker* (1977), who planned to poison the earth with lethal orchid-bearing cylinders only to repopulate it with his own superhuman race. From bullet-dispensing cigarettes to a lethal Aston Martin DB5 sports car and a revolving light fixture mounted with semi-automatic machine guns, the Bond films were generously appointed with techno-fantasies conceived and designed by Adam. A deadly autogyro nicknamed "Little Nellie" sprang from four suitcases in *You Only Live Twice* (1967). The streamlined *Disco Volante* of *Thunderball* (1965), a yacht that served as the villain's luxurious floating headquarters, transformed itself into a full-size hydrofoil able to travel at speeds of up to 90 knots. In Adam's devilish, topsy-turvy imagination, swimming pools became shark pits, and personal submarines carried H-bombs. As the real-life Q, Adam created the sexy gadgetry that embodied and defined the "Bond" persona to a far greater extent than the films' flimsy plots and only slightly less than the stars who played the title role, Sean Connery in particular. The visual foundation of many a contemporary action film and keystones of popular culture, these inventions secured Adam's unique position in cinema history and in our collective unconscious.

MENTOR MENZIES

Adam is a controlling force on the films he designs. Realizing that his decor is only as good as it appears on screen, he admits to sitting next to directors during filming so that he can advise them on the camera setups that will heighten the architectural drama of his sets. The reverse is true as well: Adam once convinced the reclusive Stanley Kubrick to make a secret late-night visit to a Bond set to weigh in on a particularly troubling lighting problem. Adam's penchant for collaboration between director and designer follows a pattern set by his mentor, William Cameron Menzies. A superb visual stylist, Menzies fashioned his own emotionally charged version of cinematic realism in the 1920s, giving Hollywood a heady dose of expressionist shadows, colors, and forms. Menzies' designs for Douglas Fairbanks's silent *The Thief of Bagdad* (1924) fused the sinuous lines of art nouveau and the comic-book fantasy of Winsor McCay's *Little Nemo in Slumberland.* In 1936, Menzies directed the British sci-fi epic *Things to Come,* placing his camera low to exaggerate the utopian grandeur of the film's cavernous, streamlined city of the future, designed by Vincent Korda. Three years later, producer David O. Selznick recognized Menzies' unique contribution to film by giving the designer Hollywood's first "production designer" credit for his Technicolored palette and striking compositions for *Gone with the Wind* (1939). As Selznick knew, Menzies was responsible for the film's visual coherence despite an extended production period and a series of directorial changes.

Menzies' capacity to manipulate movie color played a major role in Adam's aesthetic coming-of-age during the mid-1950s. Adam had just returned to London from Italy where, as an assistant art director, he had launched a fleet of Greek warships for *Helen of Troy* (1956), one of many fatuous but well-executed epics made cheaply by Americans in Europe after the end of the war. Among those attracted by the lure of overseas locations and superb craftspeople was producer Mike Todd, in London preparing to shoot his Victorian-era extravaganza, *Around the World in 80 Days* (1956). (Struggling to be seen against the film's over-the-top sets was an all-star "cast-of-thousands," including David Niven, Charles Boyer, Marlene Dietrich, Shirley MacLaine, Frank Sinatra, and Buster Keaton.) "Mike Todd was very impressive, enormously possessive, and incredibly frightening," Adam recalled after Todd hired him to design the film's European decor. "He had a suite in the Dorchester where he conducted his business like a king in his throne room, summoning people to meetings and dispensing orders at all hours and without warning."[1]

Leading Todd's regal retinue was Menzies, who served as the film's associate producer and oversaw Adam's work. The elder designer encouraged his protégé to abandon the kitchen-sink realism of postwar filmmaking. "I was able for the first time to speak of stylization on the level of color," Adam noted.[2] Working within the controlled environment of the soundstage, which he still prefers to shooting on location, Adam painted the entire Lloyd's of London set in black and white, creating stark contrast between the grayness of London and the colorful, exotic locales to follow. The film's actors were dressed in black and white too, except for waiters, who punctuated the scene in bright scarlet. For the interior of London's Reform Club, which Adam had never seen, the designer juxtaposed Georgian green walls and black columns. Adam's work on *Around the World in 80 Days* earned him his first Academy Award nomination (though he is miscredited as "Ken Adams" in the film's playful title sequence, designed by Saul Bass).

Adam was liberated. For Robert Aldrich's *Sodom and Gomorrah* (1962), few designers would have had the nerve to attempt such wild color harmonies as shocking pink and raspberry against orange and bluish-purple. In *Chitty Chitty Bang Bang*, Adam's black-and-white candy factory paid homage to bizarre Menzian angles and storybook perspectives, and the film's images of caged children surely resonated with his childhood experience in Nazi Germany.

With his newfound freedom on the set, Adam broke decisively from his Beaux-Arts architectural training. His drawings began to reject the precise delineation of the draftsman for the dramatic intensity of the filmmaker. The mature Adam works blank sheets of paper in futurist fury, shaping space with a broad Flo-Tip marker. Even when designing for a color film, he draws in black and white in an obsessive quest for chiaroscuro lighting effects.

Adam's designs follow a logic less architectural than narrative, and this enables him to work in a wide range of genres, historical periods, and literary styles. The spatial complexity and textured density of the studio-built English manor house and maze for Joseph Mankiewicz's *Sleuth* (1972), for example, mirrored the film's quicksilver cat-and-mouse antics. The viewer's eye never tires as it roams across delicate Gothic tracery, vaulted ceilings, arched screens, balconies, and furniture cluttered with mechanical dolls and clocks. It is because of this Menzian commitment to artifice in the service of drama that Adam regards *Barry Lyndon* with mixed emotions. "We did enormous amounts of research," Adam said of this collaboration with Stanley Kubrick. Director and designer pored over paintings by Thomas Gainsborough, William Hogarth, Joshua Reynolds, Jean Baptiste Chardin, and George Stubbs, often replicating specific canvasses for certain sequences, and fabricated single sets by synthesizing a number of stately British homes. "That's why it was never that exciting to me as a designer, even though I won the Academy Award for it. I felt it was much more reproductive than imaginative."[3]

In contrast, the stylized tableaux and bold colors of Adam's second Oscar-winning film, *The Madness of King George*, make up a far more inventive re-envisioning of late-eighteenth-century English court life (Adam also received Academy Award nominations for *The Spy Who Loved Me* and *Addams Family Values*).

DEADLY DOCTORS

The 1960s were chicly nihilistic. Trapped in a depleting yet constantly escalating confrontation between East and West, liberated sexually by the pill and financially by postwar prosperity, capitalist culture embraced a new pop sensibility.

Cool as a Roy Lichtenstein canvas commenting on sex, violence, and death, the cutting edge of sixties popular culture confronted previously taboo subjects. "I did a little picture called *The Trials of Oscar Wilde* in 1960," Adam remarked about the groundbreaking gay film, "in which my set budget was £15,000 from an overall cost of £250,000. But because of the budget limitations, I was forced to do a lot of stylization, rather more a theatrical approach."[4] For the funeral scene in the Marquis of Queensberry's home, on which Adam had only £450 to spend, he recycled bits and pieces of leftover decor—neoclassical pediments, double doors, a narrow French window, and a big fireplace—and with the bold simplicity of Wedgewood pottery colored everything in terra cotta and black. Adam coordinated the set to complement the actors' black costumes, and the dramatic effect was explosive. To his surprise, Adam received his first glowing acknowledgments from newspaper critics, and he won that year's top prize for art direction at the Moscow Film Festival.

Adam created his most famous set for Stanley Kubrick's *Dr. Strangelove,* the director's send-up of the ultimate no-no, nuclear annihilation. Adam was forced to invent the film's War Room from scratch, as the U.S. government considered Kubrick's black comedy anti-American and refused access to government facilities. A reinforced concrete bunker with overtones of the bombastic Nazi designs of Albert Speer, Adam's War Room loomed in deadly convergence above a giant round table where the world's leaders gathered for a game of high-stakes poker. Adam likes to recount the following, possibly apocryphal but certainly plausible, anecdote about the legendary room: "When Ronald Reagan became president, one of the first things he asked to see was the War Room, and somebody had to say 'Well...' He had expected the one from *Dr. Strangelove*."[5]

Peter Sellers's rendition of the Dr. Strangelove character—half Henry Kissinger, half Jerry Lewis—embodied for moviegoers a new absurdist antihero. The irreverent British spy played by Michael

Ken Adam, drawing for the underground command-center set of *Dr. No* (1962).

Caine in *Funeral in Berlin* (1966), another film designed by Adam, operated within a morally ambiguous demilitarized zone between the arid glass towers of the West and the war-ravaged rubble of the East. Meanwhile, Sean Connery's debonair Bond polished the image of international espionage to a deadly patina. Wry, witty, and ironic, these characters fit perfectly within Adam's Kafkaesque decors: everything from a decadent nightclub with icy metallic hues and an endless echoing corridor to a designer brain-washing machine.

Each of the seven Bond thrillers Adam art-directed pit the dashing hero against a sinister, self-obsessed villain out to control the world—often from a secluded island where natural beauty camouflages subterranean living quarters and atomic-powered laboratories that have somehow managed to spring up without capturing the attention of the powers-that-be. In the interrogation scene of *Dr. No*, the unseen doctor is a Mabusian eminence who makes his presence known through his disembodied voice. With only £500 remaining in his budget, Adam resorted to a minimalist aesthetic and created a set that is as much a signature design as those Bond extravaganzas on which he spent millions. The room is a bare space with a single door, a lone chair, and an overpowering skylight that casts a spider's web of shadows, exposing the banal anonymity of modern evil. Dr. No's

Ken Adam, drawing for the Fort Knox vaults set of *Goldfinger* (1963).

salon, on the other hand, reeked of modern glamour. Doors of copper and plastic dissolved seamlessly into thick walls of rough-hewn rock. Windows looked out on Dr. No's underwater domain, adding liquid luxury to his well-appointed machine for killing.

Dr. No established the architectural pattern for all Bond sets to come—even those for which Adam was not directly responsible. His overwhelmingly angled forms and spaces suggest the work of John Lautner. (In fact, a Lautner house, the 1968 Elrod Residence, appears as a location in the 1971 film *Diamonds Are Forever.*) "I try to be very ahead of time," Adam said of *The Spy Who Loved Me* (1977). "The Atlantis set is all curves and circles, because I think the new plastic furniture and molding is a part of our scene now, and part of the future."[6] Adam's extensive use of glass also suggests the work of Mies van der Rohe—another reverberation from the production designer's Weimar childhood. The unbuilt Adam Building of 1928 was, according to Mies biographer Franz Schultz, one of the first instances in which the architect employed a glass curtain-wall over a

Ken Adam, drawing for Spectre's hidden volcano headquarters set in *You Only Live Twice* (1966).

rectangular prism—a precursor to Mies's groundbreaking postwar skyscraper designs.[7]

Adam's Bondian fantasies, like the Howard Hughes-inspired penthouse in *Diamonds Are Forever* or the supertanker interior that engulfed whole Polaris subs in *The Spy Who Loved Me*, reveal his capacity to create an architecture of heightened reality more persuasive than reality itself. The War Room from *Dr. Strangelove* is a case in point. Another is the Fort Knox set for *Goldfinger* (1964), which was completely fabricated. "Mind you," Adam remarked, "I knew that gold is never stacked more than 2-feet, 6-inches high because it is a very heavy metal." Nevertheless, Adam dreamed up a gigantic, 40-foot-high arch with a grille, creating a golden prison that tantalizingly separates the gold from the audience and augments its seductive aura. The 40-foot stack, says Adam, "is quite impractical and unrealistic. Still, I have since received letters from people all over the world asking how we were able to shoot in Fort Knox. They believe what they want to believe."[8]

The famous volcano interior that functions as Spectre's Japanese headquarters in *You Only Live Twice* stretched 400 feet in diameter and towered 126 feet above the backlot of Pinewood Studios outside London. For years, Adam had been giving form to his childhood demons by creating spaces for Bond's tyrannical despots. His newest architectural folly offered him the opportunity to emulate the designers he so admired in his youth. The great dystopian city of Fritz Lang's *Metropolis* (1927) had been an early aesthetic touchstone. As the designer of the vast new 007 Pinewood soundstage as well as the volcano setting within, Adam finally had the facility in which to build a set of comparable scale and scope to *Metropolis*. He could now also follow in the tradition of émigré designers Lazare Meerson and Vincent Korda, who in the 1930s and 1940s brought a stylish sense of Continental grandeur to such British-made films as *Knight Without Armor* (1937) and *That Hamilton Woman* (1941). With *You Only Live Twice* Adam produced the biggest, most complex film set that had ever been built in Europe—at a cost of more than $1 million. The makeshift £500 set of *Dr. No* had become a distant memory.

CELLULOID PRISONS

Adam returned to the studio to create the evocatively reimagined Depression of *Pennies From Heaven* (1981). For Herb Ross's post-modern homage to vintage Hollywood, Adam built more than thirty sets at a cost of $2 million. The overwhelming majority of the film was shot on twelve immense soundstages located in Los Angeles: Actor Christopher Walken danced one of cinema's sexiest stripteases in a bluesy, smoke-filled bar; there was a full-size intersection of two Chicago streets, complete with an elevated train track; and a shabby schoolhouse transformed itself into an all-white confection worthy of Busby Berkeley.

Yet unlike Hollywood's Cinderella scenarios, reality kept shattering the illusions of *Pennies from Heaven*'s hapless musical instruments salesman, Arthur Parker. Played by Steve Martin, Parker is seduced, trapped, and ultimately destroyed by his own inability to live up to the myths fabricated by popular music, advertising, and, especially, movies. In one scene, a drab little bank is literally cracked open to become a celluloid cathedral of commerce. In another, Martin and co-star Bernadette Peters escape into a cinema palace based on Edward Hopper's painting *New York Movie* to see Fred Astaire and Ginger Rogers in *Follow the Fleet* (1936). Suddenly

Martin and Peters are metamorphosed into their screen idols, performing in a rooftop cabaret. But their attempt to "face the music and dance" ends with the set closing in on them.

By making the nightclub a virtual prison, the scene stands as a perfect metaphor for Adam's dark cinematic universe. Within this imaginary realm, Adam animates larger-than-life demons—whether the all-consuming media in *Pennies from Heaven*, the dark umbrella of nuclear holocaust in *Dr. Strangelove*, or the pervasive villainy in the Bond movies. To achieve these visions, Ken Adam remembers his childhood and unlocks Dr. Caligari's cabinet.

NOTES

An earlier version of this essay appeared in German in the catalog *Production Design: Ken Adam* (Munich: Kulturreferat der Landeshauptstadt, 1994), 6–13.

1. James Delson, interviewer, "Art Directors," *Film Comment* (January/February 1982): 37.
2. Gaston Haustrate, "Interview with Ken Adam," *Cinema* (January 1978): 40 (translated by the author).
3. "Ken Adam: Dialogue on Film," *American Film* (February 1991): 21.
4. Delson, "Art Directors," 37.
5. Adam confirmed this story in an interview with Michel Ciment in the latter's 1983 book *Kubrick,* translated from the French by Gilbert Adair and published by Collins in London.
6. George Waldo, interviewer, "Adam and His Creation," *Screen International* (12 February 1977): 10.
7. Ibid.
8. Peter Haining, *James Bond: A Celebration* (London: Planet Books, 1987), 131.

In 1959, Saul Bass ran the title of Alfred Hitchcock's suspense thriller *North by Northwest* across the gridded facade of the United Nations Secretariat Building.

OPENING CEREMONIES: TYPOGRAPHY *and the* MOVIES, 1955–1969

PETER HALL

IT MIGHT SEEM perverse, to the film critic and student, to decapitate the century's films of their opening and closing minutes and contemplate the offcuts as a movement. But this ignoble assortment of clips yields a colorful field of study. In a sense, the film title is to the movie as the billboard and neon sign are to architecture. It advertises the film's wares; reflects, or betrays, the director and studio's aesthetic aim (or lack thereof); and with the aid of hindsight indicates something of the prevailing state of the film industry. And like the sign, the title sequence is either ignored or disparaged by serious film students for its suspiciously utilitarian motives and close relation to advertising. Their qualms are not entirely unfounded. The standalone credit sequence came about as the products of vanity and the unexpected union between filmmakers and commercial artists. But as a form, it is capable of reaching sublime heights. It might be considered the beautiful bastard child of the medium.

The film title came of age in 1955, when director Otto Preminger unveiled his noirish junkie-thriller *The Man with the Golden Arm* with a striking monochrome graphic sequence designed by Saul Bass. To Elmer Bernstein's syncopated score and big-band orchestration, a series of white bars appear and shift on the black screen, suggesting drumsticks, then searchlights, before finally transforming into the jagged arm of the film's title. Bass called it "a sort of abstract ballet—erratic and strident."[1] At the time, this kind of prequel was unprecedented. Credits bearing the names of the movie, director, studio, and stars (not necessarily in that order) were usually rendered by lettering artists and held up unceremoniously in front of the camera at the beginning and end of the feature. But in *The Man with the Golden Arm* and, to a lesser extent, *Carmen Jones* a year earlier, Preminger and Bass turned this static procedure into an animated event. According to Bass, "there was a time when titles were very interesting, going back to the early 1930s or even the late 1920s. Then it bogged down and became bad lettering produced by firms that ground out titles. What I did was reinvent the whole notion of using a title to create a little atmosphere."[2]

The motive was undoubtedly commercial. The stark power and reductive formalism of *The Man with the Golden Arm* sequence was actually derived from Bass's previously designed poster for the film, which encapsulated in a simple "ideogram" the story of an addicted jazz drummer (played by Frank Sinatra) caught in a triangle of dependency. Rather than illustrating the ingredients of the story—a drum set, urban scene, and distraught faces of the stars would have been acceptable—Bass devised a logo with an arm thrust downward into a prison of black rectangles. It was a seminal example of his ability to identify the nucleus of a communication problem and strip away visual complexity, rendering the remaining graphic elements with a handmade, cut-out expressionist style. Preminger's reason for subsequently commissioning Bass to design the titles was to achieve a cohesive and uniform identity for the film; he famously defended the poster over the telephone (while Bass listened) to a movie theater owner upset that it did not show the film's leading man, Sinatra. "Those ads are to be used precisely as they are," bawled Preminger. "If you change them one iota I will pull the picture from your theater."[3]

If no one had thought of animating the opening credits before Preminger and Bass, it was not because the technology wasn't available. Disney's *Snow White* (1937), somewhat more sophisticated at least in terms of animation, preceded *The Man with the Golden Arm* by eighteen years. The mid-fifties, however, were a time of deep crisis and re-evaluation in Hollywood, and the need to establish the cinematic experience as something separate and superior to television became paramount. Between 1947 and 1957, American cinema lost 75 percent of its audience as families retreated to their suburban living rooms to watch TV and make babies. By 1960, 90 percent of all U.S. homes had television sets.[4] Movies had become a special leisure-time activity rather than an everyday feature of people's lives, forcing Hollywood studios to reduce the quantity and increase the quality of their productions. They also resorted to every novel technique they could lay their hands on to attract audiences. It is no coincidence that while the film industry raced to bring color, three-dimensionality, and stomach-churning smells to the silver screen, the idea of opening credits as a curtain-raiser was also born. Moviegoing was being repackaged as a special night out, a drive-in, a chance to escape the humdrum homestead, and the hyperbolic introduction contributed to the transformation.

At the same time, directors like Preminger and Alfred Hitchcock were enjoying a newfound respect in Hollywood. The end of the studio system had seen the number of independent films in production double annually between 1946 and 1956, accompanied by an increase in artistic and directorial freedom. For once, the director, in addition to the studio, had a say in how a film was promoted and packaged. The visual fanfare of a stand-alone title sequence was for directors a way of conveying the majesty of their medium. Their most obvious point of reference was the operatic overture; indeed, Robert Wise and Jerome Robbins opened their 1961 classic *West Side Story* with a still image—a Bass-designed graphic representation of Manhattan—that sits on screen for the best part of Leonard Bernstein's ten-minute overture. By today's MTV-jacked standards, it's tedious.

These early days of the film title sequence laid the conceptual groundwork for all subsequent innovation in the field. There is hardly a title designer practicing today who doesn't refer back to the work of Bass and his sixties successors. "Bass fashioned title sequences into an art, creating, in some cases, like *Vertigo*, a mini-film within a film," notes director Martin Scorsese. "His graphic compositions in movement function as a prologue to the movie—setting the tone, providing the mood and foreshadowing the action of the picture. His titles are not simply unimaginative 'identification tags'—rather they are integral to the film as a whole."[5] The mini-movie reached its apex in *Walk on the Wild Side* (1962), which today is only considered noteworthy in film encyclopedias for its credit sequence. Critics considered the relatively lengthy live-action narrative of prowling cats better than the steamy melodrama (directed by Edward Dmytryk) that followed, but that was not the designer's ambition. Better to be attached to a great film and commended for a strong supporting role than to overplay a mediocre film or be hitched to an awful film ultimately consigned to the trash heap of history.

Bass's collaborations with Hitchcock reveal a more integrated approach to the art: *Vertigo* (1958) and *North by Northwest* (1959) mark the emergence of integrated live action and graphics. *Vertigo*, with its colored spiral swirls zooming out of the eye of Kim Novak, is a frequently upheld masterpiece of the genre. The opening minutes of *North by Northwest* have a conceptual wit and efficiency reflective of the film that follows, despite typographic animation that seems clunky when compared to today's computer-generated effects. It begins with an animated sequence of lines forming a slanted grid along which the typographic credits slide. Gradually, the reflections of cars begin to appear in the grid and it transforms into the glass facade of the United Nations Secretariat Building in New York, making a seamless transition from graphic animation to architecture.

The choice of the Secretariat as the canvas for the credits is significant, because it foreshadows a key scene in the plot, set in the lobby of the General Assembly. But it is also the same structure that architecture critic Lewis Mumford derided as a symbol "that the managerial revolution has taken place and that bureaucracy rules the world."[6] With this cheeky use of Wallace K. Harrison's faceless structure as a projection screen, Hitchcock and Bass elicit the preoccupations of the era, the plight of the everyman amid the machinations of the gray organization. In *North by Northwest*, bureaucracy does rule the world. Its hero, a busy Madison Avenue advertising executive played by Cary Grant, is forced by a case of mistaken identity to adopt the persona of a nonexistent agent concocted by the CIA. Unlike James Stewart's deluded and obsessive ex-detective in *Vertigo*, Grant's character never allows the audience to believe that he is the victim of anything other than an administrative mix-up.

The film's villain is not a psychotic stalker or a flock of murderous birds, but an aristocratic art dealer and spy with ineffectual and overly elaborate methods of removing his enemies.

The sequence's strength is both its high drama (the Bernard Herrmann score is, in fact, melodramatic) and its ambiguity, setting the stage for the simultaneously camp, urbane, and nightmarish comedy-thriller that follows. At least one critic has sniggered at the phallic significance of the appearance of New York's first curtain-walled skyscraper in the opening sequence, preceding a "Freudian nightmare in which mothers, lovers, gays and cops all conspire against a man."[7] Another has argued that the sliding credits foreshadow the final scenes in which the characters cling and fall from the sheer rocks of Mount Rushmore.[8]

Such was the impact of Bass's graphics in Hollywood that a wave of look-alikes followed. Peter Bogdanovich has remarked that Preminger's use of main title designs by Bass "became almost a cliché of the mid-fifties through the sixties because of how often [they were] imitated."[9] By the time director Robert Mulligan approached art director Steve Frankfurt to create a sequence for his dramatization of *To Kill a Mockingbird*, Harper Lee's novel about racism in the South, Mulligan's expressed aim was, as Frankfurt put it, to "design a movie title that didn't look like Saul Bass had done it."[10]

The poetic short that Frankfurt created had surprisingly commercial roots. Like Bass, Frankfurt was a graphic designer who had worked at advertising agencies and was well versed in the art of distilling themes into simple symbolic forms. Mulligan and producer Alan Pakula were attracted to Frankfurt on the strength of one particular TV commercial he had art-directed, for a headache pill, which had shown a live-action sequence of a pocket watch being dissected. They wanted to evoke what Pakula called "the mysterious, secret world of childhood," by focusing the camera on the cigar box of treasures found by the central characters, Scout and Jem.[11] Frankfurt supplied the same pacing and macroscopic feel he had achieved in the analgesic ad. The subtle resonance of his sequence remains a source of reference for film title designers today. The camera pans over the contents of the box to the sound of a child humming, a watch ticking, and a marble rolling before Elmer Bernstein's score swells up and the credits appear. It has a peculiar sense of intimacy coupled with allegory—the race issues at the heart of the tale are suggested when the film title is revealed in invisible ink by a scribbling black crayon. The rendering of the actual credits, in the typeface Franklin Gothic, floating in the corner of the screen as the sequence progresses, proved a perennial solution. "I kept the type simple and in a very small form to contrast with the macro images," said Frankfurt. "I also wanted the soft emotional quality of the photography to contrast with the hard edge of the typeface."[12] In avoiding the *de facto* standard of the day, the Bass sequence, Frankfurt had inadvertently created a new default: the technique of floating credits in white over a filmed sequence is still in use three decades later.

The subsequent development of the title sequence during the 1960s reflects film's meandering growth into a mature art form. The decline of American movie audiences in the "sad sixties" and the corresponding emergence of state-supported film in Europe brought a significant change to the presentation of a movie.[13] Film noir and Hitchcockian suspense were superseded by the French New Wave, with its political satire and sexual liberation, and the Bass style of the Hollywood opening overture began to look dated. In Europe, with a few notable exceptions, the new wave of directors saw little need for the grandiose opening statements of the Hitchcock and Preminger variety, and certainly saw no need to satisfy the vain demands of actors and studios by lingering on their names at the start of a film. The titles to films such as *Jules and Jim* (1961), *The 400 Blows* (1959), and *Breathless* (1959) barely make an entrance. Bass himself concentrated increasingly on directing live action, both in the form of innovative opening sequences like that to *Grand Prix* (1966) and short films, including the Oscar-winning *Why Man Creates* (1968). Perhaps the last offspring of *The Man with the Golden Arm* was Terence Young's *Dr. No* (1962), the first Bond movie and the herald of the age of the film sequel. For the opening titles, designer Maurice Binder applied Bass-like graphic minimalism to a London pop sensibility, creating a suitable trademark for all future Bond sequels. Binder's sequence, a graphic ballet of colored circles suggesting, variously, a gun barrel, microdot, eye, and bullet hole, has enjoyed renewed attention lately with the revival of sixties modernist kitsch, notably in restaurant and retail interiors. The opening seconds, in which the dapper spy turns and fires directly at the camera, survive to this day as the Bond ID, while the addition of dancing women in silhouette (in the awkwardly spliced calypso sequence that follows) was subsequently developed by Robert Brownjohn in the opening to *Goldfinger* (1964)—cavorting female nudes in silhouette became another template of the series. The graphic packaging, in fact, became as important to the Bond brand as the formulas within the films: the suave spy, the helpless beauties, the bald villains with fluffy cats.

The tongue-in-cheek bikini thriller hit new kitsch heights in another Hollywood-funded European production, Roger Vadim's space-age *Barbarella* (1968). The technically accomplished title sequence, designed by Arcady, features Jane Fonda's famous zero-gravity striptease, in which she divests herself of a designer space suit while clouds of letters rush around her naked body like giggling schoolboys, forming the credits as they go. This naughty tribute to Jean-Claude Forest's mildly pornographic comic strip was an indication of just how far mainstream film had come from the heavy censorship of sex and nudity just a decade earlier. The typographic acrobatics, shot separately on an animation stand, are choreographed to coordinate precisely with the live action to the extent that at one point the excitable letters appear to explode on Fonda's nipples. The dance of sans-serif type is also compositionally reminiscent of the print work of Robert Massim and predates by nearly thirty years the typokinetics of 1990s television commercials.

Technically far removed from Vadim's lavish *Barbarella*, the downbeat, black-and-white opening sequence to D. A. Pennebaker's documentary of Bob Dylan, *Don't Look Back* (1967), shares some conceptual similarities. The typography becomes a kind of choric commentator; if in *Barbarella* the letterforms are adolescent in behavior, in *Don't Look Back* they serve as Dylan's alter ego, both assisting and contradicting the singer. Pennebaker's sequence, copied at least half a dozen times in subsequent music videos, shows Dylan standing in an alleyway holding giant cue-cards that he tosses nonchalantly into the street to the tune of "Subterranean Homesick Blues." At first, the cards are synched to key words in the lyrics as they are sung: "basement," "medicine," "government," and so on. But at the end of

Bob Dylan with title cards in D. A. Pennebaker's 1967 documentary *Don't Look Back*. Beat poet Allen Ginsberg stands on the far left.

the first verse there is a discrepancy when po-faced Dylan reveals a card that reads "20 dollar bills" and the voice-over Dylan sings "Eleven dollar bills/You only got ten." As the song progresses, the cue-cards become an increasingly unreliable subtitling device, carrying misspellings ("suckcess") and little maxims that don't appear in the song at all ("watch it/here they come" and "dig yourself"). As the last card, "what??" is thrown to the ground and Dylan daintily exits, the audience is appropriately prepared for the singer as he will appear throughout the film; mischievous, experimental, and constantly performing for the camera—even when pretending not to.

Pennebaker's aim with the film was to create a "working musical" rather than a documentary. "Almost all its information becomes purposely kind of abstract and tries to be musical rather than informational," he said. "What I want to tell you about is the mood."[14] The approach proved liberating. The opening song is more a prequel than a title sequence—the credits appear, rather clumsily, a few minutes later; the cue-card scene is essentially a prototype music video that functions, like Bass's mini-movies, as a curtain-raiser. The presence of the beat poet Allen Ginsberg in the background (he lingers around a trash heap) reinforces this atmosphere of free-form experimentalism, and much can be made of the implications of the poetic wordplay in the piece. Three sides of Dylan are present; the singing voice, the nonchalant actor, and the written Dylan in the form of the hand-lettered cards. (The typography itself seems to prefigure the lettering of influential designer-illustrator Ed Fella.) It could be a parody of a singer miming for the camera with subtitles (Dylan's lips never move); or, philosophically, it could suggest the relationship between objects and their signifiers (verbal and written utterances). Once the cue-cards cease to provide the correct words, however, the whole relationship between the words and their meaning is upset. Thus Pennebaker and Dylan have created the first deconstructionist pop video, and without consciously trying. "I never gave Dylan any kind of directions as to what I thought was right or wrong," said Pennebaker. "It was entirely up to him the way he wanted to present himself."[15]

Given the fun that can be had by the addition of moving type in a motion picture, it is surprising how few directors have done so, beyond the deployment of type to spell out the names of the stars, filmmakers, and bean counters. With the exception of Bass, no title designer has made a successful leap beyond the ghetto at the front and rear end of a movie; and even Bass didn't take the graphic elements of his titles with him into the main body of the film. Other than the occasional appearance of white letters indicating the time and location of a scene unfolding in a thriller (often with accompanying typewriter sound effects), type has no place in a film. There are good arguments against its use; until recently, the cost of animating letterforms had been prohibitive, and they can also be somewhat distracting to watch. With the availability of desktop animation and film editing, however, as well as a generation of screenagers accustomed to seeing type and image at the same time, this might change.

The thought of midmovie type might be horrifying to film buffs. But it needn't be that way. During the late sixties, German directors Alexander Kluge and Jean-Marie Straub used inserted text to create alienating effects, and the influential director Jean-Luc Godard dabbled with the medium for "chapter headings." Notably, in *Weekend* (1968), Godard introduced a number of typographic tricks to introduce scenes and emphasize themes in his revolutionary satire of Western capitalism. The typographic voice, ironically rendered in the colors of the French flag, is detached, cynical, and distant, introducing the movie first as: "A film lost in the cosmos/A film found in the trash." By breaking up words and letters within words over time, Godard creates a near-subliminal framework of bilingual wordplay and commentary reminiscent of commercial signs. The chapter heading "Analyse" accompanying a bourgeois wife's account of sex with her psychoanalyst is spaced to create a line break after "anal." Another heading is preceded on screen by "ss," (calling to mind Nazi stormtroopers) before it is joined by "La Lutte de la Classe" (class struggle). Even the film title, "Weekend," is broken up to emphasize the "end" part of the word, as if to highlight the *cul-de-sac* inherent in this American invasion of the French language. Few followed Godard's typographic lead in the 1970s—perhaps, as critic Pauline Kael noted at the time, this was out of a fear that "when others pick up the artifacts of his way of seeing, we murmur, 'Godard' and they are sunk."[16]

In the 1990s, however, our expectations are quite different. Godard is no longer center stage in the art-film movement, and film is no longer center stage in experimental media. For decades, the film title sequence was the torch-bearer for animated typography, but today a variety of media are competing for that position; video, Websites, even the promise of interactive television. As the great experimenters of the 1960s demonstrated, the tools of the title designer have much potential when used together with live action as a means of unloading additional information on an audience—sometimes poignant, sometimes unnecessary, sometimes even deliberately contradictory. But to move forward it is certainly not a bad idea to study the typokinetic pioneers of the fifties and sixties, to go back to the front.

NOTES

1. Steven Heller, *Graphic Design in America: A Visual Language History* (New York: Abrams, 1989), 17–9.

2. Ibid., 19.

3. Ibid., 19.

4. Andrea Gronemeyer, *Film* (Hauppauge, NY: Barron's, 1998), 109–10.

5. Martin Scorsese, *Film by Elaine and Saul Bass*, BassYaeger information sheet, 1993.

6. Paul Goldberger, *The City Observed, New York* (New York: Vintage Books, 1979), 1332.

7. Helen MacKintosh, in *Time Out Film Guide,* ed. John Pym (London: Penguin Books, 1997), 614.

8. Donald Spoto, *The Art of Alfred Hitchcock* (New York: Hopkinson and Blake, 1976), 334.

9. Peter Bogdanovich, ed. *Who the Devil Made It?* (New York: Knopf, 1998), 608.

10. Peter Hall, "Title Type," *Baseline* 17 (1994): 41–4.

11. Alan J. Pakula, quoted in thirty-fifth anniversary documentary on the *To Kill a Mockingbird: Collector's Edition* video recording (Universal Pictures, 1997).

12. Hall, "Title Type," 43.

13. Gronemeyer, *Film*, 164.

14. G. Roy Levin, *Documentary Explorations: 15 Interviews with Film-makers* (New York: Doubleday, 1971), 216.

15. Levin, *Documentary Explorations*, 217.

16. Pauline Kael, "Weekend in Hell," in *Film 68/69: National Society of Film Critics* (New York: Simon & Schuster, 1969), 32–7.

Quentin Tarantino, who frequented the Cockatoo Inn in his youth, insisted on using it in his 1997 film *Jackie Brown*.

ONLY *in* HOLLYWOOD: CONFESSIONS *of a* LOCATION MANAGER

BOB CRAFT

ANDREW NICCOL'S 1997 sci-fi thriller *Gattaca* is a story about a near future that has gone terribly awry, a time when genetic engineering has become so sophisticated that "perfect" children can be created in test tubes and those who have not been laboratorily enhanced are forced into segregated neighborhoods. How to conjure the brave new world of the film's mid-twenty-first-century settings from already extant locations? This was just the most critical of the many predicaments that confronted Niccol, production designer Jan Roelfs, and myself, the location manager, as we began work on this picture. In fact, finding locations would be the easiest—if most enjoyable—part of the job. More challenging was the negotiation of filming rights between production and property, and, later, ensuring that all ran smoothly in the field. A crew of more than one hundred people tramping through a building with heavy equipment for more than a week can do some damage. It's the location manager's job to make things right, a job that requires a judicious combination of diplomacy and dollars. And it's a job that most people don't even know exists.

When I was called in to interview for my position on *Gattaca*, Roelfs, a black-clad Dutchman with a perpetual air of European indignation and an uncanny eye for dramatic space, handed me a photograph that pictured a sleek white structure surrounded by foliage. This, he told me, is where I want to shoot. The building in question was the Marin County Civic Center, the last public building designed by Frank Lloyd Wright. If he wanted to use it, we would have to relocate the production to the Bay Area.

The civic center—designed in 1959 and composed of three circular buildings connected by long hallways—was the one building that we all felt epitomized the future reality of *Gattaca*. In the film, it becomes the headquarters for the Gattaca space program, the pride of the movie's engineered *Überclass*. Indeed, the center looks like some alien ship that has mysteriously landed on the California hillside. Its simple, clean lines conveyed just the impression we sought—a future where everything is orderly, sterile, and well planned. But not without a bit of help. Everything that interfered with the austere aesthetic Roelfs envisioned had to be removed. All signage, trashcans, unnecessary ornamentation, even the front doors were hauled off because they were, on film, jarring to the eye. And each morning we had the floors polished to a high gloss.

Shooting on location inevitably poses practical problems, and the civic center was typical in this, even if the problems it created were idiosyncratic. It rained a great deal during the spring we filmed there, and, like many of Wright's buildings, this one leaked like a sieve. More difficult was the fact that the center is a public building, open and operational five days a week, and we could not shut the whole place down—the request to do so was met by a fit of laughter and a non-negotiable answer: "Absolutely not." In an effort to control the environment, we had a number of production assistants ask people to keep areas clear while the cameras rolled. Even this proved troublesome, though, because the building is, effectively, a giant echo chamber. So not only could people not occupy certain spaces while we filmed, but they had to remain quiet and still as well. Fortunately, the movie featured two comely stars, Ethan Hawke and Uma Thurman, and the public was, for the most part, happy to gawk in silence. Still, after a week of shooting most people at the center were happy to see us go.

For Gary Fleder's 1999 film *Impostor*, another science-fiction film set in the future (it is based on the short story of the same title by Philip K. Dick), the goal was similarly to create a believable world of tomorrow. This film, however, came with a significantly smaller budget. The story opens at the home of our hero, Spence Olham, played by Gary Sinise. As the first location in the movie, Fleder wanted something with a striking visual style. For this, we chose an unusual home designed by Ed Niles with a large glass-and-steel structure and a circular living room. Built in 1990 for a Los Angeles lawyer, it was conveniently located on several acres in nearby Malibu. It was a house I had been familiar with for a long time but had avoided using for a number of reasons, most prominently the fact that the owner was not especially interested in having his house used in a film—indeed, it took a considerable payment to convince him to do so. Part of that cost was necessitated by the demand that we remove his fairly impressive collection of modern art during the shoot, not an unusual request in itself, but one that required a $25,000 cash security deposit.

Signature buildings like Wright's civic center and Niles's house in Malibu house call attention to themselves on screen just as they do in the landscape. As such, they're ideally suited for use in films where the director wants to create a dramatic visual statement. Finding such locations is, for obvious reasons, fairly simple—it's hard to miss them. Most any student of architecture, no matter how formal the education, can think of a handful of similarly "cinematic" structures with fairly little effort. And Los Angeles is filled with such buildings. But films often need to convey meaning in more subtle ways, and in these situations the screen-chewing designs of architects like Wright or John Lautner, a Wright disciple whose buildings often appear in Hollywood productions, simply don't fit the bill. Nicolas Roeg's 1992 adult-themed drama *Cold Heaven* is a case in point. The film concerns a love triangle between Marie Davenport (Theresa Russell), her husband,3 Alex (Mark Harmon), and second man Daniel Corvin (James Russo), with whom Marie has a passionate affair. The script called for the two lovers to meet at a "romantic" hotel overlooking the ocean in Carmel, and for Marie to be pictured promenading on the hotel's waterfront. To make a visual metaphor of Marie's rather unstable mental condition, Roeg wanted the hotel sited on a cliff. When combined with a relatively small budget, this request proved difficult to satisfy. The solution was the Torrey Pines Inn at La Jolla, a resort that sported impressive cliffs along which Marie could walk. But there was a catch: between the hotel and the cliffs sat an eighteen-hole golf course. Only through Hollywood magic do we see our heroine looking out of her bedroom window directly onto the cliffs and the ocean beyond.

Nature proved a bit more malleable during the production of Diane Keaton's ensemble drama *Hanging Up* (2000). Delia Ephron's script calls for one of the characters (played by *Friends* star Lisa Kudrow) to be pictured fly-fishing along a bucolic Montana river. Keaton wanted something with a bit of white water. The producers wanted it to be in Southern California. This proved to be a significant dilemma, as there are no rapidly moving bodies of water in Southern California even after a wet winter, and it had been a very dry year. My location team began the quest for our river by searching in concentric circles radiating out from Los Angeles, each day moving a bit farther from the city. We also contacted the Sierra Club, and were offered the helpful suggestion that we look in the area around Kernville, several hours north of L.A. While scouting in the region, my assistant spotted a power station on the Kern River. Eureka! With the help of Southern California Edison, we were able to divert a potion of the Kern (water being reserved to generate power) to create the largest waterfall in Southern California. We had control over 400 gallons of water per second. Not enough water? We increased the flow. Too much? We slowed it down a little. Of course, it may end up on the cutting-room floor. Only in Hollywood.

Despite its woodland excursions, Keaton considers *Hanging Up* to be her visual tribute to Los Angeles, the city in which she was born and raised, a visual counterpart to Woody Allen's classic New York films, *Annie Hall* and *Manhattan*, in which she starred. Working with production designer Waldemar Kalinowski, Keaton set out to create an almost elegiac vision of the city. In practice, this meant the use of a large number of historic buildings, including Union Station (a deco interpretation of the mission style, designed in 1939) and the Terminal Annex Post Office (1937–38, a Spanish colonial pile in exposed concrete). It's a pleasure to use such landmarks—they look great on film, and they often need the money.

Not all locations can or should be historic landmarks. Most films use ordinary places that happen to stand out for one reason or another. My *modus operandi* for finding such spaces is to drive around with my eyes peeled, sometimes with members of a production team. (A fifteen-passenger van packed with Hollywood creative types all on their mobile phones—now that's a sight to write home about!) Generally, I know in advance what I'm looking for, so I simply choose an area of town that I think might work, and off I go. There is also a happy, if competitive, collegiality in the profession. Films have been made in Los Angeles for almost a century, and for the last twenty-five years there have been location managers. It's a small world, and we often compare notes. Fortunately, there are plenty of undiscovered places still out there. Quentin Tarantino's film *Jackie Brown* (1997), for example, was shot almost entirely in a hardscrabble Los Angeles neighborhood that rarely appears on film.

Although *Rum Punch*, the Elmore Leonard novel on which *Jackie Brown* is based, is set in the author's native South Florida, Tarantino transplanted it to his own native territory, L.A.'s South Bay. (Like Keaton, Tarantino viewed his film as a visual tribute to Los Angeles, though his nostalgic vision could hardly be more different from hers.) With the aim of creating an absolutely true-to-life film reality, the director demanded that every location in the film be a real place where the scripted scene would or could take place if it were to actually happen. If this cut down a bit on creativity, it added a corresponding burden of logistical pressure. For example, title character Jackie Brown (Pam Grier) is arraigned in the Torrance Courthouse, the very court with jurisdiction over the neighborhood. The Cockatoo Lounge, where trafficker Ordell Robbie (Samuel Jackson) meets henchman Louis Gara (Robert DeNiro), is an actual roadhouse that Tarantino frequented in his younger days. (It's now closed, but we had it reopened for filming.) A cash swap is set in the Del Amo Mall, where Tarantino worked for a short time as a teenager.

In fact, Tarantino had written the Del Amo, by name, into the script. I was hired well in advance of the rest of the production crew in large part to secure its use. My assignment was pretty simple: get the mall for Quentin—no ifs, ands, or buts. Things got off to a fast start. The moment the assistant to the mall's public relations director got the phone call regarding our interest in doing a QUENTIN TARANTINO MOVIE! at her mall, she was swept away. Then she developed a crush on my assistant. Her boss was a different story. An officious woman, she wore large round glasses that always matched her outfits, and held court in an office done entirely in French baroque style. No, she had not seen *Pulp Fiction,* and what exactly was it that we wanted to do again? Eventually, I made my way up the ladder to the mall manager, a lawyer with eyes focussed on the bottom line. To him, a big Hollywood movie meant big bucks for the mall. A simple equation. But there was a complication. In the film, a character is gunned down in the mall's ample parking lot—a potential public relations problem. The owner would have to make the final decision. Now, as we learn in Sun Tzu's *The Art of War*, equal power deals with equal power, so I took care of the mall manager and let Quentin deal with the owner. In the end, we had one meeting with all of the affected parties. But the owner didn't show. In his stead came his son, who brought along a girlfriend who was a big Quentin Tarantino fan. The son was quite the Southern California scion, very laid-back and casual. They all just wanted to break bread with Quentin.

Further complications developed during the shooting of the movie. Tarantino puts a movie together in his head, shot by shot, long before the production company gets to location. For *Jackie Brown*, he devised a long tracking shot that follows Jackie as she walks seemingly halfway across the mall. Everything went fine until the very end of this sequence, when something caught the camera operator's eye. Yes, Quentin was bothered by it too. A small, mobile ATM machine sat in the middle of the mall, disrupting the symmetry of the shot.

This was the weekend before July Fourth. A big shopping weekend. A time to keep the ATM filled with money for cash-strapped shoppers. So the initial response to our request to remove it was negative. But persistence won out, and eventually the mall manager gave in and embarked on the requisite series of bureaucratic phone calls. I'm sure they all started with the phrase, "You'll never guess what those crazy film people want now." We did get the ATM removed, though we had to provide the mall with two armed guards to baby-sit the machine from the moment is was unbolted and placed on a truck in the parking lot for storage. The total cost was a little over ten thousand dollars. But the shot did look better without the ATM.

For the past several weeks I have been working on a project that is so secret I can't take the script home. Instead, I read it in the director's office. The entire film takes place in a poor factory town located by the side of a river with an old-fashioned bridge in the background. I have spent the past several weeks contacting film commissions all over the United States and Australia trying to find appropriate locations. Because I can't send them a script, I have to explain what I'm looking for. And because the production designer has only recently been hired, I've had little more than a vague idea of what that is. Do I want an old brick factory beside a picturesque river or something more gritty and industrial? Should the river be large or small? And in what kind of terrain: lush and green or barren and rocky? The production has yet to receive a green light from the studio that's backing it, and this means there is no budget—no way of knowing if we can venture beyond Los Angeles, no way of knowing when or even if we will shoot. At this point, all I can do is call more film commissions; look and dream.

Fred Astaire and Eleanor Powell dance to Cole Porter's "Begin the Beguine" on the set of *Broadway Melody of 1940*.

ESCAPE *by* DESIGN

MAGGIE VALENTINE

WHEN I WAS a kid, my sister and I stayed up late every night one week watching Fred Astaire movies on *The Late Show*. That's when I fell in love. I fell in love with Fred Astaire and the romantic way he glided instead of walked, slid instead of moved, danced instead of kissed. I also fell in love with Venice, or what I thought was Venice—the Bridge of Sighs, the shadowy silhouettes, the gleaming rails, and the polished dance floors. I thought *The Gay Divorcée* (1934) was the height of sophistication, and I imagined living in a penthouse, drinking martinis, donning satin gowns, and going to art deco nightclubs where tuxedoed bands played "The Continental" straight through the night. I thought I was learning about life.

I grew up and was disappointed by martinis, I couldn't find those clubs, and I've never had Ginger Rogers's style, although I still have a soft spot for Fred Astaire. And I'm still looking for those 1930s visions of Venice and Rio and Paris. Those streamlined sets made a lasting impression on me. Even the ship's engine room in *Shall We Dance?* (1937) was gleaming, well scrubbed, and peopled with smiling deckhands who could break into a sophisticated jazz tap at any moment. I thought it was the real thing, and I couldn't wait to travel. The sets were perfectly lighted and they matched the music. They were romantic, open, and clean, encouraging choreographed movement. People fit in perfectly. The camera took in everything as it unfolded seamlessly, inevitably. The sets were graceful and made the actors graceful, too. All in glorious black and white.

I can still separate the characters from the actors more easily than I can distinguish the sets from the places they pictured. Perhaps this is because the architecture of those sets was more beautiful than the places I knew. It was a romantic fantasy, labeled by critic Arlene Croce as the "big white set," variations of which appeared in all the Astaire-Rogers films and in other Hollywood musicals as well. Venice looked like Rio looked like Paris. This should not be surprising, as all were designed under the direction of the same man: Van Nest Polglase, who ran the art department at RKO, where nine of the Astaire-Rogers movies were filmed.[1]

Set design is generally dismissed by architecture critics who see it as artificial and derivative, shallow and false. But set design is a crucial aspect of any film—it is the art of creating vicarious experience. It is about the controlled perception of space—perspectival space, the architectural secret of the Renaissance. Ironically, set designers working in two dimensions are often more successful than architects working in three, who too often focus on the exterior object rather than spatial experience. They devote their energies to creating abstract void spaces rather than backdrops for human activity.

Sets must abbreviate but still communicate. Watching a woman descend a flight of stairs, for example, is boring in "real time." The long stairway is an important sign of place and status, but the moment is not dramatic enough for a cutaway shot. The set designer must communicate the grandness and scale of the stairway, but get the actress down in a hurry. Just as a novel, controlled by the author, may contain more truth than a history limited to events and figures, so set design can express architecture more honestly than buildings themselves, encumbered as they are by plumbing, structural requirements, and all of the other necessities demanded by clients and building codes. Indeed, the evolution of set design reveals as much about changing attitudes in architecture and place-making as it does about the processes of filmmaking and storytelling.

° ° °

Early movies were shot in actual public places, using streets and cities as backdrops. Locations were chosen not for their relevance to narratives, but for benevolent weather patterns. Los Angeles, with three hundred sunny days per year, wide-open spaces, and proximity to Mexico (should the East Coast Trust come looking for violators of its copyright), beckoned. In 1907, Francis Boggs filmed downtown Los Angeles for a backdrop in *The Count of Monte Cristo*. But it was Cecil B. DeMille's *The Squaw Man* (1914), shot in Griffith Park and credited as the first full-length feature made in Hollywood, that began the transformation of a Protestant town into Sin City. The place—Hollywood—became synonymous with the product and all that it symbolizes. A sign built in 1923 to promote real estate sales became the landmark of a city and an industry built around myth. By the 1920s, the small town of Hollywood (population 700 in 1903) had become a symbol of exponential fantasy, glamour, opportunity, faded dreams, greed, dashed hope, and corruption. The Dream Factory.

Real places used for filming soon evolved into real places built for filming. A building, now known as the Spadena House and located in Beverly Hills, was constructed in 1921 in Culver City by Henry Oliver to double as a production office (on the interior) and a film set (on the exterior).[2] The production facilities at Warner Brothers also doubled as film settings. For example, the studio tin shop was used as a prison factory in the Jimmy Cagney vehicle *White Heat* (1949). New studios sprang up. Noisy streets that posed no problems for silent filmmakers were replaced by artificial streets enclosed in soundstages where noise and weather could be controlled. The contemporary architectural parallel to this development is the replacement of "Main Street" shopping districts by gigantic shopping malls.

Studio construction crews can manufacture brick, marble, or wood, all in lightweight plastics and foam. Building 44 on the Warner lot has ten thousand architectural molds at the ready, allowing designers to create any style necessary, to modernize or antique any standing set. Walking down "Brownstone Street" on the backlot, one realizes that Murphy Brown lives next door to Lois Lane. A little paint and some new signage turns *The Music Man*'s River City, Iowa, into *Seinfeld*'s Latham, Massachusetts. Marion the Librarian

Spadena House was constructed by producer Henry Oliver in 1921 as both a film set and a business office.

lives next door to the Dukes of Hazard and across the street from Dennis the Menace. The "neighborhood" is made up of a comfortable but not too distinctive mixture of familiar architectural styles.

Such is the geography of the backlot. The "New York Street" with its fake subway entrances is just around the corner from the generic Western town. The addition of "steel" girders made from wood suggests an "el," making the standing set instantly recognizable as Chicago. *Papier-mâché* facades held upright by truss-shaped braces with people stationed on ladders convince willing believers that behind two-story faux-marble edifices are two-story marble buildings. The sets themselves become real places in the mind, just as the characters become fondly remembered friends.

Both actors and the spaces they inhabit have long been stereotyped. Jimmy Stewart was a nice guy; Bette Davis a force to be reckoned with; Jimmy Dean slightly dangerous. Dads smoked pipes.

Happy families lived on gently curving streets in two-story period revival homes with frilly curtains in the windows. In the postwar period, revivals were replaced by split-level homes with family rooms—but mom still did the housework in high heels. What made for easy recognition and ease in set dressing and filming became the perceived norm for living. The Hays Code effectively dictated standards of morality and happy endings in story lines, while the sets reinforced these standards with twin beds and middle-class decor.

The industry's ability to control the cinematic visual environment extended beyond the films themselves and into the theaters in which they were shown. From the mid-teens through the early thirties, movie palaces replaced storefront theaters and cheap nickelodeons. The new buildings had distinct presences, suggesting architecture on a grand scale while augmenting the escapist experience of a trip to the movies. They were expensive-looking and elaborate, designed to imitate exotic and unobtainable environments such as Versailles or the Forbidden City. When the lights came up in the middle of a double feature, the mood was not broken. Patrons were in a posh environment of "fine art" (the sculpture and paintings were often executed by set designers rather than architects), and waited on by uniformed attendants. Eventually, exotic revivalism gave way to modern, deco, and streamline, but the principle of escape was still primary in driving the design. Every detail, from the external pylons to the lettering on the exit signs and restroom doors, worked to create a special place, unique but recognizable.

Though the name Hollywood became synonymous with the movie business, Hollywood itself was neither the first nor the only city where American production companies undertook large-scale studio construction projects, even in Southern California. Universal built a complex in the San Fernando Valley in 1915. Culver City was host to studios for Hal Roach (torn down in the 1960s) and Thomas Ince, who began his building campaign with a Mt. Vernon replica in 1919. When David O. Selznick inherited Ince's imitation landmark, it began appearing as the logo at the beginning of each of his studio's films. Not everything he purchased would fare so well. When Atlanta burned in *Gone with the Wind* (1939), it was the leftover sets of Cecil B. DeMille's 1927 *King of Kings* that went up in smoke.

After the loss of its strong leadership, when Irving Thalberg and Louis B. Mayer were overthrown in the 1950s, MGM was considered more of a business than an artistic enterprise. Eventually it began selling off pieces of both its history and its real estate. The backlot went in 1969, the props and costumes in 1970, and the studio itself in 1987, when the company's interests shifted from Hollywood to Las Vegas and the MGM Grand displaced grand old MGM. (Since then, Las Vegas has been evolving into one continuous movie set without the movies, as gamblers and tourists move in and out of Egyptian pyramids, volcanoes, Parisian, Venetian, and New York street scenes, and King Arthur's court.)

The Warner Brothers lot, acquired in 1929, was renamed Burbank Studios when Columbia Pictures partnered with the firm in 1972, but was renamed Warner Brothers when Columbia was sold off in 1990. Twentieth Century Fox built a studio in 1927 on the site of a ranch formerly owned by movie cowboy Tom Mix. In the 1960s, they sold much of their backlot to make way for Century City, where the business is deal-making, not movie-making. Paramount is the only studio still located in Hollywood (it is the city's largest employer), and maintains its legendary facade.

In 1990, the Sony Corporation purchased Columbia Studios (the company), moved it to the recently purchased MGM site in Culver City, and tried to restore MGM's glory. The new owners achieved the *sine qua non* of artifice with the construction of a Main Street set, complete with skyscrapers, a theater, and self-promoting movie posters. The set was not created for production purposes, but to enhance the image of the lot to foreign investors who came expecting to see a set. Today, the scene is a prominent part of Sony's corporate identity, effectively stating "Sony means American movies."

Artificiality was an accepted, and apparent, component of many a film from Hollywood's Golden Age. Indeed, the "backstage story" has long been a movie staple: the camera pans back, revealing trees on wheels and false-fronted houses, a cyclorama backdrop, a wind machine and a sound crew, and a movie camera in the foreground. Art imitates art imitating life, with the ersatz not only acknowledged but celebrated. A whole genre grew out of Hollywood's penchant for telling its own stories: *Sullivan's Travels* (1942), *Sunset Boulevard*

(1950), *Singin' in the Rain* (1952), *Gable and Lombard (1976), The Player (1992),* and *A Star Is Born* (1937, 1954, and 1976) to name just a few. Most of the movies in this genre, which reveal the artificiality of movie making, in the process promote a different artificiality passed off as reality—the Hollywood Myth. Watching the movie makes one—briefly—a Hollywood insider, but it is an inside view often composed of cartoonish stereotypes. There is an obligatory scene filmed at the actual commissary, where cynical agents mix with awed newcomers just off the bus from the Midwest. Contract players dressed as cowboys, showgirls, primitive tribesmen, and a man in a gorilla suit (carrying his gorilla head), select items from a cafeteria line. Bereted directors, jaded hard-drinking writers, self-obsessed stars, and disappointed ingenues populate this mythic morality play.

Even though they know better, tourists go West to stand on the corner of Hollywood and Vine, have a soda at Schwab's, and step into the footprints of the stars they think they know. Hollywood and Vine is actually a rather nondescript corner of office buildings. Schwab's, where Lana Turner was, according to an apocryphal legend, discovered—inspiring hoards of young hopefuls to gather at its soda fountain—was torn down in 1987. The 1927 Graumann's Chinese Theatre is now Mann's Chinese Theatre, where the cement footprints of the famous and would-be famous are rotated for publicity events to promote new movies. The newest Los Angeles subway stop, which is almost on the famous intersection, displays signs and art glorifying the past while creating new Kodak moments for tourists.

The backstage story gave birth to the backlot visit. The second-most-popular tourist attraction in California (after Disneyland) is the Universal Studios Tour, a studio-inspired theme park. What started in the 1920s as a twenty-five-cent visit to the set (the price included a box lunch) reemerged in 1964 as a peek behind the scenes. I remember going on the tour shortly after it was reborn. It included a trip through sound lots and empty sets with the ever-present promise that "Quiet on the set!" might be heard, and the studio would spring to life. The *Psycho* house was a major draw, though its diminutive actual size drew amazed responses. The tour ended in the bungalows used to house costumes and makeup artists, with one lucky woman chosen for a makeover. Warner Brothers has been giving behind-the-scenes tours since 1962. Twentieth-Century Fox and Paramount discovered that studio tours were profitable in terms of public relations, and followed suit. Tours are now a major industry, generating as much money (for Universal) as many of the movies they ostensibly promote.

Eventually, the tram-ride tour through an operational set was replaced by a tour through sets created specifically for the tram. In 1965 fans were thrilled to see Cary Grant's alleged parking space. But by the 1980s it took the parting of the Red Sea, a simulated shark attack, high-rise fires, earthquakes, and tornadoes to impress increasingly sophisticated tourists. Visitors once satisfied with being in the "presence" of stars expected to be treated like stars. At Universal Studios, tourists can take home a souvenir video of themselves in cyberspace doing battle with the Forces of Evil, erected by superimposing the visitor against a pre-filmed backdrop. Not to be outdone by Disney's presence in Orlando, Universal Studios has opened its own studio theme park in Florida (where they have never had an operational studio) that includes a copy of the fake house used in *Psycho*. Visitors can take souvenir snapshots of a set where the movie wasn't filmed. The signifier has surpassed the signified—image is everything.

The latest incarnation of the Hollywood experience is Tinseltown Studios, which goes straight for the celebrity and skips the substance. Tinseltown is a restaurant in Anaheim, California (less than a mile from Disneyland), where for $45 a head ($60 for the Mogul's Package; drinks and souvenir photos extra), you are besieged by autograph-seekers, paparazzi, and reporters as you make your way down a red carpet for your own fifteen minutes of fame. The dining space is surrounded by an artificial set, including rigging, catwalks, and spotlights. Projected onto giant screens are clips of individual diners digitally inserted into their favorite movies. Pampered by waiters and hosts right out of Central Casting, lucky diners are selected as recipients of "Oggie" awards for "Best Performances." The restaurant advertises its ability to take unknown people and turn them into "screen legends." The corporate logo and the restaurant building are based on the generic studio image: a barrel-vaulted sound studio, Klieg lights, and an 80-foot water tower—symbol of Ye Olde Hollywoode.

Hollywood set design simply looked too real for the 1998 film *The Truman Show*. To achieve the level of artificiality demanded by Andrew Niccol's script (about a man whose entire life is set within the confines of a self-contained, town-size set so that it can be televised without the protagonist's knowledge), the filmmaker turned to Seaside, Florida, a real place that exudes plastic pretense. Seaside is the much-publicized New Urbanist resort town planned to project the security, scale, and feel of a Hollywood interpretation of small-town America. The Disney-backed community, Celebration, is also located in Florida. Both towns are strictly regulated by design codes that are assumed to induce codes of appropriate behavior. Social problems such as alcohol and drug abuse, crime, racial strife, unemployment—to say nothing of such public nuisances as graffiti—are ostensibly not the threats that they are in the outside world. Happy endings are guaranteed, if only you follow the rules.

With his latest entry in the *Star Wars* saga, *The Phantom Menace* (1999), George Lucas has moved in the exact opposite direction of *The Truman Show*. Whereas the latter sought an actual location that would appear artificial, Lucas created a digital world intended to convince. While many of *The Phantom Menace*'s special effects were created from conventional mattes and models, the actors also found themselves playing off characters and sets that existed only in the digital realm. The film did not push the limits of reality, but invented a whole new world with its own inherent logic. This was carried off with such finesse that the visual effects became the true star of the film, overshadowing narrative and character development.

In less than a century, we have witnessed an evolution from the set as actual place to the set as an artificial, constructed place, to real places as constructed sets. The line between the simulated and the authentic is almost hopelessly blurred. Can a real-life Truman be far behind? Probably not, as evidenced by the increasing number of voyeuristic Web cameras unleashed on an unsuspecting public. But where Truman was manipulated, we still have free will.

Good design, both for the screen and for the real world, is about giving actors control over their environments. Both art direction and architecture serve as backdrops for the stories of people living their lives. In the movies, actors—guided by a director, aided by a set designer, and enhanced by a costume designer—interpret a script developed by a screenwriter. Everything is fictional, manipulated, changeable. This is not the case with real life. If only it were. Thank goodness it's not.

NOTES

1. Like Cedric Gibbons at Metro-Goldwyn-Mayer, Polglase was listed in the credits as set designer for most movies emanating from the studio, regardless of how direct a role he played in the production. Polglase and Carroll Clark collaborated on all of the RKO Astaire-Rogers musicals from *Flying Down to Rio* (1933) to *Carefree* (1938).
2. There is currently a plan to return the house to Culver City.

TEARING DOWN *the* HOUSE: MODERN HOMES *in the* MOVIES

JOSEPH ROSA

IN RECENT HOLLYWOOD movies, modern domestic architecture has become identified almost exclusively with characters who are evil, unstable, selfish, obsessive, and driven by pleasures of the flesh. Were they still alive, this might well shock the pioneers of modernism, who envisioned their movement facilitating a healthy, honest, and moral way of life. Nonetheless, filmmakers of late have chosen modernist works as the sites for murder, gangsterism, adultery, and a catalog of other illicit and otherwise unsavory behaviors. Bad guys may no longer wear black, but they do live in white-walled modern homes.

What went wrong? If one believes Tom Wolfe's 1977 screed, *From Bauhaus to Our House*, modern design is simply anathema to the American way of living, and it therefore only makes sense that those who contest and violate American values be associated with it. The reality is actually more complicated, though it is fair to say that Americans have never fully embraced modern architecture for their homes. More to the point, Hollywood films have both reflected and shaped American views about modern domestic design.

Homes inevitably reveal something of their inhabitants' aspirations. Notwithstanding the pioneering legacy of the founding fathers of this nation, most Americans have never had a desire to "start from zero," as members of the Bauhaus suggested, at least not in terms of architecture. Americans have always been motivated to keep up with the Joneses—not to supplant the Joneses' way of life. American domestic architecture, with all of its revival styles, communicates this essential conservatism.

To the American public of the 1930s, modern architecture was anything but conservative. In fact, it was a somewhat frightening sign of progress driven by technological and scientific advance. Inasmuch, modern architecture was considered appropriate for the workplace though unsuitable for the middle-class home. Fear of the modern—mirrored both in films and in the press—focussed on the negative effects such settings could have on the family. For example, in a 1931 critique of the Aluminaire House, a prototype modern home designed by A. Lawrence Kocher and Albert Frey that was viewed by more than one hundred thousand New Yorkers, Elsie McCormick advised female readers of the *World Telegram* to be wary of the "stern, office-like effect" that would likely drive a husband to seek succor in "fluffier apartments."[1]

The elegant, urbane "moderneism" of so many films of the thirties—pioneered by such legendary art directors as Cedric Gibbons and Van Nest Polglase—soothed these fears, offering Depression-era audiences escape in sumptuous art deco fantasies. Even still, deco design, itself a far cry from high modernism, never really challenged the supremacy of America's historically based housing styles. In *Reaching for the Moon* (1931), *The Women* (1939), *It's a Wonderful Life* (1946), and countless other films of the period, a husband returns from the office to a happy, traditional home life with wife, children, and, sometimes, domestic help. Matrimony, a traditional institution if ever there was one, was appropriately set in a traditional dwelling. Conversely, modern domestic settings—invariably urban apartments—were reserved for youthful singles, the unusually wealthy, easy women, and terminal bachelors. Once married, even these characters left their modern quarters for more conventional accommodations.

In practice, there was a significant differentiation made between the portrayal of those living in apartments and those living in penthouses. The apartment-dweller was generally young, naïve, ambitious, in a precarious financial situation, and on his or her own for the first time. The penthouse was typically reserved for the wealthy, older, well educated, and unsentimental. The penthouse-dweller lived in the present and looked toward the future with little concern for the past—with the exception of its bearing on his or her social status. It was almost never the home for a married family with children, though a typical story line had a penthouse-dweller coming to his or her senses, falling in love, and relocating to a more traditional home. *Susan Lenox: Her Fall and Rise* (1931), *Dark Victory* (1939), and *Christmas in Connecticut* (1945) all feature examples of just this phenomenon.

More than anything else, though, penthouse-dwellers were rendered as eccentrics. This is best typified by Morton DaCosta's *Auntie Mame* (1958), in which the title character, played by Rosalind Russell, alters the decor of her apartment to ward off a nephew's conservative fiancée. At the beginning of the film, Mame's brother dies, leaving his young son Patrick in the care of Mame, his "irresponsible sister." The interior of her penthouse duplex on Manhattan's tony Beekman Place changes throughout the film, reflecting her whimsy. When Patrick—now in college—tells Mame of plans to marry Gloria Upson, a girl from good conservative stock, Mame goes along with it until she visits the girl's parents at their home in Darien, Connecticut. There she learns of the Upsons' anti-Semitic views and dreams of a clubby lifestyle for their daughter. Mame invites them to her place in Manhattan for an intimate dinner party before the wedding and proceeds to transform her duplex into an ultra-modern space filled with Danish design, Calder-like mobiles, and cubist art. Couches in the living room are supported by hydraulic pedestals that allow them to move up and down. Not surprisingly, the decor—coupled with appetizers of grilled rattlesnake and a cast of Mame's oddball friends—sends the Upsons and their daughter running. (Patrick ends up marrying Mame's personal secretary.)

Meanwhile, the depiction of the traditional home became ever more entwined with notions of domestic bliss. The 1944 film *The Enchanted Cottage*, starring Robert Young and Dorothy McGuire, illustrated the magical powers that a traditional setting could provide. The film's premise: love found in an enchanted cottage can mend any problem and even render an outcast couple "normal." The cottage in question is an eighteenth-century brick, shingle-roofed structure stuffed with memorabilia, including a coat of arms from the original occupant, an English gentleman. A homely girl, played by McGuire, takes a job as housekeeper and falls for a wealthy young man who was disfigured in World War II and then disowned by his society fiancée. He takes refuge in the cottage, which he had originally rented for his honeymoon. Inevitably, the disfigured man and the homely girl fall in love. While every outsider who sees them notices their flawed appearances, they see only beauty in each other's eyes.

H. C. Potter's 1948 romantic comedy *Mr. Blandings Builds His Dream House* cemented this association between traditional architecture and traditional happiness. Looking to escape the teeming metropolis of New York, Jim and Muriel Blandings (Cary Grant and Myrna Loy) embark on a mission to build their fantasy home in the suburbs of Connecticut. After a series of calamitous miscalculations (the film was remade as *The Money Pit* in 1986), the Blandings do eventually find domestic bliss in the form of a large colonial with a steeply pitched roof. Conversely, in King Vidor's 1949 architectural melodrama, *The Fountainhead,* we see a series of self-absorbed ideologs inhabiting a series of supposedly spectacular "modern" homes and apartments. In the end, the architect is triumphant, but the victory is, at best, Pyrrhic.

By the late 1940s, the technology and optimism that had ushered in modern architecture in the early part of the century had been tainted by a knowledge of the destructive power of modern science and imminent fear of annihilation from the bomb. At the same time, corporate America was busily appropriating modernism—now the "International Style"—for its own needs, stripping it of its ideological content. America faced a housing shortage, but such corporate and military associations mitigated against any wholesale adoption of modern design for the home. Not surprisingly, white-walled residences rarely appeared in films featuring loving couples. *Palm Springs Weekend* (1963) typifies Hollywood's unhappy depiction of modern domestic architecture at the midcentury. In the film, a family weekend house is trashed by teenagers who crash an unsupervised party. Elegant modern furniture is hurled through the air, destroying a wet bar and much else. Oddly, no one seems too concerned

John Lautner's 1960 Malin Residence, better known as the Chemosphere, starred in Brian De Palma's 1984 erotic thriller *Body Heat*.

about the destroyed structure. Indeed, the film's main accomplishment lay in reinforcing the equation between a hedonistic and destructive throwaway culture of weekend living and the cool look of modern design. Ironically, Hollywood elites had been cultivating a progressive school of modern architecture since the 1930s; indeed, it was the very homes they had designed for themselves—by such architects as Rudolph Schindler, Richard Neutra, and John Lautner—that were starting to crop up in their own films as the ultimate signs of sin.

If any genre has confirmed the association between dastardly doings and modern design, it has been the action thriller—in particular the James Bond series. In these films, master criminals bent on world domination inhabit remote, precariously sited modern hideaways—in the early films these were most often sets designed by the art director Ken Adam at Pinewood Studios, outside of London. On occasion, however, the Bond villains did find homes beyond the confines of the Pinewood backlot. In *Diamonds Are Forever* (1971), Bond nemesis Ernst Blofeld commandeers a house of poured-in-place concrete with sweeping views of what is supposedly the Nevada desert. In actuality it is the 1968 Arthur Elrod Residence, the *sine qua non* of bachelor pads, designed by John Lautner and located in Palm Springs. Lautner's signature California baroque aesthetic—soaring interior spaces, curving forms, dramatic vistas—is ideally suited for translation to film, and his houses appear with unparalleled regularity in Hollywood productions. And in seemingly every case, they play host to less-than-savory characters.

In both Brian De Palma's 1984 erotic thriller *Body Double* and Joel and Ethan Coen's 1998 crime comedy *The Big Lebowski*, innocent men are lured to Lautner houses where they are drugged and framed for crimes they did not commit. In *Body Double,* a naïve, would-be actor is asked by a recent acquaintance to house-sit—the house in question being Lautner's futuristic 1960 Malin Residence (better known as the Chemosphere) in Hollywood, a saucer-shaped domicile perched on a column over a steep slope. With its panoptic, 360-degree views of the surrounding landscape, the house drives a Byzantine plot in which the hapless actor becomes an addicted voyeur who witnesses the staged killing of a porn actress. In *The Big Lebowski*, the equally hapless Jeff "The Dude" Lebowski (Jeff Bridges), visits loan shark Jackie Treehorn (Ben Gazzara) who has mistaken him for another man with the same last name. Lebowski is summarily drugged while admiring the shylock's space-age pad—Lautner's 1963 Sheats House, a spectacular poured-concrete structure of triangular forms set in the mountains overlooking Beverly Hills. In both *Body Double* and *The Big Lebowski*, directors tease their audiences along with their guileless lead characters in games of architectural bait-and-switch. Lautner's striking modern designs are traps—highly seductive sites of crime and deception.

In the 1990s, filmmakers have returned dramas to modern dwellings that serve as signs for the unstable, the transitory, and the amoral. In the 1991 film *Sleeping with the Enemy*, Julia Roberts and Patrick Bergin play a married couple (Laura and Martin Burney) living in a flat-roofed, modern beach house. Everything in the home's minimalist environment is precisely placed, from the furnishings to the food in the cabinets. Shortly after the film opens, it is revealed that Martin is an abusive obsessive-compulsive who controls every aspect of Laura's existence, from the people she sees to the aesthetics of their home. This sun-filled house quickly becomes a glass prison, forcing Laura to fake her death and move to another town. In this new location she embraces her own traditional aesthetic sensibility. She rents a cottage, paints it happy colors, and puts up kitschy patterned wallpaper. The kitchen cupboards are a mess. But it's not long before Modern Martin tracks her down, fiendishly plotting to eliminate his erstwhile bride.

In Ang Lee's 1998 film *Ice Storm*, the morals of the various characters are similarly encoded by the architecture they inhabit. Set in the 1970s, the film juxtaposes two families that live near each other, examining their friendships and relationships. The Hoods live in a traditional house located on a suburban lot with a lawn; the Carvers live in a modern flat-roofed house in a wooded area. Needless to say, the traditional building is home to the more stable family. Moreover, it is the "modern" woman who seduces the "traditional" man—one of the film's central traumas. *Ice Storm* is set against the Thanksgiving holiday, but only the Hoods sit down together—on their screened-in porch—for the holiday meal.

Both families have problems—Ben Hood (Kevin Kline) is unfaithful and Jim Carver (Jamey Sheridan) is sexually inadequate—but the Hoods' troubles are for the most part normal and reparable. The Carvers, on the other hand, are completely unhinged by the infidelity of matriarch Janey Carver (Sigourney Weaver), father Jim's problems in bed, and the death of their eldest son, who is killed by a fallen live wire during an ice storm. Throughout the film, the Carvers' modern home is framed so that it can be seen in full through the woods. The camera stalks through the surrounding property, giving the impression that it is spying on the inhabitants. Inevitably, the modern house becomes the site of sexual indiscretions on the part of the adults and the children.

When it comes to manipulation and downright evil, Janey Carver has nothing on Catherine Ames, the middle-aged film-diva-cum-murderess at the heart of Robert Benton's 1998 neo-noir *Twilight*. As portrayed by Susan Sarandon, Ames knows what she wants in life and goes to great lengths to get it, mostly at the expense of others. Not surprisingly, given her nature, Ames has a taste for the modern. Along with her second husband, Jack (Gene Hackman), also a well-known actor, she lives in an opulent art deco residence (the 1929 home designed by legendary MGM art director Cedric Gibbons for himself and his wife, Dolores Del Rio). The Ameses' "country" home is Frank Lloyd Wright's 1948 Walker House in Carmel. As the film proceeds, the audience learns that Catherine had masterminded the murder of her first husband—at the Wright house—and that her foul play had been facilitated by Raymond Hope (James Garner), a retired detective now living well beyond his means in John Lautner's 1947 Polin House in the Hollywood hills. The house is Hope's undoing: even after his role in the sordid backstory is revealed, he refuses to turn himself in—"And give up this house?"—opting instead for a shootout that winds up getting him killed.

The nostalgia for a past domestic ideal has always helped to define the "good" character for the audience. In Curtis Hanson's 1998 film *L.A. Confidential*, Kim Basinger plays a high-priced call girl—a Veronica Lake look-alike named Lynn Bracken—who lives and works out of a Spanish revival house furnished in glamorous deco style. The central space of the house features a living room and bed area; this is where she conducts her business. Behind Bracken's icy persona, of course, is a warm heart. After falling in love with policeman Bud White (Russell Crowe), she invites him to spend the night and brings him into her true bedroom, which is furnished with a brass bed, floral bedding, and a pillow embroidered with sentimental maxims that reflect her nostalgia for a traditional life.

Conversely, mysterious millionaire Pierce Patchett (David Strathairn), who runs the escort service that pimps Bracken, lives in an austere modern house with a terraced garden situated on a hill near the Griffith Observatory. It's no ordinary modern box—like the Carvers' home in *Ice Storm*—but Richard Neutra's seminal Lovell Health House (1929), one of the first American houses framed in steel. In the film, the sheer size of the house is a symbol of the owner's wealth, and the modern aesthetic signifies a cool, calculating demeanor that allows Patchett to mediate between the legitimate and corrupt worlds of Hollywood.

No film better illustrates Hollywood's bizarre love/hate relationship with its modern patrimony than the formulaic action picture *Lethal Weapon 2* (1989). Much of Richard Donner's apartheid-era film—which pits L.A. detectives Martin Riggs (Mel Gibson) and Roger Murtaugh (Danny Glover) against a South African smuggling ring led by the country's racist, murdering ambassador—takes place at what is supposedly the South African Embassy. (What the embassy is doing in Los Angeles is never explained.) In actuality it is yet another house by Lautner (the 1962 Garcia Residence), a unique structure with a bowed concrete ceiling plane and perimeter walls mostly of glass. Elegantly sited on a steep hillside, the house is supported by exposed pillars that stretch to the ground below an exterior deck. These supports become a target for the film's vigilante heroes in a sequence that forms one of the most symbolically loaded images of the modern home in Hollywood history. Stymied from searching the house by the South Africans' claims to diplomatic immunity, Riggs ties a rope to one of the pillars, hitches it to his Dodge pickup, and pulls the house from the hillside—bad guys along with it.

For better or worse, filmmakers can't stay away from modernist buildings. By day they shoot their films in them, and by night they call them home. Perhaps there's something in Hollywood's collective psyche that demands to be understood as transgressive, dangerous, wild, even criminal—and it is this that has led to the unfortunate stereotyping of modern design and those who enjoy it. The silver lining? Moral content aside, modern design sure looks great on film.

NOTE

1. Elsie McCormick, review of the Aluminaire House, *New York World Telegram*, January 10, 1931.

PART THREE

VISIONS *of the* WORLD

Mr. Hulot (Jacques Tati) surveys the cubicles of a modern office building in *Playtime* (1967).

ARCHITECTURE *in a* MODE *of* DISTRACTION: EIGHT TAKES *on* JACQUES TATI'S *Playtime*

JOAN OCKMAN

1. TOWARD A THEORY OF DISTRACTION

Film has been compared to architecture almost since its inception. One of the inaugural discussions along these lines is Walter Benjamin's essay "The Work of Art in the Age of Mechanical Reproduction" (1935–36), in which the author suggests that architecture is a prototype for film because both are received "by a collectivity in a mode of distraction." Distraction, for Benjamin, following earlier definitions by Georg Simmel and Siegfried Kracauer, is a form of experience that occurs incidentally, disjunctively, and largely unconsciously—"absent-mindedly"—rather than through the alert and contemplative vision that traditionally characterizes the viewing of painting, for example. Benjamin does not deny that there is also an optical and intentional component in the experience of architecture. He is less interested, however, in "the attentive concentration of a tourist before a famous building" than in the everyday process by which built form is apprehended by the masses working in the city or the *flâneur* wandering through it.[1]

Film and architecture both mobilize spatial and temporal modes of perception. Yet insofar as film tends to be dominated by a linear and narrative structure and is perceived from a stationary viewing position, Benjamin's analogy to architecture would seem to break down. To understand the premises for his argument more fully—and its relevance to Jacques Tati's 1967 film *Playtime*—it is necessary to return to the early history of film. Benjamin is writing at a moment when the cinema as a form of commercial entertainment has not yet lost contact with its origins in the variety theater, music hall, panoramas, arcade peep shows, and other popular attractions geared to the new mass audiences emerging with the urbanized industrial working class. Unlike later cinema, designed to envelope the viewer in the illusion of a narrative fiction, the early medium depended on conventions of display or showmanship that assaulted spectators with "astonishing" sights—sensational subjects like a train crash or the electrocution of an elephant.[2] More presentational than representational, these films were accompanied by live music and shown in lavish theatrical interiors. In this context, the architectural setting enhanced the multisensory, multidimensional experience of the performance. The viewer was thereby kept, according to Kracauer, from being totally seduced by the phantoms on the screen:

> The interior design of the movie theaters serves one sole purpose: to rivet the audience's attention to the peripheral so that they will not sink into the abyss. The stimulations of the senses succeed each other with such rapidity that there is no room left for even the slightest contemplation to squeeze in between them.[3]

For early film theorists like Kracauer and Benjamin, as for the Soviet filmmaker Sergei Eisenstein, this form of entertainment was potentially revolutionary because it corresponded to the dynamic conditions of contemporary urban life. In the hands of artists, the unnerving effects of metropolitan distraction and mechanization that were implicit in the variety theater as well as in this early "cinema of attractions" could, they believed, be harnessed for more aesthetic and political purposes. The camera's insertion between the eye and the moving object, the projector's calibrated rotation, the editing operations of cutting and splicing all replicated the disjunctiveness, mobility, and above all shock inherent in daily life. Metonymically, as well as metaphorically, the cinematic medium translated the impact of industrialization into the realm of aesthetic reception.[4]

In its capacity to "see" the world in ways unavailable to the human eye, the movie camera went well beyond the still camera. Its unprecedented ability to track space-time relations enabled it to expose split-second actions and other aspects of reality that had never been captured before: "The camera introduces us to unconscious optics as does psychoanalysis to unconscious impulses," writes Benjamin.[5] This revelatory capacity to explode the "prison-world" materiality of buildings, objects, and gestures gave the cinema a moral and didactic mission, these theorists believed: that of conditioning the New Man and Woman of modernity for contemporary life. Yet it could only carry out such a task if—as Kracauer stressed—it ceased to "glue the pieces back together after the fact and present them as organic creations," radically aiming instead "towards a kind of distraction which exposes disintegration instead of masking it."[6]

Even as the visions of Kracauer, Benjamin, and Eisenstein were being articulated, however, they were already being superseded by the development of mainstream cinema. Shaped by Hollywood after World War I, the fiction film quickly became dominant, more so after the development of sound. It was a cinematic code predicated precisely on gluing the pieces back together—on narrative coherence, the illusion of spatial and temporal continuity, and the suppression of off-screen distractions. Through techniques that heightened what the French film theorist Christian Metz would later call the "impression of reality," the cinema abandoned the architectural and theatrical model in favor of a literary one, transforming the participatory space of the live theater into the now familiar black box. As far as the experience of viewing was concerned, absorption turned out to be no less "natural" a mode of film reception than distraction. Not just capitalist filmmakers but, in 1930s Germany, fascist ones seized on this insight, appropriating the new technology for blatantly propagandistic purposes. Writing "The Work of Art" a year after the appearance of Leni Riefenstahl's *Triumph of the Will* (1934), how could Benjamin fail to end on a somber note? No amount of technological optimism could dispel the realization that the new medium had as much potential to aestheticize reactionary politics as to demystify them, to mesmerize its mass audiences through the totalizing and spectacular nature of its imagery.

The utopian relationship between industrial technology and modern life would likewise be difficult to sustain in the new architecture. In the passage comparing film and architecture in his "Work of Art" essay, Benjamin tends to treat the latter as if it were an atemporal phenomenon, generalizing that the built environment has "at all times" tended to be received distractedly. Elsewhere, however, notably in his essay "Surrealism" (1929), he turns specifically to the question of modern architecture. There he suggests that the highly technical, abstract aesthetic of modern architecture has the potential to educate the masses for the changes wrought by the contemporary epoch. The poverty of sensuous experience imposed "in rooms by Le Corbusier and Oud," the shock of the new spatial and material relationships, makes modern architecture a potent instrument for overcoming outdated habits of bourgeois art and culture, and thus an effective training ground for a revolutionary engagement with modern life. "Our epoch is fixing its own style day by day. It is there under our eyes...eyes which do not see," Le Corbusier wrote in his manifesto *Towards a New Architecture.* "To live in a glass house is a revolutionary virtue *par excellence*," Benjamin answers, as if in direct response to the architect's polemic against antiquated and academic modes of perception. "It is also an intoxication, a moral exhibitionism, that we badly need."[7]

Yet the utopia of glass dreamed of by architectural visionaries from Paul Scheerbart to Bruno Taut to the masters of the Bauhaus, the "enlightened" imagination of Le Corbusier's radiant city and Sigfried Giedion's "liberated living," failed to reckon with the darker forces of modernity. After World War II the glass "house" quickly became the chosen image of a globalizing capitalism. Benjamin's intoxicating moral exhibitionism with its radical poetics of transparency quickly devolved into a controlled environment of technocratic bureaucracy. The grid became a "continuous monument"—as the radical Italian group Superstudio would depict it in the late 1960s—overreaching the world. The abstract curtain-wall facades, the anonymous language of the postwar International Style, stretched across the tensile surface of Cold War society, suturing, only superficially, its profound fissures.

What was the fate of sensory perception in this context? What effects did this totalizing environment have on the psyche and the absentminded, everyday experience of the city? With his less roseate outlook, Benjamin's predecessor Georg Simmel already foresaw the atrophy of the senses under the new metropolitan conditions. On the one hand, the urban dweller was exposed to hyperstimulation and continuous shocks; on the other, to "indifference toward the distinctions between things," a phenomenon characteristic of an economy driven by money, where "all [things] float with the same specific gravity." The contradictory combination of overstimulation and underdifferentiation would inevitably lead, in Simmel's view, to the formation of a quintessentially modern type: the *blasé* individual, to whom everything appears "homogeneous, flat, and gray."[8] Half a century later he proved prophetic. A generation of sociologists and popular writers would decry the appearance of one-dimensional organization men in gray flannel suits. As for modern architecture, its self-imposed poverty no longer appeared hortatory and liberating but sterile and reductive. Behaviorists like B. F. Skinner sought to demonstrate the cause-effect consequences of sensory deprivation: a dull environment dulled the personality. An architecture without qualities could not train or prepare, but only extinguish the capacity for experience.

In other words, the *aesthetics* of the stripped object could only end up by *anaesthetizing* the senses. In its original derivation from the Greek, the word *aesthetics* means "things perceptible by the senses, as distinct from things which were immaterial or which could only be thought."[9] By the mid-nineteenth century, however, this meaning underwent a subtle reversal. As the "truth" of sensory perception was relativized, aesthetics became bound up with theories of beauty and questions of taste. No longer describing a mode of cognition in touch with everyday life and bodily experience, it became instead an intellectual apparatus mediating reality.[10] This change coincides with the emergence of shock as one of the central pathologies of modernity. Like the new medical technology of anaesthesia, modern aesthetics now served to numb the psyche to the traumatic effects of the external environment. By privileging the visual over the other senses, by submitting experience to techniques of measurement, normalization, and control, rationalism became an aesthetic strategy for managing reality's threatening contents. As such, it would be ill-suited to opening "eyes that do not see."

In his history of modern visuality, Jonathan Crary has suggested that once the dynamics of modernity fatally undermined the authority of the senses as an instrument for apprehending reality, a permanent struggle was instigated between attention and distraction.[11] As capitalism unleashed its unending flood of new products and information into the marketplace, culture had to develop new techniques of managing and regulating their reception. The emergence of television, video, and computer imaging over the last several decades has escalated this struggle. Increasingly a function of push-button technologies, contemporary visual experience is characterized by ever more disjunctive and distracted modes of reception and, in the ensuing competition among various "channels" for audiences, ever more attention-grabbing strategies. In this context, the possibilities for transforming the contemporary experience of distraction into the critical spectatorship imagined by Benjamin and his contemporaries hardly seem good. This is all the more so with the media's thorough appropriation of the techniques of montage and shock—once staked out by avant-garde filmmakers and artists—for commercial and political purposes, from advertisements to campaign sound bites.[12]

Yet if the original analogy between the perception of film and architecture appears naïvely idealistic today, an artifact of the revolutionary social aspirations of modernism, it nonetheless remains suggestive, offering a historical reference point for a theory of twentieth-century experience.

2. FROM CHAPLIN TO TATI

Monsieur Hulot, the extraordinary character created by Jacques Tati, belongs to the lineage of great modern film clowns of which Charlie Chaplin's Tramp remains the archetype. In the role of the Tramp, Chaplin, like no other performer, found a way to mimic the fragmentation and disjunction of modern life. What was so new about Chaplin's gestures, as Benjamin pointed out in the first version of his "Work of Art" essay, was his ability to break apart the complex range of human expression into a sequence of discrete actions. "Every single one of his movements is put together from a series of hacked-up pieces of motion," Benjamin writes. "Whether one focuses on his walk, on the way [he] handles his cane, or tips his hat—it is always the same jerky sequence of the smallest motions which raises the law of the filmic sequence of images to that of human motor actions."[13] The effect is not just comic, but a particularly modern form of the comic, related to the inelasticity of mechanical things. The philosopher Henri Bergson, who believed that life was predicated on a vital impulse or *élan vital,* formulated this idea of comedy at the turn of the century: "The attitudes, gestures and movements of the human body are laughable in exact proportion as that body reminds us of a mere machine."[14]

It is instructive to compare Chaplin's comic techniques—as both filmmaker and actor—to those of Tati/Hulot. A quarter century after Chaplin invented the Tramp, Tati's Hulot displays an almost opposite set of physical features and mannerisms from his predecessor. Where Chaplin moves in small, upright jerks, Tati shuffles, strides, or lurches diagonally. Where Chaplin's Tramp is short and his pants baggy, Tati's Hulot is tall and his pants too short. Where the Tramp aspires to be a dandy, Hulot is ordinary, disheveled, a nondescript if idiosyncratic type. His talismans—pipe, hat, umbrella, suitcase—look seedy, hardly the modern *objets-types* celebrated by Le Corbusier.

Playtime, Tati's masterpiece, brings to fruition even more fundamental differences between the two clowns, reflecting the historical distance between them. The Chaplin persona, although marionette-like, never fails to retain his individuality. A victim, he is also a born rebel. On the brink of catastrophe, he responds with agility and intuitive resourcefulness. Hulot, on the other hand, is passive, deferential, absentminded. He bucks the tide with only a dim sense of purpose, even if he inevitably subverts things in spite of himself. If Chaplin's body reacts to the immediate, physical impact of mechanization, it would seem that Hulot's enacts its longer-term psychic consequences. He moves gingerly through the world, mistrustful of its materiality. Moreover, if Hulot comes off in Tati's earlier films as an innocent, bumbling eccentric, "a character," in *Playtime* he is no longer so much singular as a man of the crowd. The film could almost (as Tati himself admitted) have been made without him. Hulot's conception has been "multiplied tenfold."[15]

Indeed, *Playtime* abounds in comic instances of doubleness, mistaken identity, and false recognition—"I am not Hulot, ridiculous!" declares a look-alike character. These become a function of the film's reflective, reduplicating, disorienting architecture. The linkage between the psychological theme of the double and the alienating urban or architectural environment belongs to a long modernist tradition running from Nikolai Gogol, Fyodor Dostoevsky, and Edgar Allan Poe to Franz Kafka and René Magritte. The *Doppelgänger* or split personality acts out the contradictions between the city's superficial rationality and its underlying irrationality, between environmental forces and (human) nature. Tati's film brings to mind Gogol's St. Petersburg stories and Dostoevsky's early novellas; Hulot's ill-fitting raincoat and the bandaged nose of a character who has collided with an invisible glass wall in pursuit of a reflection recall the grotesque farce of stories like "The Overcoat" and "The Nose." (Not surprisingly, Tati—whose original name was Tatischeff—was of Russian descent.) Yet what is new in *Playtime* is that the city's surreal nature is no longer the work of the devil (as in Gogol) or the figment of a character's disturbed mind (as in Dostoevsky). Nor does *Playtime*'s atmosphere of estrangement ever have the threatening sci-fi portentousness of Yevgeny Zamyatin's dystopian *We* (1924), a sense of dread that will later also pervade Jean-Luc Godard's *Alphaville* (1965), a film nearly contemporaneous with *Playtime*. In *Playtime,* all anguish, all terror is gone. The anonymity of the city is incomprehensible, dazzling, and banal. "The absurd is presented as if it were self-evident, in order to strip the self-evident of its power."[16]

3. FROM MUSIC HALL TO FILM

It so happens that when Tati began working on *Playtime* he was also preoccupied with efforts to revive the old genre of the music hall, a form of spectacle once popular on Paris's *grands boulevards.* His own career had started there in the 1930s. In 1961, in an extended stint at the Olympia theater, he combined ballet, juggling acts, impressions from his previous films, and a small supporting cast that included the oldest clown in France and a goat. He called his new form of entertainment ciné-music-hall. Three years later he rented the Lux cinema on the rue de Rennes to show a colorized and resonorized version of his first major film, *Jour de Fête* (1948), accompanied by live music, ballet, and large-scale architectural decorations. Although it was unsuccessful commercially, Tati took his cinematic variety show to Strasbourg, Lille, and Lyons.

In *Playtime,* however, the external props are gone. The architectural setting of the film itself has become the spectacle. Taking as its slim narrative pretext a visit to Paris by a group of provincial American tourists, the film opens with their arrival, literally out of the blue, in a place that is not a place, but rather a monochrome purgatory of glass and metal, a glistening, antiseptic environment. The location turns out to be an air terminal. Thus is set in motion the strange choreography, the *ballet mécanique,* that marks this film as excessive, outside the bounds of normal space-time relations, a heterotopia. It initiates the viewer into an "other" order, a time of aesthetic play, cinematic time—*playtime.* Right-angle blocking patterns, an unsynchronized polyglot soundtrack, and the sly insertion of cardboard cutout figures among the "real" actors heighten the atmosphere of Bergsonian mechanistic comedy and general distraction.

The film's big joke is that the tourists never arrive in the historic and symbolic center of French and world culture. Rather, they pass their compressed holiday in its hypermodern simulacrum, a fact they hardly seem to realize:

> The story: a group of foreign tourists arrive on a visit to Paris. In landing at Orly, they find themselves pretty much in the same airport as the one they left in Munich, London, or Chicago. They climb into the same autobus they would have climbed into in Rome or Hamburg, and arrive on a highway lined with street lights and buildings identical to those in their own capital city. They find themselves back in that style of architecture that is designed to keep you in a constant state of crying, "Watch out! Watch out!"[17]

Into this same inhospitable, post-urban milieu stumbles Hulot, literally ejected from a moving bus. He has an appointment to meet an official in one of the glass office buildings, a rendezvous that, owing to a series of miscues and architecturally orchestrated mishaps, never quite gets consummated. Like Lautréamont's famous meeting of disparate objects on a dissecting table, the paths of Hulot and the American tourists cross in chance ways throughout the film. Circumstances eventually prompt an evanescent "relationship" to bud between Hulot and one of them, a diffident young woman bemused by everything she sees, distinguished from her comrades by her air of independence and blithe sense of humor.

In addition to the air terminal, the film's major settings are the lobbies and interiors of several interchangeable high-rise buildings. Office spaces, convention hall, hotel, housing block, supermarket, drugstore/snackbar, and a new restaurant metamorphose into each another as oneiric elements of an unmappable pedestrian and vehicular milieu. Tati had originally intended to rent Orly airport or a large supermarket or bank building for the shooting of the film. When none of these proved available for the lengthy project, he decided to contruct his own *grand ensemble* from scratch. He located a site east of Paris near Vincennes and collaborated on the design with the architect and set designer Eugène Roman. In July 1964, with a construction crew of one hundred and a dozen supervising technicians, a studio-city 15,000 square meters in area (about four city blocks), entirely of glass and steel, began to take form.[18] Five months later it was complete. Four stories high in actuality, the buildings were designed to give the illusion of being skyscrapers. They were equipped with central heating, escalators, and enough electrical power to light up a town of fifteen thousand people. Neon signs illuminated the facades. In addition to the fixed constructions there were several facades on rails that could be rolled around to create varied perspectives and ensembles. The paved streets were outfitted with lamps, traffic lights, parking meters, and dozens of automobiles for simulating dense traffic and parking. Parallel to this Potemkin city was concealed an extensive production center: offices, studios, film lab, restaurant, traffic control station, underground sewer system. When asked why he had constructed such an elaborate set—delaying production and putting the film well over budget from the start—Tati replied that the costs were comparable to what other filmmakers would have spent to hire stars. He preferred, as in his previous films, to draw much of his cast from nonprofessional actors, selecting them for their physical types rather than their experience or box-office allure. Most of the women in the tour group, for example, were wives from a nearby American army base. In *Playtime,* people were "extras." Architecture was the *vedette.*[19]

4. NEOBOURGEOIS SPACE

Playtime's comic assault is directed against the reduction of spatial and cultural experience to a totalizing global language of technobureaucracy and consumerism. Even the proud French language has submitted: "How do you say 'drugstore' in French?" an American tourist asks Hulot. "*Le drugstore.*" In historical terms, the arrival of the American tourists was already a *fait accompli* in 1967. Like the rest of Europe, France had been invaded by American culture two decades earlier by way of World War II and the postwar Marshall Plan, and Americanization was the price paid for liberation. Among the commodities exported by the United States were not just refrigerators and washing machines, televisions and Coca-Cola, but also corporate architecture (the International Style having at this point, *mutatis mutandis*, become an American product) and the Hollywood film (dominant since World War I, but now, through new credit agreements, with virtually total control over the European market). In his previous film, *Mon Oncle* (1958), Tati had satirized the infatuation of the new French class of technocratic managers and their wives with the American way of life. The "ultramodern" suburban architecture and domestic gadgetry of the Arpel household and the Taylorization of M. Arpel's Plastac factory parodied the intense desire for up-to-dateness on the part of this forward-looking, acquisitive class. Yet at the time *Mon Oncle* was made the postwar changes in everyday life had not yet been smoothly integrated. A distinction remained between the old ways and the new, and the new had a propensity to self-destruct. The film shuttles back and forth, not without sentimentality, between the modernistic milieu of the Arpels and the quaint village locale in which the family's socially misfit, chronically unemployable uncle, Hulot, has his garret.

In *Playtime* all such traces of uneven development are gone. Tati hermetically confines his view to the brave new world of the *grand ensemble*, now totally colonized by the forces of capitalist modernization. Appointed guides shepherd compliant flows of people—*blasé* businessmen, excited female shoppers, camera-toting cadres of Japanese tourists—through controlled grids and labyrinthine cubicles of space, channeling, prodding, organizing, counting. Orthogonal movement patterns govern the lines of flight, as when Hulot stumbles into a "room" only to find himself riding upward in the cab of an elevator. By this point, Tati insinuates, the French have even surpassed the Americans at their own game, exhibiting their advanced level of civilization in not just their mastery of technology but their penchant for culture. At an international trade fair of domestic goods—a parody of the annual Parisian Salon des Arts Ménagers—the Cartesian obsession with order is matched by the native French flair for fashion. Chic salesladies and dapper salesmen demonstrate the latest consumer products—a vacuum cleaner with headlights, eyeglasses that need not be removed while applying mascara—to the frowsy group of American visitors, whose orgasmic "oohs" and "ahs" give utterance to what Henri Lefebvre so exquisitely characterized as the "domestic sublime."[20]

In fact, the decade between the making of *Mon Oncle* and *Playtime* was decisive in transforming France from an insular, agrarian, and empire-oriented society into an urban, industrial, and decolonized nation.[21] The face of Paris, "capital of the nineteenth century," was permanently reshaped during these years by a sweeping new wave of Haussmannization. Between 1954 and 1974, 24 percent of the buildable surface of the city was subjected to demolition and redevelopment, and entire districts were razed and reconfigured in the name of urban renewal. The transformation of postwar Paris into "neobourgeois space" entailed a whole new geography of inside and outside, city and suburb, social modernization and ethnic segregation. Subjected to successive rent increases, more than two-thirds of the population of Paris moved out of the urban center. By 1969 the *grands ensembles* that sprang up around the periphery, built by a technocratic Gaullist regime and notorious for their shoddy construction, lack of amenities, and "morbid geometrism," housed one-sixth of the inhabitants of the greater Paris region and were as familiar a part of the metropolitan landscape as the historic monuments.[22]

5. ABSENCE

In *Playtime* it is Paris itself that has been decentered and displaced to the periphery. The only traces that remain of *vieux Paris* are ephemeral signs and simulacra—an old woman picturesquely selling flowers on a street corner in front of a glass slab, place names like "Champs Elysées" and "Hôtel de Ville" emblazoned on moving buses, the dreamlike images of the Eiffel Tower, Sacré Coeur, and the Arc de Triomphe fleetingly reflected in a swinging glass door. The surrogate city of *Playtime* is an arbitrary system of signs and images where information has replaced both nature and history. Arrows, maps, posters, photographs, and advertisements proliferate, tendering incomprehensible or insipid messages. The rare glimpse of sky is deadpan, Eastmancolor blue.

Tati's film has undeniable thematic affinities with the school of French semiology and structural linguistics with which it is contemporary. Yet the surrogate city of *Playtime* is not a structuralist object lesson. If anything, it is an implicit critique of that worldview. One might, in fact, take the film as a kind of punctual inversion of Roland Barthes' essay "The Eiffel Tower" (1964). Barthes reads that great nineteenth-century monument as the iconic center of a reciprocating optical system at the heart of Paris, at once receptacle of all gazes in the city and universal point of view. As such, he writes, it functions as a signifier free of any fixed referent, a pure and empty sign, "ineluctable, *because it means everything.*"[23]

The *grand ensemble* of *Playtime,* on the other hand, is an empty center that means nothing. Its quintessential architectural ritual is celebrated in a brief nighttime scene in which a crew of workmen struggle to install a heavy glass curtain-wall panel on a second-story facade while a cluster of onlookers watch intently from a dark street corner. It calls to mind a cartoon in which a man looks uncomprehendingly at a huge crowd doing obeissances to an unremarkable boxlike monument inscribed with the letter *N* and asks, "Is Nothing sacred?" In *Playtime* the gaze returned by the mirroring metal-and-glass architecture communicates no more than the redundant routines and incessant traffic flows, the fetishistic, overwrought consumerism, the absurdity of excessive logic. With its desecrating humor the film dethrones the very values on which structuralism, like the *grand ensemble* itself, is founded—rule-governed systems of classification, idolatrous worship of method, denial of the efficacy of human agency.[24]

The film theory of Christian Metz, Barthes' collaborator and the primary exponent of a semiotics of the cinema in the 1960s, emerges from this same historical milieu. Analyzing film as a language of signification, Metz argues that the "impression of reality" that film elicits in the spectator derives above all from the spectator's experience of "being there"—that is, being hermetically isolated from any other reality, an illusion heightened by the fact that films are animated by moving images.[25] As such, the cinematic experience begins not in a mode of distraction for Metz, but in a primal scene of voyeurism. The darkened movie theater, in which the spectator's body remains relatively inert and attention fixates on the shadow play of the screen, encourages a state of absorption and credulity close to a dream. In contrast to Benjamin and Kracauer, Metz considers this intense illusion of presence or presentness to be what makes the cinema unique as an art form, something for the filmmaker to exploit rather than resist. Metz's theory of film turns on the distinction he draws between the cinema and the theater, "whose too real vehicle puts fiction to flight." The fact that early cinema still had theatrical components and lacked sound only betrayed its immaturity in his view, not its "natural" state. In a subsequent book, *The Imaginary Signifier* (1977), Metz elaborates and revises his concept of presence in psychoanalytical terms, developing a theory of identification between the spectator and the film derived from Jacques Lacan's description of the mirror stage. He argues that what distinguishes film from all other arts is that its illusion of presence is founded on a *double* lack or absence: it is not just a matter of its being a fiction or a surrogate for reality (the case with any form of representational art, like the novel or painting), but also, in physical terms, of being a uniquely phantasmatic art form, in other words, a spectral projection of light. "[That which is] perceived is not really the object, it is its shade, its phantom, its double, its *replica* in a new kind of mirror." This concept of presence, or more precisely of the phantasm of presence, leads Metz to consider "narrativity" or "sequencing" the hallmark of modern cinema, and to criticize the emphasis on the individual shot and montage in early film theory as an "erector-set" notion of the medium.[26]

Playtime implicitly renegotiates these contradictions between the experiential model of the early film theorists and Metz's psycholinguistic theory of illusionism, casting doubt on the assumption that film can conjure up an impression of reality by means of a coherent story line. The underlying and pervasive trope in *Playtime* is absence or lack or emptiness: the absence of a "real" Paris, the lack of substance at the heart of a consumerist society founded on nothing but exchange value, the emptiness of glass architecture. In this sense, *Playtime*'s architecture becomes a self-reflexive metaphor for insubstantiality, for the ephemerality of film representation itself. The lack of reality inherent in late-twentieth-century architecture is, in a literal sense, superimposed on the lack of reality intrinsic to film—on celluloid.

This multilayered impression of unreality is conveyed above all through *Playtime*'s dialectic of attention and distraction. Hulot is Benjamin's distracted spectator *par excellence*. Reconnoitering in a not always predictable or explicable environment, he becomes a foil for the world's strangeness. In this sense, he functions, at least potentially, as a surrogate for the audience's collective gaze: all of us, suggests Tati, are a little bit Hulot. At the same time, Hulot's antic mode pushes distraction to such a point of comic exaggeration that he makes us excessively conscious of our own bodies. Ultimately, his awkward gestures and foolish reactions release us from our empathetic identification with him. We become cognizant that the filmmaker-actor Tati has invented the gags of the character Hulot for our amusement, and are thus reassured of our difference from this odd, absentminded clown. We laugh, and with laughter our bodies are explosively liberated from the optical tyranny of the movie screen. In like manner, Tati discourages our identification with the on-screen situation through his treatment of the other characters in *Playtime*, whose mannequinlike behavior and mechanistic affects are even less fleshed out, holding us "safely" at arm's length, keeping us from being "sucked in" by the film.

In prohibiting his audience from a state of complete absorption in the film and from an identification with its protagonists, Tati not only subverts the conventions of characterization and narrative, but exploits a variety of purely cinematic devices—spatial, temporal, and acoustic—that invite a distracted reception. Among these he uses the device of peripheralization to activate the edges of the frame and empty its center. The effect of this device is heightened by the conceit of filming *Playtime* in 70-millimeter format conventionally reserved for panoramic action films. In *Playtime* the wide format actually causes the viewing experience to change depending on whether one is seated in the center or at the edges of the movie theater. It also serves to emphasize the film's lack of dramatic action, its central vacuum. Trivial tics and gestures take on outsize importance. Long shots (in both distance and duration) stretch space and time across the frame's empty center, as in a sequence where the camera records Hulot and the concierge of a glass office building waiting as a man traverses a long, empty corridor heralded by the resounding clatter of his own footsteps. The emergence of the figure from the perspectival vanishing point, out of nowhere as it were, plays with the optics of disappearance, while the decentered action and unsynchronized sound militate against focused vision. The protraction of the shot provokes an aleatory, roaming mode of viewing (similar to that experienced in Michael Snow's classic film *Wavelength,* also made in 1967). In other instances, minor disturbances and comic business occurring simultaneously in various planes within the frame counteract the illusion of depth, creating a curious spatial effect akin to entrances and exits from the theatrical wings of a wide stage. The eye moves around the field saccadically, its scansion bucking the predisposition to centralized vision, as if arresting the linear advance of the film reel.

Tati foils our conventional notions of time much as he decenters our sense of space, elastically compressing and extending it, breaking up narrative continuity by creating simultaneous foci, as in a three-ring circus. For Tati, the rhythm of interruption and ellipsis reflects the nature of daily life:

> It's always like this in life. Someone arrives, parks his car, disappears, you forget, he reappears an hour later, etc. It was interesting to base an entire construction on [this notion of time]. It is evident that this demands an entirely different form of attention on the part of the spectator.[27]

Playtime thus proceeds, like Hulot himself, according to the erratic, errant, absentminded nature of attention, or, one could say, the competing claims of attention and distraction. The film's arbitrary sequence of events is offset by its curious repetitions and "recognitions." Minor characters, identifiable by their idiosyncratic physical traits, appear in multiple contexts, reinforcing the film's uncanny atmosphere of doubleness.

The soundtrack is likewise structured to intensify the effects of disjunction and distraction. *Playtime* was not only postsynchronized, but originally released with stereophonic sound (a decision that, together with the 70-millimeter format, made the film commercially unviable, because few theaters at the time were equipped to accommodate such requirements).[28] The staggering, multilayering, garbling, exaggeration, and inappropriate absence of sound produces a palpable gap between hearing and seeing. At the trade fair, a door that can be slammed shut "in golden silence" not only pokes fun at the ersatz nature of modern materials ("It looks like wood, it feels like wood, but it is not wood"), but alludes to the synthetic nature of acoustics in the cinema, which, since the invention of the "talkie," have been no less contrived than its optics. Tati repeatedly plays the game of confusing boundaries and viewing positions by synchronizing an "exterior" sound with an interior scene—or vice versa—as in a sequence in the air terminal in which the roaring sound of an airplane's engines makes it seem as if the plane had actually entered the building, or the whimpering of a dog in a passenger's travel bag that becomes audible only after a character's gaze has landed on the bag.

Silence, or lack of sound, functions as another kind of empty center. In a sequence that takes place at a high-rise housing block, the camera views the domestic scene taking place inside a ground-floor living room from outside the building's curtain-wall while the soundtrack exaggerates the background noises of the street to the point of cacophony. The pantomimed presentation of the dialog occurring inside the building makes us aware of the camera's voyeuristic position. The domestic interior becomes a vitrine—a shopwindow for consumption both by pedestrians and automobile passengers in the film and by cinematic spectators in the audience. Likewise, the sound barrier that prevents us from hearing the inhabitants' conversation relates the "outside" of the street and the "outside" of the audience.

6. FOURTH WALL

Just as the camera remains outside the curtain-wall looking in, so the audience is always on the other side of the screen looking in, separated by an impenetrable fourth wall—notwithstanding the appearance of transparency. In myriad ways, but above all by the extended analogy he develops between glass architecture and film, Tati calls attention to the grand illusion of filmmaking. At once frame, mirror, and window, glass architecture wreaks havoc with materiality just as film does, except inversely: whereas film calls forth what is unreal, glass tends to dissolve what already exists. Its quixotic qualities of transparency, opacity, and reflectivity make it an analog for the unreality and absence at the heart of film itself.

Playtime thus conflates and confounds the "nothing" of cinema and the "almost nothing" of glass architecture. People crash into transparent planes pursuing reflections, or else they are obliged to take roundabout routes to avoid them. Conversely, they wait obediently while a doorman ushers them through a nonexistent door (the shards of the real plate-glass one, having been accidentally shattered by Hulot, later to serve as ice for cocktails). Like the inappropriate affects of the characters, so too the glazed architecture inhibits identification, keeping the viewer, literally and figuratively, at a distance. *Playtime* constantly makes us aware of the liminal experience of doors, windows, and thresholds. The exacerbation of boundaries transmutes the physical operation of crossing from one space into another into the metaphysical one of entering into an illusionistic world.

The analogy goes further. Just as film calls forth a world that did not exist before, at least temporarily, so too does architecture, delimiting unbounded space into inside and outside, positive and negative quantities. In film, the medium of artifice is light projected through matter (celluloid). In architecture, it is matter projected or "thrown" into light (in the Heideggerian sense of being launched into the world, or the Corbusian one of architecture as the "exact, correct, and magnificent play of volumes in light"). Tati plays with this phenomenological inversion in *Playtime*. Reciprocal shots of daytime and nighttime architecture call to mind the relation between a film negative and its projected image. *Playtime*'s opening shot—of the exterior of a curtain-wall building reflecting the sky, vacuous save for a few clouds—already establishes the ambiguity of day and night within the film's suspended temporality; the light makes it unclear whether it is dawn or dusk. The image is also a visual pun on the double meaning of the word *temps* in French—at once *time* and *weather*.

In later shots, the generic window-wall becomes a metaphor for the movie screen itself, its extruded architectural technology multiplying it *ad infinitum*. Meanwhile, from inside, the window frame, like the camera lens, is an optical instrument that positions the viewer and constructs the gaze. Tati subverts—or inverts—this convention when the American tour group, riding in a bus back to the airport, experiences a sensation of vertigo upon looking out of the bus window at a workman perched precariously atop a ladder washing a hinged pane of glass on a passing building. (Tati achieves this "illogical" effect by tilting the camera, precipitously skewing the eyeline of the tourists.) The ribbon window of the bus becomes yet another metaphor for the strip of film. So does the facade of the housing block in a remarkable sequence in which the activity inside the apartment block is viewed from the street through its picture windows. In a prolonged shot, Tati centers the frame on a vertical partition that separates an apartment Hulot is visiting from another apartment that is its mirror image. The insistent mullion in the frame's center delineates the thickness of the wall section—deep enough to accommodate back-to-back television sets, into which the occupants of the adjacent apartments gaze oblivious to each other. The interstitial space of the wall section is another empty center, analogous to the space between the frames of a strip of film. The film would almost seem to have "skipped some sprockets"—a displacement causing the frame's edges to end up in the center of the screen.

7. PLAY TIME AS GAY TIME

Almost precisely at the midpoint of *Playtime* a major change in rhythm occurs. More accurately, there is a gradual crescendo from the previous slow, nonprogressive, ping-pong tempo to one of total chaos. This acceleration culminates in one of the most antic and extended cadenzas in film history: *Playtime*'s restaurant scene. Here, the jumpy right-angle blocking patterns of previous scenes give way to convoluted arabesques of movement, and little by little the empty center of the frame fills up with a seething, writhing mass of dancing bodies. This change is initially signaled by a neon arrow that also reads as a question mark while directing a crowd of arriving diners into the Royal Garden restaurant, opening for its first night of business.

The Royal Garden—whose name and crown insignia travesty the *luxe, calme, et volupté* of another royal French garden, Versailles—is the setting for a scene that propels *Playtime* from surrealist ballet into the realm of myth, for the enactment of a ritual triumph of anarchy and the body over the forces of regimentation and control. This epic struggle is, once again, figured by architecture, which is submitted to literal deconstruction at the hands of an increasingly convivial and drunken crowd of revelers. The figure of the architect appears for the first time in the film—having heretofore been another absent presence—a harried-looking, bow-tied little Frenchman rushing around with a set of blueprints trying to ready the fashionable premises for the evening's opening as he ineffectually attends to its malfunctions. His foil turns out to be one of the restaurant's guests, a boisterous businessman, at once ugly American and lord of misrule. Hulot, who eventually enters the scene, becomes the inadvertent agent of the premises' demolition, as he reaches up to the ceiling to touch something, causing it to collapse.

The carnivalesque disorder of the restaurant scene calls to mind a Rabelaisian banquet as well as the eating orgy in Luis Buñuel's *Discreet Charm of the Bourgeoisie* (1972). Against the latter's vicious critique of bourgeois consumption, however, *Playtime* offers, at least temporarily, the gentler image of a materialism rooted in the body. It allows for a notion of what Mikhail Bakhtin has called "gay time" in reference to the saturnalian imagination of Rabelais, where the banquet's function is always to move things "toward a better future that changes and renews everything in its path":

> We will not understand the spirit of grotesque feasting if we do not take into account the deeply positive element, the victorious triumph inherent in every banquet image of folklore origin. The awareness of a purely human material bodily power fills this genre. Man is not afraid of the world, he has defeated it and eats of it. In the atmosphere of this victorious meal the world acquires a different aspect; it becomes an abundant harvest, a superabundant increase.... [The banquet spirit] travesties and debases the purely idealistic, mystic, and ascetic victory over the world.[29]

8. BEYOND THE SPECTACLE

In 1967, the same year *Playtime* was released, Guy Debord, cofounder of the International Situationist movement, published *The Society of the Spectacle*. In that book Debord condemns late capitalist society as a gigantic spectacle in which the commodity form has come to dominate every aspect of daily life, reducing social relations to a collection of false images to be contemplated and passively consumed. Tati's film shares many targets and tactics with the radical French polemicists of the sixties, from Henri Lefebvre to the Situationists. His poetics of distraction and play are reminiscent of the Situationists' experiments with the *dérive,* a mode of achieving authentic experience and liberatory cognition through "psychogeographic" drifting. A kind of Situationist moment occurs in *Playtime*'s restaurant scene when Hulot attempts to show a drunken character his way back to Paris on a map, and the character ends up tracing out his route in the veins of a faux-marble column. Just as the actions of the Situationists are credited with anticipating the student upheavals of 1968, so the anarchic free-for-all in the Royal Garden restaurant seems to augur the "explosion" to occur one year later in French society.

Yet if *Playtime* subverts structuralist orthodoxy, it also eschews Situationist avant-gardism. It is significant that the film does not end triumphally in the shambles of the Royal Garden. Nor does it reconstruct upon its ruins some utopian fantasy of a new and better world. Instead the film proves to be even more prescient than the Situationists with respect to the "events of May" and their aftermath. The restaurant scene winds down from its frenzy to a lyrical "morning after." The bleary-eyed revelers stumbling out of the restaurant at daybreak (to the anachronistic sound of a cock's crow) encounter a fresh crew of workmen repairing the streets, the urban workaday already under way. The sociality of the Parisian cafe is reconstituted, if wanly, in a new "drugstore/snackbar," where coffee and newspapers still serve familiar, restorative functions. The tourists climb back into their bus, preparing to depart for home, having completed their "Parisian" tour. An ever-so-delicate piece of business between Hulot and his giggling American acquaintance concludes with his purchase of a couple of gifts for her, Proustian memoirs of their ephemeral romance. Lilting carousel music plays as the tour bus enters a rotary jammed with the usual traffic and pedestrians amid good-humored jockeying and honking. Children appear for the first time. Amid the glass architecture an ice cream vendor's sign conspicuously displays the pun *glaces*. The merry-go-round of the traffic—another metaphoric film reel—freezes for a moment until someone puts a coin in a parking meter, starting it up again. Finally the bus vectors onto the highway, disappearing into a night sky illuminated by street lamps and winking building lights, rounding out the accelerated day-night cycle and completing the loop of the film.

On the brink between modernism and postmodernism, *Playtime* is a kaleidoscopic reflection on the experiential conditions of late-twentieth-century architecture and the mass subject that inhabits it. The character of Hulot is a collective but nonutopian embodiment of the Benjaminian viewer, receiving architecture, an experiential correlate for film, in a mode of distraction. He personifies the contradictions between the confused eye and the panoptic eye, literally mobilizing the gaze, glazed over from looking without seeing.

In a 1967 interview concerning the film Tati stated, "The satire is not on the places but on their utilization. People believe they are 'crushed' by the *grands ensembles.* But if they knew how to observe, they would perceive that life there is the same as everywhere else."[30] If *Playtime* has a didactic message to impart, it is about adaptation, the way human beings habituate themselves to their environments, find a bit of happiness. Sentimentality? Possibly. Certainly it is a form of guarded optimism, but based on neither Luddite nostalgia nor illusions of cyborg salvation.

> I don't claim to have the right to pass judgment on architecture today. I content myself with making a film on my epoch. Enormous buildings are constructed in our time. Of glass, nothing but glass: we belong to a civilization that needs to encase itself in glass!...But if at first the inhabitants of the new city feel lost, little by little they habituate themselves to it. They gradually efface its ultramodern stage effects, ultimately rendering it human.[31]

The body with its idiosyncrasies and tics is, in the end, a holdout, a constant—at least for the time being. The relationship between architecture and film is a paradigm of the relation between physical experience and the advancing forces of dematerialization and virtualization. The world goes forward while the body goes around. Humor, rooted in a play between the animate and the inanimate, is among the most potent instruments of deconstruction. The ironic, endlessly fascinating mirror disappears for a moment once one gets close enough to breathe on it, effacing its representations with a cloud of breath.

NOTES

An earlier version of this paper was published in *Any* 12 (1995), 20–7. I am grateful to Pellegrino d'Acierno and Bob Slutzky for their comments on its development. Thanks also to Miranda Robbins and Mark Lamster for their editorial suggestions.

1. Walter Benjamin, "The Work of Art in the Age of Mechanical Reproduction," in *Illuminations,* trans. Harry Zohn (New York: Schocken, 1969), 239–40. It should be noted that Benjamin fails to distinguish in his essay between the daily experience of the urban worker and the privileged gaze of the leisurely stroller.
2. See Tom Gunning, "An Aesthetic of Astonishment: Early Film and the (In)Credulous Spectator," and Miriam Hansen, "Early Cinema, Late Cinema: Transformations of the Public Sphere," in Linda Williams, ed. *Viewing*

Positions: Ways of Seeing Film (New Brunswick, NJ: Rutgers University Press, 1994), 114–33; 134–52.

3. Siegfried Kracauer, "Cult of Distraction: On Berlin's Picture Palaces" (1926), trans. Thomas Y. Levin, *New German Critique* 40 (winter 1987), 94.

4. As Benjamin writes in his notes to "The Work of Art": "The film is the art form that is in keeping with the increased threat to his life which modern man has to face. Man's need to expose himself to shock effects is his adjustment to the dangers threatening him. The film corresponds to profound changes in the apperceptive apparatus—changes that are experienced on an individual scale by the man in the street in big city traffic, on a historical scale by every present-day citizen" (250). For a valuable interpretation of Benjamin's theory of experience, see Miriam Hansen, "Benjamin, Cinema and Experience: 'The Blue Flower in the Land of Technology,'" *New German Critique* 40 (winter 1987), 179–224. For an early statement by Eisenstein on the origins and psychological effects of the montage technique, see "Montage of Attractions" (1923), in Sergei Eisenstein, *Film Form and the Film Sense,* trans. Jay Leyda (Cleveland, OH: World Publishing Co., 1968), FS 230–3.

5. Benjamin, "The Work of Art," 237.

6. Kracauer, "Cult of Distraction," 95–6.

7. Walter Benjamin, "Surrealism: The Last Snapshot of the European Intelligentsia," in *Reflections,* trans. Edmund Jephcott (New York: Harcourt, Brace, Jovanovich, 1978), 189; Le Corbusier, *Towards a New Architecture* (1923), trans. Frederick Etchells (New York: Praeger, 1960), 89; Benjamin, "Surrealism," 180.

8. Georg Simmel, "The Metropolis and Mental Life," trans. Edward A. Shils, in *On Individuality and Social Forms: Selected Writings* (Chicago: University of Chicago Press, 1971), 329–30.

9. Raymond Williams, *Keywords: A Vocabulary of Culture and Society,* rev. ed. (New York: Oxford University Press, 1985), 31.

10. See Susan Buck-Morss, "Aesthetics and Anaesthetics: Walter Benjamin's Artwork Essay Reconsidered," *October* 62 (fall 1992), 6, 18, and in entirety, 3–41.

11. See Jonathan Crary, "Unbinding Vision," *October* 68 (spring 1994), 22.

12. Cf. Hansen, "Early Cinema, Late Cinema."

13. Walter Benjamin, notes to "The Work of Art" (first version, 1935), cited in Susan Buck-Morss, *The Dialectics of Seeing: Walter Benjamin and the Arcades Project* (Cambridge, MA: MIT Press, 1991), 269–70.

14. Henri Bergson, "Laughter," in *Comedy,* ed. Wylie Sypher (Garden City, NJ: Doubleday, 1956), 79.

15. See Jacques Tati, interview with Paul Carrière, *Le Figaro,* June 1959, cited in Marc Dondey, *Tati* (Paris: Editions Ramsay, 1989), 188.

16. Theodor Adorno, *Über Walter Benjamin* (Frankfurt: Suhrkamp, 1970), 54.

17. *Playtime* production dossier, cited in Dondey, *Tati,* 190 (my translation; the last phrase is "pour vivre 'garde-à-vous!'").

18. With regard to the set of *Playtime,* see Armand J. Cauliez, *Jacques Tati* (Paris: Editions Seghers, 1968), 77–9, and Dondey, *Tati,* 190 ff.

19. Tati also planned to leave the set of *Playtime* standing after he finished shooting the film as a permanent studio-city to be used by other directors. Ironically, it was torn down to make way for a new autoroute.

20. Henry Lefebvre, *Critique de la vie quotidienne,* vol. 2 (Paris: Arche, 1958–81), 88; cited in Kristin Ross, *Fast Cars, Clean Bodies: Decolonization and the Reordering of French Culture* (Cambridge, MA: MIT Press, 1995), 89.

21. This is the subject of Kristin Ross's book, cited in the previous note. She characterizes Tati as "the greatest [film] analyst of postwar French modernization," (30).

22. The phrase "morbid geometrism" is cited by Ross in *Fast Cars, Clean Bodies*, 76, in reference to the writing of Alain Robbe-Grillet, but it is an apt characterization of the architecture of the new housing projects. Of the transformation of Paris, Manuel Castells, an eyewitness, wrote, "Paris is not Paris anymore. Less than 16 percent of the 9,400,000 Parisians live within the administrative limits of the city. For the others, their home is the *banlieue,* the ring of suburbs built around the historic city during the accelerated metropolitan growth of the post-1945 period. The suburban landscape is dominated by the *grands ensembles,* an image that since the 1960s has become as characteristic of Paris as the Eiffel Tower." Manuel Castells, *The City and the Grassroots: A Cross-Cultural Theory of Urban Social Movements* (Berkeley: University of California Press, 1981), 75.

23. Roland Barthes, "The Eiffel Tower," in *A Barthes Reader* (New York: Hill and Wang, 1982), 237. Barthes' italics.

24. For a historicized interpretation of structuralism and intellectual thought in France in the 1950s and 1960s, see Ross, *Fast Cars, Clean Bodies,* 176–96.

25. Christian Metz, "On the Impression of Reality in the Cinema," in *Film Language: A Semiotics of the Cinema,* trans. Michael Taylor (Chicago: University of Chicago Press), 3–15.

26. Christian Metz, "Identification, Mirror," in *The Imaginary Signifier: Psychoanalysis and the Cinema,* trans. Celia Britton, Annwyl Williams, Ben Brewster, and Alfred Guzzetti (Bloomington: Indiana University Press), 45; Metz, "The Cinema: Language or Language System?" in *Film Language* 34: 42.

27. Jacques Tati, interview in *Cahiers du Cinéma* 199 (March 1968), 42; trans. in Lucy Fischer, *Jacques Tati: A Guide to References and Resources* (Boston: G. K. Hall, 1983), 42.

28. *Playtime* was a financial disaster for Tati. Besides its unconventional format and soundtrack, the film was deemed uncommercial because of its excessive length and slow pace. To get *Playtime* distributed, Tati was forced to cut twenty minutes from the final version.

29. Mikhail Bakhtin, *Rabelais and His World* (1965), trans. Helene Iswolsky (Cambridge, MA: MIT Press, 1968), 296.

30. Jacques Tati, *Télérama,* 17 December 1967, cited in Cauliez, *Jacques Tati,* 77 (author's translation).

31. Jacques Tati, cited in Cauliez, *Jacques Tati,* 106 (author's translation).

the CONSUMING LANDSCAPE: ARCHITECTURE *in the* FILMS *of* MICHELANGELO ANTONIONI

MITCHELL SCHWARZER

IN DAY-TO-DAY experience, the sight and feel of buildings is subject to extreme shifts of attention, duration, and familiarity. We experience buildings on pragmatic excursions, in the rounds of routine, and via flashes of discovery. In the representation of architecture (through drawing, model, or rendering), by contrast, the approach to buildings is abstract and ideal. With film, the experience of architecture is more directed than in everyday situations and less focused than in architectural representation. In a dark auditorium whose seats point toward a fixed screen, great demands are made of a viewer's attention and vision. Images of buildings unfold off reels in a linear sequence, yet this succession is guided not by the steady flow of experienced time but by the choices of the filmmaker. The camera has the capacity to associate buildings with a great many objects and events, moods and atmospheres, locations and relations. Film brings architecture into focus only to disperse it within the hubbub of life.

No filmmaker has used architecture to greater effect than Michelangelo Antonioni, who studied architecture before becoming a film director and remained fascinated by the built world throughout his career. Many of his films depict famous buildings or sites, and several feature architects as characters. Nevertheless, the larger

Lidia (Jeanne Moreau) and Giovanni (Marcello Mastroianni) separated by a pillar in *La Notte* (1960).

statement Antonioni makes about architecture has less to do with buildings designed by famous architects than with the expanses and particles of building and landscape. Following in the tradition of Italian neorealism, Antonioni first picked up on the acute observations of the Italian poor as they anxiously wandered through cities and the countryside. In *Il Grido* (*The Shout*, 1957), shot mostly out-of-doors, his camera chronicled the events of a road journey along the Po River, and established a connection between the starkness of the landscape and the futility of the characters' actions.

In the tetralogy of films that followed, Antonioni undertook a sustained critique of the lives of affluent and middle-class Italians. In *L'avventura* (*The Adventure*, 1960), *La Notte* (*The Night*, 1960), *L'eclisse* (*The Eclipse*, 1962), and *Il deserto rosso* (*Red Desert*, 1964), the director explored architecture and the urbanized landscape as the physical soul of modern humanity.

Unlike such celebrated "architectural" films as *Metropolis* (1926), *The Fountainhead* (1949), and *Blade Runner* (1982), the architecture and landscapes explored by Antonioni are real. And unlike most directors, who confine their renderings of real settings to title sequences and small interludes in plot, the forms and spaces of architecture and the city stalk the viewer throughout this tetralogy. In fact, since Antonioni is so unconcerned with plot, character development, and dialog, he shifts the viewer's attention to the wide-open confinements of the modern *mise-en-scène*. Architecture both contributes to the events taking place among actors and acts independently with other objects in motion and in space. Architecture is protagonist and antagonist, nucleus for the slow collapse of perception into a space between the actors' lines, a visual language with a power all its own. As Frank Tomasulo has noted, for Antonioni, architecture "enunciates themes of ancient vs. modern, nature vs. culture, atheism vs. Catholicism, woman vs. man, and even socialism vs. capitalism."[1]

In the opening credits of *La Notte*, Antonioni explicitly announces that architecture will serve as much more than a background. We first see a noisy street, bursting with traffic and the ornamental excesses of a late-nineteenth-century facade. A sudden cut transports us skyward to the unoccupied and sharply defined upper terraces of Gio Ponti's Pirelli Tower of 1957, Milan's tallest building. In these first two shots, Antonioni establishes the oppositions of turmoil and order, of crowds and silence, and of historicism and the modern movement that run throughout both this film in particular and the tetralogy in general.

From the tower's summit, the camera begins a slow descent down the facade. This scene has been often interpreted as a commentary on the fall from the high ideals of modernism to the earthly chaos that modernism sought to eliminate. But beyond this metaphor, Antonioni fixes architecture as a means of constructing the mood of the film. As the camera gradually makes its way down the sheer walls it looks head-on at the building's glass and steel surfaces, creating an analogy between the shots on a reel of film and the stories of a building. Both reflect the city with varying degrees of opacity; despite the tower's monolithic stature, we see that the windows of some floors are transparent, whereas others are cloudy, and others still are divided by venetian blinds. Midway down the building, the camera abruptly pans ninety degrees and looks out toward the city. The shot is a split image divided between the camera's view of the city and the camera's view of the city as reflected by Ponti's building. Architecture becomes object viewed and frame for viewing.

With the first scene of *L'avventura*, Antonioni introduces what will be one of his central themes: the destruction of tradition and community by the forces of industrial society. A year before Pier Paolo Pasolini's *Accatone* (1961) chronicled the seedier side of the Roman demimonde, Antonioni had already unveiled the calamity of Italy's burgeoning urban periphery. We first see Anna, the protagonist who will later disappear on the island of Lisca Bianca, walking out of an old walled garden into a noisy and vacuous urban space. There, on unpaved ground in view of nearby construction sites, she meets her father, who has just commented to a workman that his peaceful villa will soon be torn down to make way for a modern housing development. Seconds later, as a background of menacing housing projects is scanned, Anna's father remarks on the growing distance between him and his daughter. The collapse of family occurs amidst the demise of a family home. Antonioni's vision is not completely despairing.

Positioned (for a moment) over Anna's left shoulder is the dome of St. Peter's Basilica, the seat of the Papacy and the center of the Catholic community. An archetypal image, the dome serves as a counterpoint to the present chaos in both architecture and society, hope out of the distant past.

Soon afterward, Anna, her boyfriend, Sandro, her friend Claudia, and a group of decadent acquaintances take a yacht trip around the Lipari Islands in the Mediterranean Sea. Despite the idyllic setting, they are almost universally afflicted with modern maladies of the emotions—*ennui*, anxiety, restlessness, and disorientation—and these are set against the tumultuous gray of the sea, the brilliant sunlight, and the jutting rocks of the islands. After arriving on Lisca Bianca, Anna vanishes without explanation and is never seen again. In the subsequent disinterested search for her, we see several times the pyramidal shape of a volcano on the nearby island of Stromboli. In one sense, the volcano may be read as a metaphor for the inner flame that might (or might not) still burn within the souls of Anna and her friends. In another, as a mountain that has existed for millions of years in the form of one of architecture's most potent archetypes, a pyramid, Stromboli is a counterpoint to the corrupting specter of indifference and indolence displayed by the human characters. As is the dome of St. Peter's, the pyramidal mountain is a symbol of humanity's connection to lasting meaning. Together, such archetypes contrast with the chaotic foreground scenes in which they appear, and provide a measure of hope that there is perhaps divine guidance in the modern world after all. A similar device is later used in *La Notte*, where the camera views a tragic scene in a hospital room from behind the round, steady head of a silent mother. For a brief moment, motherhood provides a foundation of meaning and security in a world where words no longer provide answers.

Antonioni again and again poses the upheavals of modernity against the order of religion, family, and nature. Toward the end of *L'avventura*, the troubled Sandro, an architect who has sold his creative soul to become the pawn of a real estate developer, intentionally knocks over a bottle of ink onto the drawing of an architectural student. The drawing, following the intricate details of a shell niche on the Sicilian Cathedral of Noto, is a reflection of a lingering aspiration for beauty within modern society. But inasmuch as Sandro has renounced the search for beauty elsewhere in his life, he is driven to destroy it here. Interrupting the inevitable confrontation between the angry student and the embittered architect is the sudden appearance of a linear procession of children emerging from the door of the cathedral, among them, perhaps, a future artist.

Antonioni is skeptical, however, of attempts to create archetypes in modern times. Claudia and Sandro's Sicilian search for Anna and their own developing relationship leads them to a ghost town outside of Caltanisetta. Composed in cubic geometries, with simplified classical forms like blind arches and blank pediments, the town's vacant abstraction looks like a facsimile from the paintings of Giorgio de Chirico. Yet, if the painter's metaphysical dream was to re-establish an archetypal language of geometric forms, this town, constructed during the fascist era of Benito Mussolini, is an unrealizable fantasy of community and a relic of dangerous dreams. While Sandro wonders why such a well-built place was never occupied, Claudia remarks on a similar town in the distance—or is it, as Sandro interrupts, a cemetery?

The inability of modern-age designers to achieve idealized dreams of pure geometric cities is highlighted throughout *L'eclisse*. Much of the film is shot on the southern outskirts of Rome, in the EUR (Exposizione Universale di Roma) district, the same locale where Federico Fellini had shot a disturbing murder-suicide in *La Dolce Vita* (1960). Intended by Mussolini's architects and postwar planners to be a utopian city that would replace the congestion and chaos of old Rome, the neighborhood where translator Vittoria lives appears much more like a cemetery for the living. The streets are silent, devoid of stores, people, cars. The inhabitants that do appear seem robotic, mechanized into routine, and out of touch with their physical surroundings. They walk in the middle of streets and alongside playfields where the only action is a rotating sprinkler. This city of white slab buildings, flat grassy fields, and empty roads is as much a failure as the ghost town depicted in *L'avventura*. The archetypes designed in the godless times of modernity are dreams for illumination that shed only darkness.

° ° °

If archetypes cannot be created in the modern era, what about a return to history? Throughout the tetralogy, Antonioni sets the frosty architecture of the modern city against the earthtones of architecture's past. Characters often project their most vital desires onto old buildings and public spaces, and onto memories of their youth associated with objects unspoiled by modernity's infertile conventions. For example, it has been frequently observed that in a hospital scene in *La Notte*, the view of the protagonist Lidia from her dying friend Tomasso's bed opens out through a window onto an old, intricately designed building. Seen from elsewhere in the room, however, without Tomasso's loving gaze at Lidia, the view takes in sleek gray modern buildings that hover menacingly over the polychrome grain of the old building. In *L'avventura*, Sandro and Anna's only sensual moment occurs in an older building, their union consummated by the crisscrossing lines of a ceiling's parabolic vault.

Similarly, the only bright moment of *Il deserto rosso* occurs when housewife Giuliana, worried over the loss of sensation in her son Valerio's legs, tells him a story of a little girl who lives alone on a tropical island. In contrast to the drab surroundings of Ravenna's industrial quarter where they live, the island's beauty lays in the fact that modernity hasn't yet reached it. As Seymour Chatman writes:

> It is interesting to note the textural difference between the beach scenery in the story she tells to her son and the surfaces of her life in Ravenna. Everything near her home is smooth, hard, and cold to the touch, a medley of modern materials—steel, glass, and plastic—whereas the sand and sandstone of the fantasy beach are warm and soft-looking, resembling nothing so much as the limbs and breasts of lovers embracing in the sea.[2]

Is this connection to unspoiled nature and historic architecture anything more than a dream? Can we live in the past? Or do images of the past come clattering down on the present?

In a powerful scene in *L'avventura*, Sandro and Claudia view Noto's cathedral square from the roofscape of a nearby church. What begins as a romantic ramble through a monument of architectural history ends up highlighting the dimness of Sandro's past and future. At first, Sandro is inspired by the panorama before him, an enormous plaza enclosed on its principal side by a long facade articulated by pilasters, urns, towers, and a central pediment and dome. He comments stirringly on how the baroque was planned with extraordinary freedom as a stage set for its times. These bright thoughts lead him to reflect on how he'd like to be an architect again, a creator of ideas instead of profits. But despite Claudia's encouragement, Sandro quickly demurs from his enthusiasm. Beautiful things don't last long in a transitory age, he sadly reflects; whereas new buildings once persisted for centuries, now they have lifespans of only ten to twenty years.

Then, incredibly, after only a few seconds, Sandro impulsively asks Claudia to marry him. Trapped between ropes that pull the great church bells above their heads, Claudia is a caged animal. Sandro, who does not see the possibility of lasting architecture, clearly does not believe in the permanence of marriage. Architecture's fragmentation presages social disintegration—neither cupolas nor couples will last long in his world.

At the all-night party that concludes *La Notte*, Antonioni likewise expounds on the impossibility of permanence. The industrialist Gerardini wants writer Giovanni to come work for him, to pen a history of his company and then direct the firm's public relations office. After telling Giovanni that his garden already contains more than one thousand roses and many valuable statues, Gerardini goes on to reflect that his commercial enterprises themselves are works of art. Only he, the grand capitalist, can create solid design, a lasting monument to the times. Although Giovanni wants to differ, he labors sentences whose words end in affirmation. Yes, he sadly reflects, the free artist or architect is today an anachronism; the times indeed are in the hands of industrialists.

Earlier in *La Notte*, Lidia embarks on a great journey through modern Milan, from its center to its periphery, but fails to escape from its grasp. Her journey begins at a downtown party celebrating her husband, Giovanni's, new book. Trapped between cocktail glasses and overflowing pretense, she flees the social game that the dying Tomasso had never learned to play. In a flowered dress, she begins her great walk through the anonymous streets of the modern city, a journey in search of renewed love for a wayward husband who now resides in the anteroom of fame. Along the way, Lidia encounters numerous people but is unable to connect with any of them. Instead, her encounters are with buildings and machines, dissonant sirens and jet planes, rows of uniform windows and balconies, a canvas of forms and sounds opaque to her heart. She is trapped once again, not by ruthless people but by the harshness of modern architecture, by the restless shadows and cutting shapes cast by smooth-skinned buildings.

Modern architecture not only cuts people off from each other, it also cuts them off from the past. At one point on her walk, Lidia looks in on a site where an old building is being demolished. There she discovers and comforts a solitary weeping child. As she leaves the gloomy confines, Lidia gently touches the remaining wall of the building. The cracked paint easily peels off. Mother "protector" has abandoned both child and architecture.

Seeking to rid herself of the repetitive, clamorous loneliness of the modern city, Lidia takes a taxi to a spot on the outskirts of the city where she and Giovanni had once enjoyed romance. But what must have once been a quaint town reached by railroad has been engulfed by the fringe of metropolitan development. The small pavilions and train station are abandoned. The hotel is run-down and the fields overgrown. The old magic is gone. Having found no deeper meanings or stability, the event that most captivates Lidia is a bottle-rocket launching, another feeble attempt at escape.

Not all of Antonioni's characters seek to escape their lives. Several live comfortably within the pretenses of the present. In *L'avventura*, Antonioni juxtaposes the empty lives of the rich with the monumental weightiness of the palaces, churches, and ancient villages they frequent yet blithely ignore and even degrade. One palace is now a police station; another has become a hotel and the setting for interminable parties. Their apathy toward their heritage is clearly reflected when, during the search for Anna, one member of the group finds an ancient vase in a crevice. While at first they all marvel at its beauty, the vase is suddenly and carelessly dropped. After lamenting its loss for only a couple of seconds, the characters nonchalantly move away from the shattered pieces.

In *L'eclisse*, the past offers no comfort whatsoever. Much of the film alternates between the modern environment of EUR and the old city of Rome. Yet the contrast here is not one of modern alienation and traditional community. To the contrary, the scenes in Rome's narrow streets and, especially, at its stock exchange reinforce the notion that the commodification and senselessness of modern life has penetrated every nook and cranny of the historic city. In a tradition that reaches back to the neorealist films of Vittorio de Sica and Roberto Rossellini, the old cities of Italy have become stages for depicting the struggle for survival.

If Italians labored just to find enough food following World War II, by the early 1960s their struggle transcended material survival. Now, the characters battle psychic breakdown. This is reflected in *L'eclisse*, at Rome's stock exchange, when Vittoria tries to speak with her mother but is repeatedly rebuffed. The bedlam of commodity trading has taken over modern life; Vittoria's mother is only interested in financial gain. The incongruous consequences of Italy's newly won material prosperity are screams of stock prices and orders, rushing hands, constantly ringing telephones, and the loss of time for human conversation.

Setting the hell of capitalism within a giant columned space adds poignancy to Antonioni's commentary. This hypostyle hall is no longer a sacred grove, the center for community it would have been in the past. Instead, the thick columns of the stock exchange stand as mute reminders of an ancient world covered by the sands of accumulation. In a frequently analyzed shot, the columns actually divide Vittoria from her potential new lover, Piero. Here as elsewhere in Antonioni's films the life and solidity of historic buildings are bent and broken by the derangements of modern society.

Throughout the tetralogy, Antonioni uses architecture to emphasize his themes of alienation and isolation. Walls, in particular, illustrate the ability (or inability) of his characters to relate to each other. For Antonioni, blank walls—whether concrete, brick, or stone—often symbolize mute feelings, an inability to express oneself or connect with others, metaphors for a distanced soul. Walls, of course, are also notoriously prey to multiple meanings. Are they a means of support

Sandro (Gabriele Ferzetti) and Claudia (Monica Vitti) before a peeling wall in *L'avventura* (1960).

or are they a fortification for defense? Does their traditional stone or brick impenetrability contribute to social isolation or a focused interior life? Does their modern transformation into transparent curtains by steel and reinforced concrete frames free people to engage with the outside world or expose people to their disadvantage?

In *L'avventura*, Patrizia and Claudia represent the walled and the unwalled, the one who accepts social conventions and the one who tries to stay true to her individual emotions. Patrizia, the wife of a real estate developer, is immersed and surrounded by the social pretenses of the well-to-do. While her yacht is anchored off gorgeous island caverns, she prefers to play puzzles and nuzzle her little dog in the boat's lower cabin. Later, toward the film's conclusion, Patrizia admits to Claudia that she feels comfortable at meaningless social gatherings; what she cannot stand are islands where she is surrounded by emptiness.

Claudia is the unwalled. She is still in touch with—yet troubled by—her visceral emotions. On the boat, it is she who intently watches a dolphin thread waves in a rhythmic dance. She is also the only one who really cares that Anna has disappeared. And, she is even willing to love Sandro, who already on the island had substituted Claudia (for the missing Anna) as the goal of his search. It is Claudia's flickering spark of life that makes the final scene of the movie so difficult. After Sandro's inevitable infidelity to her, she ends up forgiving him and, therefore, admitting that she too must join society and its hypocrisies. In the closing shot of the film, as Claudia comforts the scoundrel Sandro, the background of the frame is evenly split between a wall of the villa on the right and an open shot of Mt. Etna appearing as an island over the Gulf of Catania. Can individuals live unwalled like mountains or islands, distanced from conventions they abhor, yet separated from others? Or, shall individuals (as Claudia now seems to be doing) accept the confinements of walls, of claustrophobic and superficial modern society, but at least belong to something?

In *Il deserto rosso*, Giuliana, because of a mysterious industrial accident, takes the path that Claudia did not take, that of trying to find her true feelings outside of the walls of social convention. But she has taken this path because she is no longer sane. Corrado, the engineer Giuliana meets through her husband, is attracted to her madness much as he is to great engineering challenges. She is a project for him, an objective terrain to be researched and reconstructed. Corrado has made the opposite choice of Giuliana, accepting the compromises and dislocations inherent in modern society. Like the other principal male characters in the tetralogy, he is entangled in the circumstances of modernity. Whereas Giuliana wants to connect to everything around her, but cannot, Corrado pointedly remarks that he only travels with a couple of light suitcases because the world is his home. In a sense, both have become the social islands feared by Patrizia in *L'avventura*, but social islands of a different tenor. Throughout the film we witness Giuliana walking inches away from walls hoping for some imaginary support; Corrado, his soul at ease in the global world, walks in the middle of the street, unburdened.

Giuliana's greatest hopes rest on an implausible plan to open a gallery on a deserted downtown street where there is obviously no potential clientele. The walls of her gallery are bare; unable to relate to the world, she is incapable of filling them with art. Similarly, throughout *La Notte* blank walls reveal troubled spirits, as when Lidia rests alongside the hospital's exterior wall after seeing Tomasso for the last time, or when the psychiatric patient who seduces Giovanni in her hospital room is pictured like a rabid animal against the expanse of a stark white wall.

The blank walls of modernist architecture were polemical statements, the realization of a functionalist aesthetic that sought to reveal the materiality of pure surface and banish the pretense of historical ornament. In Antonioni's films, however, these all-too-honest walls are often contrasted to their disadvantage with premodern walls. Modernity's sterile surfaces lack the textural depth of Noto's baroque facades in *L'avventura* or the rhythmic monumentality of the ancient Hadrianic columns attached to Rome's stock exchange building in *L'eclisse*. Modern walls, like islands, refuse social hypocrisy but at the risk of alienation and madness. Antonioni thus likens ornament to an acceptance of social pretense whereas modernist asceticism ends in isolation.

During the 1920s, Le Corbusier had announced that steel and reinforced concrete construction represented a revolution in the history of the window. Windows could be elongated to fill the space between the members of a structural frame. Transparent glass could replace opaque walls and bring light and air into a building. Enshrined as one of his "Five Points" of architecture, the strip window was expanded by other architects into a glass curtain-wall where interior and exterior became a unified visual realm. In the work of architects like Richard Neutra, the view through expansive plate glass onto nature was understood as one of modern architecture's great contributions to the spiritual and aesthetic well-being of humanity.

For Antonioni, however, this great contribution yielded consequences unintended by its proponents. In *L'eclisse*, when Vittoria pulls open the curtains revealing the strip windows of her apartment, as if to relieve her soul in a view of nature, she is confronted instead by a water tower whose form resembles an alien spaceship or atomic mushroom cloud. Similarly, in *Il deserto rosso*, a strip window in Giuliana's home reveals a dizzying view onto giant ships plowing through a harbor. If modern architects envisioned the strip window offering a healthful gaze onto nature, for Antonioni those windows exacerbate the anxiety of being held hostage in a world of entwining mechanical objects.

In all four films, Antonioni's principal characters are well off. Survival is not an issue for them. As a result, their material possessions are something other than necessities governed by a logic of use. They are playthings, distractions, masks, even uninvited guests with minds of their own. Apartments, streets, and urban spaces teem with an ungodly dance of vacuous particulars, artificial lights, droning appliances, racing automobiles, and smoke-plumed factories. The sounds of objects and machines are a speech unto themselves, a technological yet archaic rumble that obscures human dialog. In this storm of engineered objects the rhythm of human relationships is terminally interrupted.

The numbing effect of materialism on the human condition is the principal theme of *L'eclisse*. A tundra of pointless material accumulation and real estate development shrouds everything. The film opens much the way it ends, through a slow-moving panorama of objects in disarray and human relations in decline. The only difference is that the object incantations of the opening scene have a counterpoint in the collapsing relationship between Vittoria and Riccardo. By the end, human relationships are beyond a state of collapse; consumerist materiality submerges anonymous people in its gray final music.

The first shot in *L'eclisse* is of a table lamp illuminating an apartment cluttered with objects. Through a scan of these objects, absent any dialog but filled with the disturbing drone of an electric fan, Antonioni establishes a mood of disarray in human relationships and a connection between that disarray and those objects. We quickly see that Riccardo's arm had been part of the first shot, although it appeared an inanimate object. Predictably, Vittoria cannot connect with this lifeless lover, nor can her own lifeless consciousness offer any verbal cause for her disconnection. Yet the reasons surround them, the paintings, vases, trinkets, razors, and manuscripts that pull people apart from each other and from themselves.

If Vittoria is torn apart by the demands of objects, her attempts to connect with objects end obscenely. In a friend's apartment, she is astonished by the collection of emblems and trophies from Kenya pasted onto walls and inserted into cabinets. In a trance, Vittoria assumes the character of these objects, becoming an African dancer, complete with darkened face cream, hoop earrings, and a spear.

Vittoria unwittingly relinquishes her soul to the exhibition of engineered objects and loses everything. Whereas men are more or less able to dissolve themselves in the modern spectacle's material fantasies and fetishes, the principal women in Antonioni's films are always ill at ease. Vittoria's counterpoint is Piero, the floor man at the stock exchange who aspires to material possessions and financial gain. He is comfortable navigating the rocky shores of capitalistic opportunity. When someone steals his automobile and plunges it into a pond, the automobile is pulled by cranes from the waters. The material world replaces the materials that are lost.

The material world of *L'eclisse* ends in a set of images in which people are more dead than alive. Set in the haunts of EUR, the final scene is bereft of dialog. Instead, the camera scans a patchwork of unresolved built shapes and natural forms, mechanical objects and human figures, a city dissolving into silent noise, an abstract art. In the twilight approaching evening, humans are objectified and objects animated. We see the crooked lines on the face of an old man and the clean sharp lines on the balcony of a modern apartment building; water floating in a tank and then flowing toward a drain; a nondescript corner where a building's scaffolding indicates a state of impending demolition more than renovation.

If the mood is serene, it is deeply disquieting, an elegy to our ability to discover meaning in things and hence in ourselves and each other. Ian Wiblin describes the strange beauty that emerges from Antonioni's random arrangement of buildings and objects:

> Finally, a bus comes and goes, its braking interrupting the quiet of the scene, adding an almost violent edge that jars with the emptiness,

> the lack of activity. The urban space has eventually won out over the characters and the narrative thread has finally been dissolved.[3]

The film ends amid the blinding light of a streetlamp. But unlike Alexander MacKendrick's *Sweet Smell of Success* (1957), where blinding lights energize New York City and its people, Antonioni's last frame is monochromatic white. Amid an energy created solely by machines, humanity is eclipsed.

It is logical, given the ending of *L'eclisse*, that the ominous shadows cast by industrial technology are the subject of the last film in the tetralogy, *Il deserto rosso*. Shot in the ancient city of Ravenna, Antonioni never allows a glimpse of the old city and its magnificent Byzantine architecture. The action, or inaction, is set on the industrial barrens alongside the Adriatic Sea, marshes that have become dumping grounds where giant ships move eerily through channels cut into the land. The modern world's Stygia, it is a place of droning noises and sudden sounds, of earth that releases white vapors, a place by the sea where seafood must be bought from elsewhere because the waters now taste of petroleum.

Giuliana wanders through these infernal haunts over the course of the film, frequently accompanied by a dense fog that fades the human figure and spirit. Although the terrain has been constructed by men, people are forced to walk between tight passages, under hovering cranes, and alongside plumed releases of gas. Giuliana's engineer husband seems hardly human; he differs little from the giant machines he controls at work and the gadgets and robots with which he fills his son's room. At the beginning and end of the film, we see Giuliana and her son trying to negotiate a ground made barren by grime and filth, furtively eating sandwiches under skies whose yellow poisonous smoke, she tells her son, the birds have learned to avoid.

Nature and humanity assaulted and defeated, machines disclose a new order of dazzling forms and lascivious colors. The great ships move like dinosaurs in a prehistoric swamp, hulking-edged shapes in a murky bowl. Giant transmission towers point antennae out into space, the interests of machines having shifted already from our world. In the way this landscape is modeled, there are bits of newfound beauty. As Diane Borden writes:

> One danger of the architectural wasteland is that is can be transformed into a "beautiful object." The factories of Red Desert become works of abstract art when Antonioni paints pipes, walls, and machines orange, blue, and yellow; places the actors in sculpted positions within the mechanical constructs of the shot; and shoots fog, steam, and belching sulfur to create an atmosphere that is almost magical.[4]

The machine architecture of *Il deserto rosso* can be seen as boldly expressive where the human landscape has become mute, a composition of formed power and chromatic range where the slab architecture of human residence has become reductively regular and white. In Corrado's hotel room, walls, furniture, and bed are all of an austere white. The power station is a hodgepodge of brilliant color. Both the formal complexity and fantastic colors of the machined environment have surpassed the reductive logic of modern architects.

Antonioni's overriding interest in the tetralogy is the enervating numbness of modern life, the defeat of the human spirit amid material affluence and technological progress. This preoccupation with the extraordinary failure of modernity continues in Antonioni's subsequent English-language films, although these films are more plot-driven and attentive to the popular and revolutionary culture of the sixties.

Architecture does not play a large role in *Blowup* (1966). Set in London, the film begins as a jeep of merry mimes drives around the austere plaza of Peter and Allison Smithson's Economist Building and quickly cuts to a column of morose workers emerging from a brick factory. Beyond these scenes, however, *Blowup* is a film about the vagaries of perception. Through a story about a fashion photographer's accidental shooting of a murder, the landscape becomes a terrain where the real and unreal, the seen and the unseen, are blurred.

In *Zabriskie Point* (1970), the architecture of America is subsumed by signs: signs on billboards, signs on trucks, signs on taxicabs, benches, and buildings. Anticipating Robert Venturi's *Learning from Las Vegas* (1972), the signscape of Antonioni's Los Angeles takes on the sonority of a boombox blasting nonstop random messages. This visual bombardment reaches a crescendo at the film's conclusion in the Arizona desert, where a sumptuous modern house explodes in slow motion over the course of six minutes—in a psychedelic sky show, clothes, books, furniture, and Wonder Bread wrappers dance the last dance of consumer culture. *The Passenger* (1975) begins in another desert, the Sahara of North Africa, before moving to scenes in Germany, London, and Spain. In Barcelona, Antonioni films the entrance and rooftop of Antonio Gaudi's Casà Mila and Park Güell, contrasting their variegated and polychrome textures with the flat emotions of his characters. As in *L'avventura*, the protagonist, for no apparent reason other than acute modern *ennui*, decides to disappear. The difference is that he assumes the identity of another man, a gun runner for African revolutionaries, and later dies as a consequence of this game in a Moorish-style courtyard hotel, eerily evocative of the fascist ghost town in the earlier film. The relentless materialism that degrades buildings and cities has finally turned people into disturbed facsimiles of one another.

In all the films, but especially those of the tetralogy, Antonioni makes use of the laconic aspects of modern architecture to accentuate the muteness of the modern individual. Ideas are conveyed not as much by revealing conversation or facial expression, both of which are typically lacking, but by situations in which the threadbare emotions of people are conveyed on the razor-edged corners of balconies or the implacable expanses of smooth walls. The films are a sequence of collages that confront the disturbing affinities between the modern urbanized landscape and the modern mind. As Antonioni himself writes: "The best results are obtained by the 'collision' that takes place between the environment in which the scene is to be shot and my own particular state of mind at that specific moment."[5]

Like later directors, such as Terrence Malick in *Badlands* (1973), Antonioni filmed landscape as an echo of the alienation inherent in the modern age. Apartment buildings, power stations, and new towns billow as barren mental breezes, accumulating the blankness of material accumulation, twisting with the false seductions of technology, or whispering dangerous dreams of nostalgia. Asphalt avenues and curtain windows reflect the estrangements of modern subjectivity, and are bathed alternatively in monochrome flatness, blinding contrasts of sunlight and shadow, the white cream of moonlight, or the sudden flashes of a thunderstorm. Not just columns and walls, but also screens, balconies, and windows separate people as they attempt to see or speak to one another. A figure on a balcony overlooking an interminable forest, cut in half by an angular shadow, and seen furtively by another person through a doorway, such are the frames by which Antonioni animates modern architecture and landscape into a corollary of the disintegrating modern mind.

Antonioni's viewpoint should not be reduced, as some critics have tried, to a blanket rejection of the modern world in favor of the past. Granted, his camera consistently and deliberately falters on the threatening hiss of power stations, on the apathetic acquisitions of individuals, and on the neurotic shadows of tall buildings. Yet, over the course of the films, such images pile atop and around one another, and compress the human characters into slow-motion trances that are themselves intensely captivating. The plotless stories, the desultory rhythms, and the lugubrious visual contents wage offensives on two fronts. For Antonioni, modern architecture is menacing but exact; it is monotonous but exquisite. Modern architecture is Antonioni's grand metaphor for the turbulence, tedium, and sublimity that make up the age.

Indeed, Antonioni seems to have a romantic belief in the insights to be gained from juxtaposing the longings of the modern mind with the disharmonies of the modern landscape. As Mira Liehm states: "He used the immediate significance (presence) of things to reach beyond their mere objectivity and create out of their phenomenal existence a Proustian metaphor of oblivion."[6] Perhaps that is why so many of his films end at dawn or dusk, that time of luminary transition when the sharp glare and clear lines of the marketplace world are diffused and the anxiety of human emotions softened.

At the conclusion of *La Notte*, Giovanni and Lidia walk onto a great lawn that opens onto a distant view of the horizon. As they wander in the misty morning air, absorbed in their individual thoughts, the two figures are set against single trees, fragments of the larger woods that define what is actually the fairway of a golf course. At this hour, the space is not a playing field with rules and routes any more than Giovanni and Lidia are individuals with purpose. Instead, the vista evokes the romantic sublime, a panorama onto an infinite space where their troubled souls may roam freely together. Lying together in a sand trap, Lidia reads aloud an intensely passionate letter Giovanni had written her years earlier. He is moved by the letter, so much so that he asks who wrote it. His mind has become obscured by the dense fog that envelops the trees and fairway, the irresolute atmosphere of the modern condition that swallows illusions of individuality and community in great gulps.

NOTES

1. Frank Tomasulo, "The Architectonics of Alienation: Antonioni's Edifice Complex," *Wide Angle* 15 (July 1993): 4.
2. Seymour Chatman, *Antonioni: Or, the Surface of the World* (Berkeley: University of California Press, 1985), 113.
3. Ian Wiblin, "The Space Between: Photography, Architecture and the Presence of Absence" in *Cinema & Architecture: Méliès, Mallet-Stevens, Multimedia*, ed. François Penz & Maureen Thomas (London: British Film Institute, 1997), 106.
4. Diane Borden, "Antonioni and Architecture," *Mise-en-Scène* 2 (1980): 25.
5. Michelangelo Antonioni, *The Architecture of Vision: Writings and Interviews on Cinema*, ed. Carlo di Carlo and Giorgio Tinazzi (New York: Marsilio, 1996), 27.
6. Mira Liehm, *Passion and Defiance: Film in Italy from 1942 to the Present* (Berkeley: University of California), 178.

Two figures silhouetted against the desert in the title sequence of *Split Second* (1953).

SHADOWS *in the* HINTERLAND:
RURAL NOIR

JONATHAN F. BELL

A BLEACHED, CRACKED, and apparently infinite stretch of desert fills up the entire screen during the opening titles of Dick Powell's 1953 film noir *Split Second.* Eventually, two small figures appear on this abstract field, running toward the screen. Their fatigued gaits indicate that they have been running for a long time, but from where—or from what—we cannot see. What they are headed for we do not know either: the two men disappear into the foreground without giving us a clue as to who they are. Our brief encounter with these two strangers is unsettling. How is it that out of this sun-baked landscape they remain faceless, rendered completely in silhouette? Here are two icons straight from a film noir textbook, but clearly far, far away from the pervasive noir environments of under-lit, rain-soaked city streets. Once these two are gone, we remain watching the same unblinking desert, wondering what we have just witnessed.

Film noir settings are primarily and typically urban; the alienation and paranoia in the hearts of these films are made manifest through their depictions of the American city in the late 1940s and 1950s. Worn down and cynical about their lives in these centers of corruption, greed, and crime, the characters in films noir are powerless to do anything except perpetuate these conditions. The emptied streets and deteriorating buildings of the inner city—signs of the middle-class flight to new and rapidly expanding suburbs—provide a stark architectural environment through which these fatalistic stories wind.

Some city dwellers do escape, however, and bring their picnic baskets of angst out onto the open roads of rural America. A relatively small list of films within the classic noir cycle are set primarily outside of an urban area, including *Detour* (Edgar G. Ulmer, 1945), *The Postman Always Rings Twice* (Tay Garnett, 1946), *Out of the Past* (Jacques Tourneur, 1947), *Key Largo* (John Huston, 1948), *Gun Crazy* (Joseph H. Lewis, 1949), *On Dangerous Ground* (Nicholas Ray, 1952), *The Hitch-Hiker* (Ida Lupino, 1953), and the aforementioned *Split Second.* These films present portraits of Americans uncomfortable and unfamiliar with the countrysides in which they find themselves. Open, mountainous, or deserted environments assume noir characteristics ranging from the claustrophobia of a foggy swamp in *Gun Crazy* to the flat-out nihilism of the Nevada desert at the end of *Split Second.* These landscapes, atypical in the noir cycle, also remained foreign to most Americans in the mid-twentieth century. After World War II, the nation's population gravitated toward metropolitan areas, driven in no small part by an explosion in suburban residential construction. This served to create a general perceptual abandonment of the great open spaces that lay between the nodes of major cities. Filmmakers who worked with the combination of noir elements and rural locales—landscapes still most closely associated with Westerns—therefore found rich new territory in which to explore traditional noir themes.

In his 1972 essay "Notes on Film Noir," the writer and director Paul Schrader essentially opened critical interest in the film noir cycle, which, in the broadest dates attributed to the production of such films, stretched from 1941 to 1958.[1] The noir look and tone could be seen as developing from several artistic precedents (German Expressionism, American "hard-boiled" crime fiction of the 1930s, and postwar cinematic realism with its location shooting and available-light cinematography), all of which converged during this period. Schrader argued that film noir was not a "genre"—a group of films adhering to (in noir, particularly urban) "conventions of setting and conflict"—but a cycle of films unified by a series of cultural and stylistic elements used to convey a specific mood and tone. Noir, because it exists independent of a genre, can inhabit the stories and settings of genres such as Westerns, road movies, gangster movies, or science fiction. Schrader's description of noir as a historically and stylistically based cycle allows for a broader understanding of films from this period than a genre-based system of identification allows, and makes it possible to classify as "noir" certain films that venture outside the urban setting.[2]

Rural noir serves as a blanket term to designate those films within the cycle that are not primarily set in urban environments—desert landscapes, farms, mountains, and forests all qualify as settings for consideration. Diverse as these landscapes are, this set of films uses them in surprisingly like-minded fashion to achieve a counterpoint to the ubiquitous noir city. While most of the rural noirs contain characters and themes common to urban noirs—*femmes fatales*, unredemptive violence, ambivalent protagonists, fatalist narratives—and otherwise operate well within the "noir" rubric, they are unique in that they offer a series of social, spatial, and visual readings of an American landscape that had been rapidly changing. Several "urban noirs"—Stanley Kubrick's 1955 *Killer's Kiss*, for example—use romantic visions of America's distant hinterland to thematize escape from the city. Here, an idealized rural world is treated as a beacon to ensure that amidst the darkened urban alleys, there is some "light left to cast shadows."[3] It is also useful to consider how these films, while their narratives remain city-bound, similarly address conceptions of the rural environment.

Three-fifths of all new housing in America in the later part of the 1940s was built in the suburbs. In a seven-year span between 1940 and 1947, about sixty million people—one half of the American population—moved to new homes.[4] The demographic shift around the country was remarkable: people from the countryside were relocating to urban and suburban areas, and people who had previously lived in city centers were now moving to the suburbs. In 1956 Christopher Tunnard and Henry Hope Reed described this as a "Mad Hatter" pattern of relocation: "Like the Mad Hatter at the tea party, who moved around the table using only the clean teacups and leaving the dirty ones behind him, we Americans move on to new land once we have exploited the old." The centers of cities were becoming primarily the realms of business, and were decreasingly viewed as desirable habitats.[5]

As film noir characters were darting through the dirty teacups of abandoned downtown America, mass-scale housing developments were under way in the outskirts of most major cities. Long Island's Levittown (built between 1947 and 1951), where approximately seventy-five thousand residents lived in 14,700 virtually identical homes, epitomized this postwar suburban expansion. If the "ideal retreat" out of the city involved the pursuit of peace, stability, and privacy, then perhaps the new suburban housing stock being erected in places like Levittown also appealed to those who were migrating inward. Suburbanization—or "rurbanism," as it was called in one journal in 1951—combined in the minds of Americans the pastoralist notion of owning land and a house with proximity to urban centers of culture and commerce. The proliferation of such developments prompted the watchful historian and critic Lewis Mumford to write that "the ultimate effect of the suburban escape in our own time is, ironically, a low-grade uniform environment from which escape is impossible."[6] Regardless, new housing predicated on "willful spatial isolation or 'quarantine'" from the city was extremely popular among middle-class white families.[7] This demographic group was, of course, Hollywood's target audience, and film noir codified precisely those anxieties about city life that were causing the exodus to the suburbs. But however effectively it represented a paranoid urban society, film noir did not seek to placate that audience. Noir was noir, and no escape was the norm.

The postwar sprawl described by Mumford fueled American fascination with and romance for the truly rural. In 1966, John Brinckerhoff Jackson, the preeminent commentator on the American landscape, observed that Americans had long possessed a "firm belief, passed on from generation to generation, that there is and always will be a part of the world remote from the city where we can retreat and find ourselves. The more the city expands and absorbs us, the firmer the belief in a rural paradise becomes.... However we look at it, this hinterland is held to be the great antidote, spiritual as well as physical, to the evils of the city." Jackson, however, observed that the reality of the contemporary rural landscape was quite different from the popular conception. Jackson's postwar landscape was one where industrial processes had been applied to agriculture, where the ability to imagine oneself inhabiting this land was thwarted by the absence of human-scale reference points. Rural landscapes were emptying as small-scale farms gave way to "engineered landscapes." Agribusiness had largely replaced what was once familiar in the countryside. In a letter to the editor of the journal *Landscape* (which Jackson had launched in 1951 to bring attention to the "human geography" of rural areas), one disillusioned, transplanted urbanite wrote that it should be made clear to "city and country dweller alike, what a sick and unhappy place the American countryside has become; sick physically, economically, socially; spiritually sickest of all.... Country living can be absolute hell, and frequently is."[8] The evidence presented by the rural noir films support the findings of this unhappy writer, who had left the city to find his or her retreat.

While Jackson was busy describing America's deserted countryside, others were using images of that countryside to describe the nation's metropolitan areas. Suburbs were "cultural, economic, and emotional wastelands," cities were "asphalt jungles," downtown streets were "canyons"; Jean-Paul Sartre wrote an article in 1946 entitled "Manhattan: The Great American Desert." It is useful to extend this metaphor to the analysis of rural noir films. With urban and suburban environments understood as conceptual deserts and wastelands, what more could one expect of the real thing? The answer is a resounding, noir-inflected, Nothing. As film noir historian Robert G. Porfirio has written: "The Hemingway hero may withdraw to the sanctuary of the country or a café...as a way of assuaging his pain and finding some order in his life. The noir hero does likewise, but he has far fewer resources to work with. There is no 'country' left, only the modern wasteland of such cities as New York, San Francisco, and Los Angeles."[9]

When characters in films noir attempt to locate this countryside, they invariably fail to find the retreat that they expect. *The Hitch-Hiker*'s Roy Collins and Gilbert Bowen (Edmond O'Brien and Frank Lovejoy), two wartime buddies who leave their families in an Arizona city, ostensibly to go fishing in the mountains, are emblematic of such attempts. Their fishing trip is actually a ruse—the two switch course for Baja, California, where they hope to relive some of their prewar carousing. As if on cue, they pick up Emmett Myers (William Talman), a murderous hitchhiker who commandeers their car into the Mexican desert. Myers becomes a symbol for the two men's folly—the itinerant demon conjured when the two men stray from their families and the city. Their fate in the desert typifies a noir treatment of rural locales: the "paradise" the characters enter is host to the same threats as the "modern wasteland" they have left behind. In the noir landscape, the idea of a peaceful fishing trip, country drive, or hiking retreat is fraught with deadly consequence.

The Hitch-Hiker illustrates the model of a "retreat" from the city, in which the exile is a self-imposed search for that elusive rural paradise that instead leads to a foreign landscape whose Arcadian promises are quickly obliterated. The other primary model at work in these films is the "escape," in which characters are compelled to flee the city. The escapees may not have the same false optimism about the countryside, but nonetheless view the getaway as the solution to their urban dilemmas. Usually—though not always—escapees are "villains." (In film noir, the distinction between heroes and villains is rarely clear, complicating the motivations for flight. The noir "hero" is often morally ambiguous, cowardly, untriumphant, and, by the end of the film, dead. In *Gun Crazy*, for example, the protagonists are thieves, murderers, and—as the title makes clear—extraordinarily trigger-happy.) Both a "retreat" and an "escape" as seen in film noir posits the idea that there is a qualitative difference between the city and the country. This idea is invariably either proven false or, at best, remains unanswered over the course of the film.

Stanley Kubrick's *Killer's Kiss* literally frames the idea of a retreat by setting its opening and closing sequences in New York's Pennsylvania Station. At the opening of the film, we see Davey Gordon (Jamie Smith) waiting for a train that will be his deliverance from an unsuccessful boxing career. He is returning to his uncle's horse farm in Washington State, where he has been promised that "out here, everything's about the same." In this optimistic moment, Kubrick (who is also the cinematographer, editor, co-writer, and co-

Jim Wilson (Robert Ryan) and Pop Daly (Charles Kemper) in pursuit of a killer in *On Dangerous Ground* (1951).

producer) films Davey from a low angle gazing across McKim, Mead & White's vast iron-vaulted monument. Davey's voice-over then interjects and begins his tale, told in flashback, of cramped tenements, dangerous women, and lowlife violence. When the story closes, we are returned to Penn Station, but the ambiguous ending leaves open the question of whether or not Davey successfully breaks free of the city's hold.

An inversion of the *Killer's Kiss* story arc occurs in Nicholas Ray's *On Dangerous Ground.* Jim Wilson (Robert Ryan) is a cynical and brutish cop in an unnamed city. After Wilson instigates a series of violent incidents, his chief sends him away from the big city for a "restorative" murder investigation in the mountains (how his jurisdiction extends into the mountains is never explained). Once in the snowy countryside, Wilson is grudgingly treated as "the city cop"; his desire to return to his life as a city loner is only eroded after he befriends a blind woman (Ida Lupino), whose brother he has just chased to his death. *On Dangerous Ground* is perhaps the only rural noir in which the countryside positively affects a character, however marginally. Wilson, upon completing the case, actually returns to the city before finally deciding to retreat back into the mountains (foreshadowing, perhaps, Robert Ryan's acting career in Westerns).

John Huston's *Key Largo*, although not specifically set in the "country," brings together in the remote title location both a retreater and an escapee. Frank McCloud (Humphrey Bogart) comes to visit the family of his dead wartime friend because "life on land has become too complicated." His intention is to move on from the family's hotel where he is staying, but the simultaneous arrivals of a hurricane and a group of Chicago gangsters force him to remain. Where McCloud has left his newspaper job in New York in pursuit of a life less complicated, gangster leader Johnny Rocco (Edward G. Robinson), a wanted criminal from Chicago, is now en route back to that city after a period of exile. Their paths cross in Key Largo—the "antidote" to the cities—which proves to be a more destructive place than either of the two great metropolises.

The "escapees" illustrate a paradox of inhabiting the city: it is both the perfect locale in which to disappear and the most likely place to be found. In films noir we hear again and again of the city swallowing up its inhabitants. The quintessential statement of urban anonymity comes from the murderer Willie Garza (Ted de Corsia) in Jules Dassin's *Naked City* (1948), as he mutters to his pursuer: "This is a great big, beautiful city. Just try an' find me!" In *He Walked By Night* (also 1948, directed by Alfred L. Werker and an uncredited Anthony Mann), the police scour Los Angeles for "a shadow of a man—mysterious, elusive, deadly, hidden away somewhere in the vast city." And in Edgar G. Ulmer's *Detour*, Al Roberts (Tom Neal) quickly finds himself in need of getting out of the Arizona desert. Roberts, a pianist who was hitchhiking from New York City to Los Angeles, unexpectedly finds a corpse on his hands. In a loopy attempt to prevent what he is sure will be his arrest for murder, he dons the dead man's clothes, dumps the body in the desert, and drives off in the deceased man's car. In voice-over, he tells the audience he must get to some city where he can "be swallowed up....In a little town I might be noticed, but in a city I should be safe enough."

Yet the city is also a place of notoriety, where (in the noir world) the "one chance in a million" always seems to come through. For escapees, the city becomes a place of undesirable attention and instantaneous communication: we see montages—as in *The Naked City*—of telephone switchboards relaying news across town. The need to escape Chicago brought Johnny Rocco to Key Largo in John Huston's film; a similar need befalls the main character in Jules Dassin's 1950 noir *Night and the City*. The unscrupulous Harry Fabian (Richard Widmark) spends the last portion of that film trying—unsuccessfully—to escape his pursuers and leave the city. The unofficial all-points-bulletin placed for Harry quickly has the entire London underworld on the lookout. He can't hide.[10] In *Out of the Past*, it is the smallness of the city—the knowledge that around every corner lurks precisely that which one fears to face—that forces Jeff Markham (Robert Mitchum) to flee San Francisco. In the mountainous town of Bridgeport (349 miles from Los Angeles, a road sign tells us), Markham settles down, complete with a new identity, in the hopes of erasing connections to his former life. According to film noir convention, a retreat or escape to the countryside is either impossible, disillusioning, or ill-fated. And so it is for Markham, who is quickly pulled back into the web of deceit and intrigue from which he had sought to remove himself.

Noir's moods and tones are achieved with specific visual motifs as well as narrative ones. Within the urban noirs, city streets are typically rendered as series of fragmentary perspectives. Long, dark shadows, intensified by sharp camera angles and stark lighting, limit lines of vision: the inhabitants of film noir cities can be justifiably claustrophobic. The opening up of broad vistas in the rural noirs can be seen as a deceptive visual counterpoint to the labyrinthine city. Once placed in a wide-open space, the landscape allows characters a feeling of power, a grasp of totality through visual surveillance. These characters may have a delusional sense that they can encompass and control such space. However, noir filmmakers tend to use

Jeff Markham (Robert Mitchum) before the gate of Whit Sterling's Tahoe mansion in *Out of the Past* (1947).

formal devices within these landscapes to close off that space and create claustrophobic environments similar to those found in the city. Thus, when noir steps into the countryside, the shadows and dead ends associated with urban scenarios return in a new guise, proving that the same forces are at work in rural locales.

In the films in which broad vistas figure prominently—notably *Out of the Past*, *On Dangerous Ground*, and *The Hitch-Hiker*—they represent the folly of a safe retreat. These vistas are used to most consistent effect in *Out of the Past*, where mountain views serve as symbols of a pastoral life aspired to by erstwhile private eye Jeff Markham. After crossing too many people—a failed assignment leaves his client robbed of his money and mistress, and Markham's former partner dead—Markham makes a new life for himself pumping gas in a bucolic town. The first glimpse of Markham in the film emphasizes his new immersion in the landscape: he is shown in extreme long shot, walking along a wooded lakeshore. Of course, his past catches up to him, and Markham is soon summoned by his former client, Whit Sterling (Kirk Douglas), to Sterling's Tahoe house. Director Jacques Tourneur frames this fateful transition in Markham's life by showing Markham's silhouette, back to the mountains, pass reluctantly through the prisonlike gate of Sterling's mansion. Later, *femme fatale extraordinaire* Kathie Moffatt (Jane Greer)—the subject of the original trouble—wistfully admonishes Markham, "Remember the mountains?" as Tourneur again teasingly frames those mountains in the background. But Markham's past has fated him not to return. Tourneur uses the mountains as a symbol of a getaway, but they cannot be reached.

Rural noir filmmakers often constructed visual parallels to the dark alleyways, blind corners, and expressionistic shadows that externalized the threats of the city. Take, for example, the botched cliffside murder scene in *The Postman Always Rings Twice*, in which a car containing Nick Smith and Frank Chambers (Cecil Kellaway and John Garfield) plummets into a foggy abyss as Cora Smith (Lana Turner) barely clings to a rockface. Director Tay Garnett creates a claustrophobic and acrophobic *mise-en-scène,* forcing Cora to edge her way up the cliff through a narrow rock channel. At the top of the cliff stands the district attorney, who awaits her for questioning. The rock channel is the guarantee of her apprehension, and parallels the use of constricted spaces that culminate urban chase scenes in films such as *He Walked By Night* (the Los Angeles sewers), or *Killer's Kiss* (a Times Square alley, a mannequin warehouse). Ida Lupino's *The Hitch-Hiker* has similarly constructed scenes, only played out on desert topography. To avoid detection by patrol cars and helicopters scouring the Baja desert, the three main characters crouch in brush shadows and squeeze between narrow rock fissures. And in *Gun Crazy,* director Joseph H. Lewis closes his film by eliminating almost all visuals as the two exhausted main characters await their pursuers in a dense, fog-filled mountain swamp. Six years later, the same director would transfer this eerie visual device into the city in *The Big Combo* (1955), which ends—again with a shoot-out—in a similarly foggy airplane hangar.

Long stretches of road through vast deserted territories also, ironically, foster claustrophobia. In fact, the fatalist characteristics of the noir cycle actually work better in such linear environments than in the grids of city streets. The road to the horizon is a loaded symbol. In rural noirs, it tends to represent the only course, a preordained destiny from which no escape is possible. One can survey the future by looking down the road and see nothing but a continuation of the same dry, empty landscape in which the film is already enveloped. The road is the opening image of *Key Largo*: the "concrete causeway" that is literally the only path connecting the Florida Keys and will necessarily bring the divergent characters together. In *The Hitch-Hiker*, road maps play a role in orienting the characters, who are literally and figuratively lost in the desert. The propelling geographical vector in *The Hitch-Hiker* is the Baja peninsula itself, a narrow finger of land that extends to the south via Santa Rosalia, Mexico. With the border patrol behind them and only one chance to catch a ferry to the mainland at Santa Rosalia, the characters have little choice as to their destination.

The conflation of fate with linear movement is most clearly exemplified in Edward G. Ulmer's *Detour*. As protagonist Al Roberts drives his way across the desert, the first person he picks up is, inevitably, the only one who knows his secret and is capable of (and quite intent on) destroying him. Ulmer frames this scene so their meeting is inevitable: Roberts refills his car in the left foreground, and the road stretches off to the right. In the middle ground, directly between Roberts and the road, stands Vera (Ann Savage). He cannot proceed without confronting her. In the rural landscape, there is no one chance in a million—the odds are reduced to one in one.

The narrative themes and visual conventions that were established within urban noirs were ultimately quite transferable into readings of the vanishing American landscape in the rural noirs. This point is made clear in *Split Second*, when dancer Dorothy Vale (Jan Sterling), is picked up at a desert rest stop by Nevada newspaperman Larry Fleming (Keith Andes). In laconic noir fashion, Dorothy asks her ride why he doesn't move to the city. "I like the country. 'The West—where men are men'," he replies. Her response: "Men are men anywhere."

J. B. Jackson's entreaties to turn critical attention to the American countryside were in fact being concurrently addressed by a small number of Hollywood films within the classic noir cycle. As both city centers and rural regions emptied into suburbs, these films found means of exhibiting warnings to an American public about their physical and psychological environments. The primary message was that there was no place left to go. The same essential conditions seem to pervade both the iconic noir city and the neglected hinterland. As Johnny Rocco proclaims to his captive audience in *Key Largo*, "I was too much for the big city to handle!" Like Rocco, a number of filmmakers in the late 1940s and early 1950s felt the same about noir themes, finding in forays into the American countryside alternate means of expressing the dark, unique visions that haunted postwar America.

NOTES

Special thanks to M. Christine Boyer, for introducing me to the subject of noir and urbanism and encouraging me in its pursuit; Lisa Dombrowski, for her discussions with me and guidance on the film analyses; and Sarah Zurier, for many invaluable proofreadings and tireless support.

1. Those years are marked by the releases of *The Maltese Falcon* and *Touch of Evil*, respectively, but it is probably a bit facile to say that individual films "opened" and "closed" the cycle. The term *film noir* was first coined in 1946 by Nino Frank, a French critic.
2. Paul Schrader's essay first appeared in *Film Comment* (spring 1972). It has been reprinted in several collections, including *Film Noir: A Reader*, Alain Silver and James Ursini, eds. (New York: Limelight Editions, 1996). The term *noir* has by now been folded into the common film-classification lexicon, and has become somewhat separated from its historical usage. For an account of this, see Todd Erickson's "Kill Me Again: Movement Becomes Genre," (1995) in that collection.
3. Mike Davis, *City of Quartz* (New York: Vintage Books, 1992), 45. Davis is offering a critique of James Ellroy, the contemporary "noir" author, who (according to Davis) leaves no light to relieve the dark world of his fiction.
4. Edward Dimendberg quotes city planning authority Mel Scott's statistics in "Film Noir and Urban Space," unpublished dissertation, University of California, Santa Cruz, 1992, 84, n. 10.
5. Christopher Tunnard and Henry Hope Reed, *American Skyline: The Growth and Form of Our Cities and Towns* (New York: Mentor, 1956), 184; on suburbanism in general, see Kenneth T. Jackson, *Crabgrass Frontier: The Suburbanization of the United States* (New York: Oxford University Press, 1985).

6. " 'Rurban,' according to the *Country Gentleman*, is a word coined to describe the new kind of communities developing throughout the United States.... Farm population is declining, and at the same time people employed in towns and cities are moving out into the country and commuting as far as fifty miles by car to work." *Landscape* 1, no. 2 (autumn 1951), 37; Lewis Mumford, *The City in History* (New York: Harcourt, Brace and World, 1961), 486.

7. Dimendberg, "Film Noir and Urban Space," 33. Dimendberg characterizes these developments in an analysis of Stuyvesant Town in New York City.

8. John Brinckerhoff Jackson, "An Engineered Environment" (1966), in *Landscape in Sight: Looking at America*, Helen Lefkowitz Horowitz, ed. (New Haven: Yale University Press, 1997), 225; "What We Want," unattributed letter to the editor, *Landscape* 1, no. 3 (winter 1952): 2.

9. Robert G. Porfirio, "No Way Out: Existential Motifs in the *Film Noir*" (1976), in Silver and Ursini, eds., *Film Noir: A Reader*, 92.

10. That this American-produced and -directed film is set in rubble-filled postwar London brings into ironic focus the director's own forced exile from the United States—Dassin had been recently blacklisted by the House Un-American Activities Committee.

WRETCHED HIVES: GEORGE LUCAS *and the* AMBIVALENT URBANISM *of Star Wars*

MARK LAMSTER

ARCHITECTS HAVE LONG dreamed that given the proper freedom, authority, and budget they might reform society. The making of a better world was one of the primary objectives of the modern movement, grounded as it was in the socialist politics of the early twentieth century, and it is a goal that continues to resonate with architects and town planners today. George Lucas, the billionaire movie mogul, has similarly made no secret of his intention to foster a more moral universe through his creative practice—his *Star Wars* films, with their transparent plots of good versus evil, were specifically designed to provide a generation of TV-addicted children with a firm ethical grounding. It therefore seems fitting that Lucas, who has described himself as "a frustrated architect," has often used architecture as a means for conveying his ideas about appropriate communal behavior. And like those of Le Corbusier or Walter Gropius or even the Walt Disney Corporation, the architectural environments he has created—both in the real world and in his films—are ideologically loaded.[1]

Lucas has no reason to feel frustrated as an architect; the world's top-grossing filmmaker has more buildings to his credit than many Fellows of the American Institute of Architects. Lucas micromanaged the design and construction of Skywalker Ranch, the expansive Marin County compound of nearly 3,000 acres that is home to Lucasfilm, the flagship and linchpin of his moviemaking empire. Boasting a Victorian-style mega-manse, numerous outbuildings (including stables and its own fire station), a man-made lake, and enough underground parking to ensure that cars don't disrupt the views, Skywalker Ranch exudes a sense of bucolic bonhomie. "At the Ranch you get the sense that some all-controlling intelligence has rubbed itself over every element for a long time," wrote the *New Yorker*'s John Seabrook after a visit to the compound in 1996. There is no question as to just whose controlling intelligence is doing the rubbing. Lucas, ever the storyteller, even fabricated a history for the ranch, propagating an ersatz legend in which the property was originally the estate of a railroad baron.[2]

Lucas, who readily concedes that his preferred form of government is benevolent despotism, oversees his fiefdom as the altruistic seigneur he finds so appealing as a political paradigm. "I find myself with this little country," he told the *New York Times*'s Orville Schell in 1999. "It's got about 2,000 citizens, and they are very complex. Some are very loyal and some of them are very dissatisfied. Some are very good in terms of obeying the laws of the land and some aren't. It's a mini version of the larger society." The nostalgic design of Skywalker Ranch at once reinforces and disguises the feudal nature of the corporate empire Lucas commands. (He is the sole shareholder in his various companies.) "Lucasland" is tightly guarded, and its codes of conduct are passed on from the sovereign's inner sanctum. But the bearded Lucas, famously disheveled in his typical uniform of flannel shirt and blue jeans, is no Sun King; the ranch's lolling landscape and Victorian charm foster a laid-back, commodious atmosphere that supports the brand of collaborative effort demanded by filmmaking and digital-era corporate culture. "I like the esthetics of the Victorian age," says Lucas, "things that are homey and kind of Midwestern—a very warm, fuzzy kind of reality."[3]

Lucas's Marin County neighbors have not always seen him as such a benign presence. In 1985, he undertook a major expansion of Skywalker Ranch, acquiring three adjacent parcels of land but concealing his ownership of two of those tracts. Lucas's deputies then attempted to bully the Marin County Board of Supervisors into waiving a zoning regulation that would have cost the filmmaker several million dollars to accommodate. The dispute was eventually resolved, but not before exposing the Lucas empire as a corporate power willing to flex its muscle against the community's elected establishment. It also left Lucas somewhat embittered. In 1990, his sympathetic biographer, Dale Pollock, wrote: "Like any king, Lucas feels beleaguered in his castle, surrounded by hostile forces who fail to understand the singular importance of his vision."[4]

Lucas's penchant for honeyed architectural landscapes is often veiled in his films—the environments he has conjured for the *Star Wars* series are, by and large, anything but warm and fuzzy. The opening installment, *Star Wars* (1977), spends most of its time shuttling between the desert planet of Tatooine and the Empire's Death Star battlestation, a moon-size machine for killing. In the following two films, *The Empire Strikes Back* (1980) and *Return of the Jedi* (1983), scenes unfold on an ice planet, a swamp planet, a forest planet, an asteroid (in a monster's belly), a floating Gotham, and yet another Death Star.

These environments are neatly divided into the natural and the man-made, and coded to their inhabitants' stations in the moral universe of the series: the innocent Rebel Alliance is time and again pictured amidst the natural world, while the evil Empire is fascistically resplendent in its technological terrors. Yoda, the Rebel's ancient troglodytic guru, lives in a swamp; Darth Vader, the Empire's dark knight, inhabits a mechanical cocoon on the Death Star. The opposition between these two worlds could hardly be more blunt, and Lucas uses all available tools to call attention to it. In one especially portentous sequence, midway through *Jedi*, Lucas uses a wipe cut to shift from the lacquered flight deck of the Death Star, where Vader has just received the Emperor amidst Nazi-like columns of stormtroopers, to the steamy slough of Dagobah, where Yoda counsels Luke in a scene roughly cribbed from Akira Kurosawa's *Throne of Blood* (1957, itself a *Macbeth* adaptation). The Rebels inhabit colorful worlds of creamy pastels, blues, and greens, while the *Empire*'s gigantic warships are mercilessly black and white. Subtlety has never been a hallmark of Lucas's filmmaking, and it's just as well; moralizing fables are not well served by understatement.

From the desert of Tatooine to the ice plains of *Empire*'s Hoth to the forest of *Jedi*'s Endor (where teddylike Ewoks live in tree stumps), the persistent identification of Luke and his Rebel mates with the natural world marks them as prelapsarian innocents, in effect justifying their battle against fallen father Darth Vader and the Empire he serves. Architecturally—and Oedipally—this infantilization is signaled by an obsessive fascination with caves, as if Luke were somehow trying to return to the safety of the womb. When we first encounter the young Skywalker in *Star Wars*, he is living with his adoptive parents, the Larses, in a complex of caves and domed structures on their isolated Tatooine homestead, filmed on location in the Tunisian desert town of Matama. In the final scene of the film, shot in a Mayan ruin in the Guatemalan rain forest, Luke and the Rebel forces gather in their caved headquarters to celebrate the allied victory in a scene borrowed from Leni Riefenstahl's 1934 Nazi propaganda *Triumph of Will*.[5]

That Lucas traveled to the farthest reaches of this planet to set the other worlds of his Star Wars galaxy ensured that they would be unfamiliar to all but a few experts in non-Western architecture, contributing to the fantastic nature of his grand epic while reinforcing audiences' suspension of disbelief. (These lessons were unfortunately lost in 1999's *Episode 1: The Phantom Menace*, which bursts at its very seams with—if we are to believe the "long ago and far away" prescription—anachronistic period architecture and statuary clearly of this earth.) Lucas's identification of so much indigenous, Third World architecture with the innocent and even the primitive carries with it disturbingly paternalistic, if not racist, overtones. These become overt in *Jedi* with the Ewok sequences—where the Pygmy-like forest dwellers overcome a battalion of the Empire's crack stormtroopers—but reach their most egregious in *Menace*, in which the Rasta-tongued Gungans, forced underground, inhabit some slippery Atlantis while the humanoid Naboo live on the planet's surface in an epic imperial city. (When the Jedi character Qui-Gon claims that these two cities live in a giant "symbiotic circle," it seems little more than New Age mumbo-jumbo, given their physical disparity and the general lack of contact between them.)

All three films in the initial *Star Wars* trilogy open, famously, with prolonged shots of the Empire's fearsome star destroyers interminably sliding across the screen. Lucas's Rebels are constantly on the run from the faceless villains who operate out of these awesome ships, from which the natural world has been thoroughly banished—there are no plants in the Empire. And these behemoths are but preludes to the Empire's Death Stars, entire planet-cities devoted to destruction. Together, these terribly beautiful ships define what can be characterized as an Interplanetary Style—an on-screen corollary to the so-called International Style of design that stripped the modern movement of its ideological bearings. Frigid, sleek, authoritative, and potent, they are the *Star Wars* analog to the corporate facades of New York's Park Avenue. When an Imperial general arrogantly declares that the (first) Death Star "is now the ultimate power in the universe," we can see just how far from its ideals modernism has fallen and, reading more deeply, are confronted by the very hubris of its reformist impulses.

Aesthetically and conceptually, the architectural spaces of the Empire are derived from Lucas's first feature film, *THX 1138* (1971, itself based on *THX 1138:4EB*, a film Lucas made while teaching at the University of Southern California film school four years earlier). *THX 1138* is set in an Orwellian, subterranean world of shiny black-and-white spaces and masked paramilitaries, where the populace is controlled through mind-numbing drugs and constant surveillance. In the film, modern design is inextricably associated with sterility and villainous power (much of the footage was shot in Frank Lloyd Wright's stark Marin County Civic Center). It culminates as the character *THX*, played by Robert Duvall, escapes from the frigid, monochrome modernity of this brave new world, climbing from a tunnel to witness a spectacular, panchromatic sunset in his first moment above ground.

Another obvious design source for Lucas's Imperial environments—and for much of the trilogy's appearance, in particular its special effects—is Stanley Kubrick's *2001: A Space Odyssey* (1968). But in contrast to Kubrick, who added pathos to his film by humanizing *2001*'s *Discovery* spacecraft and its operating system, HAL, Lucas took pains to dehumanize and sanitize the Imperial ships of the *Star Wars* saga—even the Death Star's vermin are mechanical—leaving audiences with little cause for remorse upon their inevitable destruction. There are but a handful of anomalous scenes: in *Star Wars*, Luke, Leia, Han, and Chewbacca plunge into the bog of a Death Star trash compactor and are attacked by a sludge-monster; at the opening of *Jedi*, Vader arrives at a partially completed Death Star, where work seems hopelessly behind schedule. In a scene that can't help but appeal to architects, Vader breathily dismisses the admiral-in-charge due to his "apparent lack of progress" and proceeds to take over the job as *Über*foreman, making him something of a galactic Robert Moses.

Between the natural worlds inhabited by the Rebels and the technological war machines of the Empire are a series of more conventional urban spaces. Lucas invariably depicts these environments as corrupt, duplicitous, and dangerous places of base individualism best viewed from safely elevated positions. Our first confrontation with one of these urban environments comes roughly midway through *Star Wars*. From a dramatic escarpment on Tatooine, Luke and Obi-Wan look down on a frontier settlement nearly invisible on the sandy plain below. "Mos Eisley space port," intones the old Jedi. "Never will you find [a] more wretched hive of scum and villainy." Without recourse, the two descend into the town, where they are exposed to segregation, smuggling, and homicide—among other misdeeds—before making their escape under fire in the Millennium Falcon.

Empire's Cloud City, a floating mining colony that hovers above the planet Bespin (conceptually indebted, as are many of the mechanical units in the series, to Archigram's work of the 1960s), is another of Lucas's perilous towns. Here, the slick Lando Calrissian makes a Faustian bargain with Vader that ostensibly guarantees his city's freedom from Imperial rule. Of course it does not—instead, Han winds up freeze-dried and a trap is set that pits Luke against his newly revealed father, costing him his hand. Forced to explain his duplicity, the overwhelmed bureaucrat claims, "I got my own problems," having earlier cited "supply problems" and "labor difficulties." Though Lando eventually joins the Rebel team and intervenes on his friends' behalf, the city he administers is nonetheless a place that forces unseemly compromise.

Like his namesake, Luke, filmmaker Lucas is a child of the desert. "A simple, small-town boy" according to his biographer, Lucas was reared in Modesto, California, by a notoriously conservative father whose warnings about "big-city hucksters" and the general turpitude of cities—and Hollywood in particular—clearly rubbed off on his son (witness Lucas's secluded ranch). It is difficult not to see the dim vision of the city propagated by the *Star Wars* films as a product of this upbringing. But it also takes its place in a rich American tradition of anti-urban thought that finds its esteemed progenitor in Thomas Jefferson. Indeed, Obi-Wan's admonition in regard to Mos Eisley suggests Jefferson's more general declaration, "I view large cities as pestilential to the morals, the liberties, and the health of man." It should also be kept in mind that when *Star Wars* was conceived, during the early and mid-1970s, America's urban cores were rife with conflict and crime, bankrupt, and betrayed by the federal government. A cascade of contemporary films depicted urban life—particularly in New York—as an uphill struggle against freaks, druggies, and criminals. At the apex of this "genre," which includes such notable films as *The French Connection* (1971), *The Taking of Pelham One Two Three* (1974), and *Dog Day Afternoon* (1975), is Martin Scorsese's *Taxi Driver* (1976), a film Lucas was intimately familiar with: his wife, Marcia Griffin Lucas, edited it while her husband was hashing out the story for his great space epic. Indeed, Lucas had become a Hollywood sensation by directing a counterpoint to these films, *American Graffiti* (1973), a nostalgic rumination on his suburban youth.[6]

Though Lucas regularly depicts them as dangerous, dystopic places, cities are also undeniably alluring to him. Lucas himself departed Modesto to make his name as a young filmmaker in Los Angeles and, later, San Francisco. Similarly, in *Star Wars*, Luke itches to escape the humdrum farming life of Tatooine; in *Empire*, he rushes off to Cloud City against the wishes of his mentors Yoda and Obi-Wan. But the most blatant indication of Lucas's paradoxical affection for the city is the lavish care he has expended on the production of his films' urban spaces. With their sky-hugging towers and swarming streets, cities are a visual playground that Lucas can't resist. Indeed, the 1997–98 re-release of the Star Wars trilogy in an enhanced "special edition" was by his own account driven, at least in part, by a desire to add detail to the Mos Eisley and Cloud City sequences.

Lucas's majestic visions of cinematic urbanism reach their most grandiose realization in *Episode 1: The Phantom Menace*, the sprawling "prequel" to the original three films. *Menace* begins with the blockade of the planet of Naboo and its outlandish capital, where monumental buildings in a disconcertingly wide range of period styles parade along triumphal avenues. Most of these visually impressive buildings are computer-generated pastiche, though the centerpiece, Naboo's marble-flooded palace, was shot in the neoclassical Palazzo Reale of Caserta, a distinctly non-urban royal summer residence outside of Naples. In *Menace*, the palace's period veneer runs only skin deep; in one of the film's concluding episodes, Jedi knights Obi-Wan and Qui-Gon engage in a vicious light-saber battle with evil Darth Maul that somehow leads all three to the inner core of the palace, a mechanical space of catwalks and plunging modernist perspectives. It is yet another example of what might be called the Foundry Principle; that action-picture cliché—reaching back to the 1960s but *de rigueur* since James Cameron's 1984 thriller *The Terminator*—of setting final, apocalyptic altercations in vast industrial spaces.

From Naboo, *Menace* returns to Tatooine and, defying historical possibility, a souped-up Mos Eisley far more developed than in any of the three films of the original trilogy (ostensibly set in the relative future). Lucas's new old Mos Eisley features a Berber-style slave village, and, more impressively, a magnificent stadium of cylindrical bastions and massive grandstands. A bravura orchestration of computer-generated design, the stadium is the most elegant of Lucas's on-screen architectural creations, rivaled only by a droid army that systematically deploys from a series of treaded vehicles in the film's culminating battle sequence.

But it is with *Menace*'s Coruscant that Lucas most clearly reveals his conflicted vision of the urban world. Like Empire's Cloud City, Coruscant is a retro-futuristic metropolis where nothing seems to go right for the forces of good. The nostalgic inspiration of both cities should be familiar to anyone acquainted with the cinematic gothic of Fritz Lang's *Metropolis* (1926), the chiaroscuro urban fantasies of 1920s visionaries Harvey Wiley Corbett and Hugh Ferriss, or, reaching even farther back, the prewar publications of Moses King. With its extraordinary vistas of ragged skyscrapers and its streams of floating vehicles, Coruscant is the most sophisticated realization of yesterday's future ever committed to film—eye-candy on a most elaborate scale. Even Lucas's characters are awed: "The entire planet is one big city!" exclaims a gaping Obi-Wan as he approaches the vast planetopolis. It is the exclamation of a tourist, an out-of-towner enthralled but overwhelmed by the big city (one half-expects Obi-Wan and his mates to land their ship in front of a cosmic Hard Rock Cafe). Not surprisingly, the trip is an unmitigated disaster; Obi-Wan defies the Jedi Council's admonition not to train young Anakin Skywalker in the ways of the Force (the result being his future transformation into Darth Vader). More seriously, the Naboo's desperate queen is manipulated into a political gambit that renders control over the interplanetary Senate to the man who will become the Rebel's ultimate nemesis, the Emperor. Though the Naboo manage to vanquish the forces of evil at the close of the film, the seeds of future disaster are set, and we are left to wonder just how much conceptual distance separates the latent hostility of Coruscant and the outright evil of the Empire's manufactured moon, the Death Star.

Lucas has promised two more pictures to fill in the temporal gap between *Menace* and the original *Star Wars* film. Perhaps he will take one of these as an opportunity to illustrate his vision of an ideal, civil society. In the meantime, he has a more concrete outlet for his architectural imagination: in June 1999, a Lucas proxy paid $250 million for the right to develop a "digital arts center" on a 23-acre parcel of the Presidio, the landmarked former military base that sits in the heart of San Francisco's Golden Gate Recreation Area. The initial proposal calls for buildings to house various Lucas enterprises (including the special-effects operation Industrial Light and Magic), 15 acres of public space, and underground parking for fifteen hundred cars. Sequestered in the park's luxurious greensward, the complex will be at once a part of the city and separated from it, a lasting marker of its patron's urban ambivalence.

NOTES

1. On Lucas and morality, see John Seabrook, "Why Is the Force Still With Us?," *The New Yorker*, 6 January 1997, 48; and Dale Pollock, *Skywalking: The Life and Films of George Lucas* (New York: Samuel French, 1990), 144. On Lucas as architect, see Charles Champlin, "The Last Maverick: Inside George Lucas' Empire," *Los Angeles Times*, 15 May 1988.

2. Seabrook, "Why Is the Force Still with Us?," 44–5.

3. Orville Schell, "George Lucas: A Galaxy of Myth, Money and Kids," *New York Times*, 21 March 1999; Schell, "I'm a Cynic Who Has Hope for the Human Race" (interview with George Lucas), *New York Times*, 21 March 1999.

4. Eric Ingram, "The Marin Empire of George Lucas Is Under Attack," *San Francisco Chronicle*, 25 May 1985; Pollock, *Skywalking*, xv.

5. On *Star Wars* and infantilization, see Peter Biskind, "Blockbuster: The Last Crusade," in *Seeing Through Movies*, Mark Crispin Miller, ed. (New York: Pantheon, 1990). For filming locations, see Pollock, *Skywalking*, 132, 176.

6. Pollock, *Skywalking*, 4–5; Jefferson is quoted in Kenneth T. Jackson, *The Crabgrass Frontier: The Suburbanization of the United States* (New York: Oxford University Press, 1985), 68; on Marcia Griffin Lucas and the editing of *Taxi Driver,* see Pollock, *Skywalking*, 138.

BURSTING *at the* SEAMS: ARCHITECTURE *and the* FILMS *of the* BEATLES

ERIC ROSENBERG

THE BEATLES' 1970 film *Let It Be* concludes with the four band members performing on a wood-planked temporary stage assembled on the roof of their record company's London headquarters. Though no one realized as much at the time, it would be their final live performance, and one of the last instances in which the beleaguered musicians would unite behind a common purpose. For Beatles fans, it is an iconic scene, comprised of footage of the band interspersed with shots of the four or five facades that front the supporting and surrounding buildings and stretch to the ground below.

The Beatles' appearance above the street, in the open air, and without permit was just one more small subversion of authority that took its place alongside a host of similar moments in their careers. One thinks of John's comment about the Beatles' popularity relative to that of Jesus, of the numerous drug busts, of John and Yoko nude on the cover of *Two Virgins*. More to the point, the moment that brings *Let It Be* to a close places these four immensely popular British musicians in a particularly meaningful space: above Georgian Savile Row, a largely eighteenth-century enclave in the Burlington Gardens section of London known for its high-end tailors.

No longer contained by the buildings below, an act of ascendancy takes place in the face of dissolution—the thrust of the film, however unintentional, is the story of the group's demise. Now merely atoms in the universe, sparking only occasionally, the Beatles

Paul, George, Ringo, and John make a break for it in *A Hard Day's Night* (1975).

and their music waft into the ether, untouchable in this ecstatic moment. In turn, their public conglomerates—with great difficulty—in clottish fashion at street level, on corners, along the sidewalk. The group's constituency can reach them only by climbing utility ladders that reveal, frame by frame, the indecorous undersides of the facades below. Only one member of the audience at a time risks the dangerous climb. In the moment of their own fragmentation, they are afforded only a random, haphazard quality of attention.

An early prefiguring of this awkward yet moving epiphany comes in the Beatles' first film, *A Hard Day's Night* (1964). Roughly a third of the way through the story, the group is bursting at the seams of managerial confinement. This is denoted time and again by the placement of the group in claustrophobic spaces where they are choked by a press of hysterical fans. The group is in constant search of release. Locating a fire escape, they flee a regional television studio where they are to tape a performance for a cheesy local variety show.

Virtually tumbling down an iron lattice staircase, the four screaming males are seen only from below in fragments that signify the imprisonment from which they run but can't hide. Accompanied by their recent hit "Can't Buy Me Love," they descend on an enormous open field adjacent to the studio. There, they come to a square section covered by a large slab of concrete, presumably hiding some sort of industrial or electrical material buried below. From above, however, this space looks in its abstract play of light and dark patches like nothing so much as a partially articulated map of the world. On top of and around this slab, the Beatles lose themselves in a performance of silly, mock theatrics meant to secure their collective identity as jokers bent on world domination.

It is an extraordinary moment, anarchic yet constructed, frameless yet framed, threatening yet embracing. Despite seconds of near levitation and aerodynamic lift, the scene secures the group to the ground—a point made especially apparent, if paradoxically, at the end of the episode. With barely a hint of transition, the pandemonium ends and the band, collecting itself and straightening out, exits the field as per the shouted, angry eviction of a groundskeeper who identifies the turf as private property. In an instant the Beatles' world conquest, ebullient as it seems, is marked as a blow against capitalism and is doomed to failure. It is too late. The world is already parceled, possessed, inaccessible. The need, evinced in *Let It Be*, for dissolution, for absorption into the heavens, for death, is forecast. The impossibility of transcending space and architecture by way of their own corporeal manifestation of rebellion, freedom, creativity, and irrationality makes just that much more necessary the force of their greatest resource—their music. It is their most dangerous tool—dangerous because of its abstraction, its ineffability, and yet its materiality—and their last and only resort.

The three major release, live-action films that chronicle the Beatles' existence through the 1960s (*A Hard Day's Night*, *Help*, and *Let It Be*) tell the group's story primarily through their music, propelled by only the most skeletal of narrative structures. Story is recognizable but hardly intrusive as compared to sheer aural and visual force. As a result, the group's ability to project itself as in control—as the maker of its own destiny—is carried, with varying degrees of success and failure, elation and poignancy, by the use of spatial, architectural, and urban settings.

The rapidity with which the Beatles climbed the ladder of global success and fame precluded their being associated with any one place. Certainly they were British. Liverpool was their city of origin, London and its environs their home after success—few could forget these markers. Later, John Lennon, in life and in death, would become indelibly associated with New York City. But for every association that derives from such specificity of location, there is an equivalent recollection of a global or universal or timeless significance meant to belie the stasis that might obtain by way of particular geographical reference. For well over a decade, the group was seemingly everywhere, omnipresent. It is therefore ironic that the Beatles' cinematic fortunes provide a deeply associative notion of space, location, and architecture.

It is difficult not to think of *A Hard Day's Night*, *Help*, and *Let It Be* as parables of the band's maturation, corresponding as they do to the early acquisition of fame, international worldly domination, and an internalized, hermetic process of disintegration. In the films, each of these quite real moments in the history of the band is made to correspond to an equally real architecture that reinforces the idea of a teleological development from birth to death, rags to riches, local to global to universal.

Filmed by director Richard Lester in grainy black and white, *A Hard Day's Night* is reminiscent of so many contemporaneous kitchen-sink dramas devoted to capturing a working-class milieu of hope and desperation. The absence of color sets the mood for a virtual litany of references to a class-confined life on the run, hemmed in by limits. *A Hard Day's Night* is a story of making ends meet, of containment and release, of narrow corridors, confined spaces, of deceit and other evasive measures made necessary by invasive fans, managers, and professional handlers. "I thought I was supposed to be getting a change of scenery and so far I've been in a train and a room, a room and a car, and a room and a room," says Paul's frustrated grandfather, played by Wilfrid Brambell.

With these words, he deflates the breakneck excitement of Beatlemania, circling and highlighting its deadening monotony.

The four musicians confined in a pullman car as their fans go wild outside in *A Hard Day's Night*.

Ringo is only able to fight this enervation by donning a disguise and "parading" around the outskirts of an anonymous southern city (to the tune of "This Boy") in his famous tragicomic walkabout. There he finds himself, nonetheless, completely unable to reassimilate the practices of everyday life that until recently must have been second nature to him. A riverbank, a pub, a police station—spaces in which Ringo would have once found anonymity unavoidable—are presented generically. Now, as a Beatle, he demonstrates the increasing inadequacy of these settings to provide shelter from his own celebrity. They no longer represent the normalized, constrained standards of authority, regularity, collectivity, individuality—even the rebellion he is momentarily attempting to recapture.

The process of discovery facilitated by *A Hard Day's Night* is one in which the Beatles, rather than transcending the world of their origins, continually find themselves homeless, without shelter. For every moment of hilarity, there is a second of poignancy that signifies some type of vanishing experience. Comfortable in their train compartment, they lose its hermetic safety to a member of the upper-middle class who insists on sharing the space and imposing his expectations for quiet and boundaries. Imprisoned in a freight car by their manager, they are forced to vacate and evade massive crowds as they reach their destination. Settling into a luxurious hotel suite, they are commanded to answer fan mail and refuse social invitations. Social discourse on the largest scale thus wins out over the desire to wring from their hotel room a sense of comfort and protection, a place of safety from the masses, a space wherein a private language might be better facilitated. Later on, eager to enjoy the perks of a catered press conference, they are denied access to material sustenance at every opportunity, and any possible command of space is obliterated by a crush of interviewers. Finally, free to enjoy a nightclub, having disobeyed their manager's orders to stay at the hotel, they are hauled away from the fun when their escape is discovered.

Passing from space to space, from setting to setting, the Beatles are continually denied the association with shelter that might define identity. As a result, these places, in their necessary failure to hold and protect the group, assume a beauty in the repeated momentary quality of their inhabitation. Perhaps the most extraordinary example of this is witnessed in the opening moments of the film, when, making their way to a train, we see John—shadowed almost imperceptibly by Ringo—through the window of what appears to be the station's cafeteria. Peering out to his right, his face pressed against the glass, he avoids the viewer's glance while searching for a clear path, his other two mates, or some sign as to his next direction. Seeing none of these, he retreats into the station. In this movement, the deep recesses of the cavernous room hold a loneliness, an ambiguity, even an ambivalence of motive and desire that render a mundane architectural space as mysterious as a café in nineteenth-century Paris.

For a moment, architecture's sometimes complimentary, sometimes contradictory roles—to serve its own intentions and those of its inhabitants—are made painfully clear. Lennon's gentle, tentative gaze radiates a desire for protection and embrace, a vantage point from which to survey the outside world. But the cafeteria does not provide for his desires, supporting, at best, a neutrality and coldness that marks the station's role as a hostel for those in transit, for the temporarily homeless. Lennon moves through a space that is all exposure and repulsion.

The film being a friendly vehicle of self-promotion, however, it may be easier to argue for such visual interests in terms of reflection rather than repulsion. Mirroring and the vicissitudes of window-gazing take the measure of space in some of the film's most affecting visuals. An uncanny moment occurs as the camera focuses for an instant on a photo booth in the train station. As we read and digest the advertisement for instant photos, the curtain hiding the interior is pulled back, revealing three of the Beatles—John, George, and Ringo—peering out to ensure that the coast is clear to continue their mad dash for transport, escape, and safety. In the instant that they—and most prominently John, the curtain puller—stare out, a mirror to the right of the curtain meant for grooming shows a horde of kids running by the booth, unawares.

The Beatles' frozen moment is caught within the space of concealment by a type of disposable architecture. Here is a spot of Robert Venturi's Las Vegas in the middle of London. The booth is a "building" designed to house no one for more than a few minutes, for no longer, in fact, than it takes to "snap" their image. This is a shelter no one could expect to "last," to stand for more than a metaphoric minute. It is a ruin from the start. The booth and the Beatles in it, disfigured without Paul, are thus a canvas against which the flying, running, stumbling desires of children are ignited, given image themselves, in the face of the Beatles' containment. This is the other side of their predicament. It is a moving and lovely juxtaposition of innocence and growth, the chaotic possibilities of youth and the already static limits of maturity. It is also a deeply generous and somewhat melancholic gesture, afforded by and from the safety and compromise of shelter toward those passing through and on the outside. It is as if to say that this is as much your moment, perhaps even more so, than it is ours. Youth find their feet, for an instant, in the image of their idols' encasement.

The vignette also serves as a kind of pop-culture version of Diego de Velázquez's *Las Meninas*. Like the Spanish master's painting, this shot seems, however briefly witnessed, an iconic moment, yet one destabilized by its own visualized uncertainties. The architectural skeleton of the photo booth is reduced to an image fleetingly projected and just as rapidly exchanged for another and then another, all meant to reinforce the same narrative. The trappings of status shift over time, but the limits to freedom and representation are ever enforced, sometimes bursting the seams of spatial confinement and other times contracting to meet the constraints of a given setting.

Such themes are nowhere more evident than in the Beatles 1965 film *Help*, their second and the second directed by Richard Lester. Now international mega-stars, their reach extends around the globe, enmeshing them in intrigues and escapades worthy of a James Bond adventure. As a result, shelter can now mean anything: a customized group of row houses, for example, converted on the interior into one shared apartment distinctly but unobtrusively divided into living spaces redolent of each Beatle's "personality"—a sunken bedspace for devilish John, an organ that rises from beneath the floor for angelic Paul.

As the Beatles are established as cultural icons, the spaces they inhabit become emblems of their iconoclasm, physically reconfigured from bourgeois norms to the point of postmodern parody. Over the course of ninety minutes we find the group occupying, chronologically, their townhouse, a recording studio, Salisbury Plain (both above and below ground), Buckingham Palace, the Alps, and the Bahamas. The moral of the story is that they have already begun to outlive this mortal coil—no space on earth is adequate to their needs or can contain their being. The end of the film has them splashing around in the surf amidst a religious ruin—a stone Buddha—as if returning to some kind of primordial sea species through prehistoric reinvention. This then becomes the only way to imagine a space of security and completion at the end of time, the end of the film.

From Stonehenge to the sea, it is a tale of exacerbated evolution, an evolution made necessary by the constant harassment of those seeking a piece of the Beatles—a disparate collection of Occidentals and Orientals who succeed time and again in taking advantage of architecture's radical inadequacy to provide shelter for the group. The movie's convoluted plot finds Ringo and his mates hunted by a vaguely Eastern collection of mystics tracking down a ring that the drummer received in a fan's letter. Also chasing the ring—and its bearer—are a pair of "scientists" out to marshal its extraordinary physical properties for their own nefarious purposes. Meanwhile, Scotland Yard, Buckingham Palace, and other powers-that-be work vainly to protect British interests in the form of the world's most popular rock band. In *Help*'s mythology, science and religion (West and East) are posed as nemeses to art, which is left to wander rootlessly, searching for a proper home that it will never find.

All of this is, of course, fantasy. And what better way out of fantasy than reality, if only to assert the absolute of one's being. Thus came *Let It Be*, by all accounts a colossal disaster born of a weary impulse to film the group as is, warts and all, in the making of an album from start to finish. Now, the imagination can only cough up three settings in which to situate the group: the cavernous Twickenham film studios, the basement recording studio at their record company's Savile Row headquarters, and on the roof of this same building. A microcosmic movement is implied, from birth in the womblike, neutral-white fish tank of Twickenham—occasionally bathed in amniotic-colored lights—to burial in the basement of Savile Row, and ascendancy to heaven from the roof above.

Along the way the Beatles replay their roles in hermetic isolation—they are always removed from the social world. Space and architecture are almost invisible players. Particularity of place and design are barely registered until the end of the film, when the group attempts for a moment to transcend its confinement. This constitutes a radical departure from *A Hard Day's Night* and *Help*. Now, at the end, nondescript interiors house these four psychologically drained figures. The feeling of oppressive proximity created by entrapping walls is ever present. In response, despite increasing friction and antipathy, the Beatles continually huddle together, as if always around the proverbial campfire, scouts till the end. Whether in cavernous Twickenham or the cavelike basement studio of Savile Row, two spaces that could not be more dramatically different in scale, appearance, and atmosphere, the group clings to itself. Self-preservation in the face of social alienation is the goal. They form a physical unit as the psychological, emotional one begins to fail. Their sheer materiality, proximity, and momentary identification as like beings are what will have to carry them to the roof, shedding the built environment as they lose themselves, left only to instinct and the senses.

This sounds somewhat apocalyptic, but it is unavoidable. *Let It Be*'s visuals and the reality they purport to document can no longer offer any kind of solution to a problem. The problem would be: How to maintain the propulsion of a commodity and its aesthetic in the event of its enervation, an enervation that now seems the result of the failure to find a space that will properly nurture the collective and its component parts? This is not an enervation of sheer creative practice—the music of *Let It Be* and the last album the group would record, *Abbey Road*, are in their best moments as rich as any of the group's career. Rather, for these four individuals working together, pure creativity cannot be separated from its external manifestation in capital and consumption.

Only in the process of separation, as the Beatles remove themselves from the interior of Savile Row, shedding along the way the accretions of their own history, offering their music to the heavens and the street below, do they, for a moment, recapture something of a sense of origin. This is the fiction of a pure connection to their intention, making music. It is an origin, however, that is utterly dependent upon history, in this case place and its material characteristics, and the resistance of that object which defines their contemporaneity: their audience. As the camera pans the facades below, it becomes apparent that it is the impassive Georgian architecture—stolid, immovable, preserved—against which the Beatles push, but from which they catch a spark as well. They stand atop a built environment, a foundation transcended at last, but one that simultaneously marks the group as past. Along the way, the social and the commercial are sacrificed, the crowds, if not diminished, are farther away than ever; they disperse into anonymous traffic as much as they congeal at corners. As the sixties end, it is the Rolling Stones who have the last words: "Gimme Shelter." For the Beatles, that demand was obsolete—they were history.

ACKNOWLEDGMENTS

THIS BOOK WOULD not have been possible without the support of publisher Kevin C. Lippert. I thank him for his faith, generosity, and constant sage counsel. My colleagues at Princeton Architectural Press received the initial proposal for this project with enthusiasm and encouragement, and have subsequently offered no end of support. For suffering my presence on a daily basis with humor and good cheer, and for creating an atmosphere that makes my arrival at work each morning a pleasure, I thank Eugenia Bell, Jan Cigliano, Jane Garvie, Caroline Green, Beth Harrison, Mia Ihara, Leslie Ann Kent, Annie Nitschke, Lottchen Shivers, Jennifer Thompson, and Deb Wood. Clare Jacobson has a ready answer for every editorial question; Sara Moss was saddled with the onerous task of procuring images for this book, and did so with consummate skill; Cathryn Drake ensured the text was error-free. For her exceptional design, editorial acumen, endless patience, and neighborly disposition, I owe a special debt of gratitude to Sara Stemen.

The contributors to this volume have given of themselves beyond any reasonable expectation. All signed on to this project when it was more rumination than reality, and have stuck with it as other commitments have imposed themselves. I thank them all for their time, effort, and ideas. In addition to providing his own contribution, Philip Nobel spent many an hour helping me formulate my thoughts about architecture and film—often over beer and bourbon. Mary

McLeod and M. Christine Boyer supported this project when it was in its infancy. Every neighborhood should have a video store with as deep a selection and as friendly a staff as Movie Place, where architecture and film meet on New York's Upper West Side.

These acknowledgments would not be complete without recognition of my parents, Hal and Jane Lamster, and my grandfather, Brandon D. Stone, for a lifetime of support and encouragement. Lastly and above all, I thank Anna Kuchment for her grace and intelligence, and for always knowing the right words.

CONTRIBUTORS

DONALD ALBRECHT is an independent curator and the author of *Designing Dreams: Modern Architecture and the Movies*, *The Work of Charles and Ray Eames: A Legacy of Invention*, and *World War II and the American Dream.*

JONATHAN F. BELL is a Providence-based architect and writer.

BOB CRAFT has been a location manager in the film industry for more than a decade, and has worked with such noted directors as Blake Edwards, Diane Keaton, Peter Medak, Quentin Tarantino, and Nicolas Roeg.

BOB EISENHARDT is a New York-based documentary filmmaker. His 1983 film *Spaces: The Architecture of Paul Rudolph* was nominated for the Academy Award for best short-subject documentary. He received one of his three Emmy Awards for directing *Spaces.*

PETER HALL is a senior writer at *ID* magazine and co-editor of *Tibor Kalman: Perverse Optimist* (Princeton Architectural Press, 1999).

MARK LAMSTER is a senior editor at Princeton Architectural Press.

NANCY LEVINSON is an architect and co-editor of *Harvard Design Magazine*.

PHILIP NOBEL is a New York-based architecture writer. His work appears regularly in *Architecture, The New York Times, Metropolis*, and numerous other publications.

JOAN OCKMAN is director of the Buell Center for the Study of American Architecture at Columbia University, where she also teaches history and theory of architecture. She is editor, with Edward Eigen, of *Architecture Culture, 1943–1968: A Documentary Anthology*.

JOSEPH ROSA is curator of architecture at The Hines Architectural Center, Carnegie Museum of Art, in Pittsburgh, and the author of *Albert Frey: Architect* (1990; Princeton Architectural Press, 1999) and *A Constructed View: The Architectural Photography of Julius Shulman* (1994).

ERIC ROSENBERG is associate professor in the Department of Art and Art History, and director of the American Studies Program at Tufts University.

MITCHELL SCHWARZER is associate professor of architectural history and theory at California College of Arts and Crafts in San Francisco, Executive Editor of *Design Book Review*, and the author of *German Architectural Theory and the Search for Modern Identity* and *Architecture and Design: San Francisco*.

MAGGIE VALENTINE is professor of architecture and interior design at The University of Texas, San Antonio, and is the author of *The Show Starts on the Sidewalk: An Architectural History of the Movie Theatre, Starring S. Charles Lee*.

CHRISTINA WILSON received her Ph.D. in architectural history from the University of Virginia, where she wrote her dissertation on the work of Cedric Gibbons.

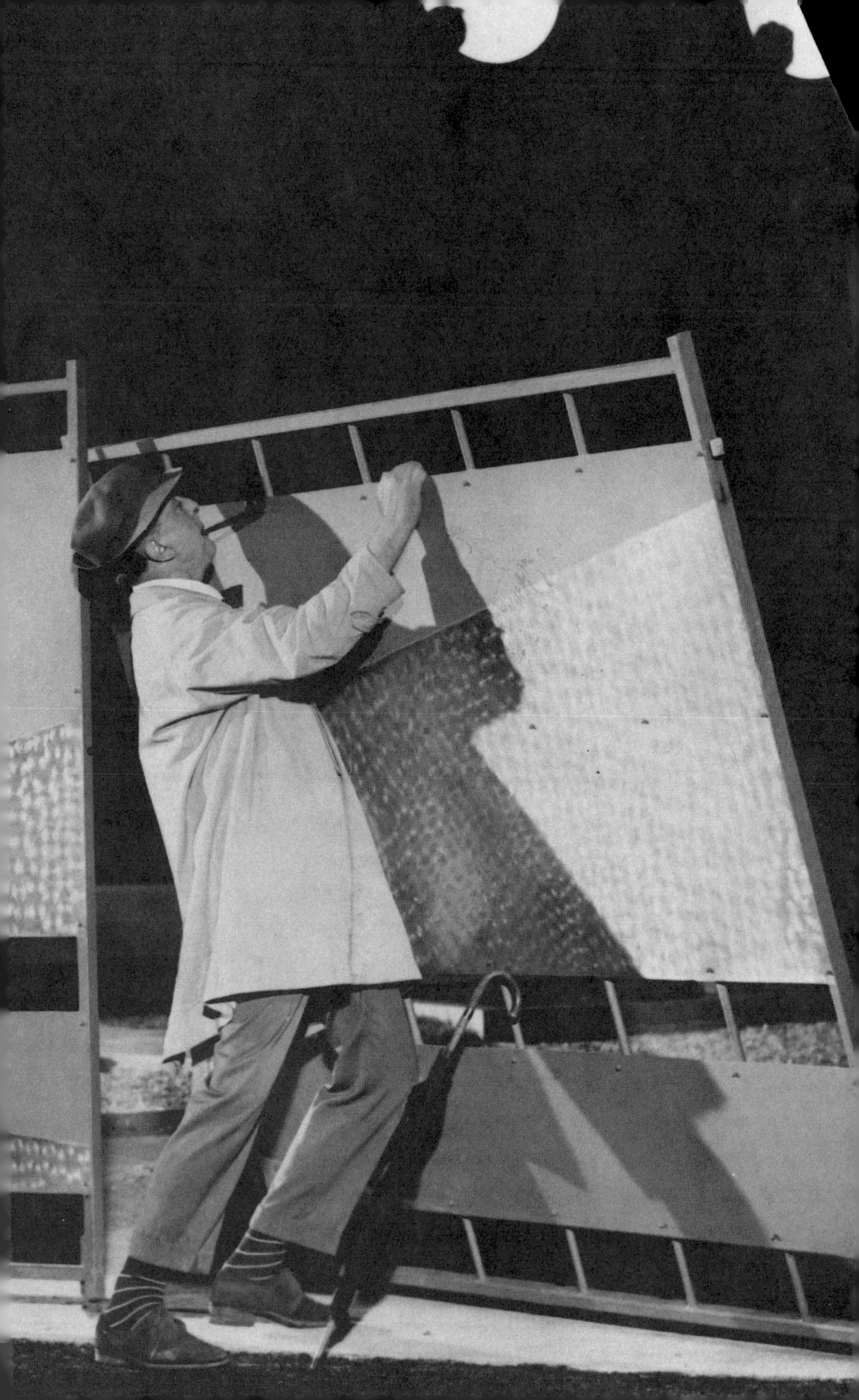